CW00542909

To the Twelfth Infallible Imām al-Mahdi;
May he accept the present work!

To the living memory of all those who aspired to have the grace of paying ziyārah (ritual visitation) to Karbalā but could not make it.

To those who enjoy hearing such marvelous names as Imām al-Ḥusayn, Karbalā, and Ashurā, and their eyes get brimmed with tears out of ardent devotion.

From Medina to Karbala
In the Words of Imam al-Husayn

Ayatollah Muhammad-Sadiq Najmi
Translated and annotated by
Dr. Muhammad-Reza Fakhr-Rohani

SUN BEHIND THE CLOUD
PUBLICATIONS LTD

بسم الله الرحمن الرحيم

Published by
Sun Behind The Cloud Publications Ltd
PO Box 15889, Birmingham, B16 6NZ
with
Imām al-Ḥusayn's Sacred Sanctuary
Karbalā, Iraq

First published in paperback 2012
This second edition published in paperback 2013

A CIP catalogue record for this book is available from the British Library

ISBN (Print) 978-1-908110-22-0

www.sunbehindthecloud.com

Contents

Part Three: In Karbalā

Abbreviations

- A.H., (in dates, *anno Hegirae*) Arabic-cum-Islamic lunar calendar
- b., (Arabic *ibn*) son of
- bt., (Arabic *bint*) daughter of
- d., (followed by dates) died
- qtd., quoted
- r./eigned
- Sh./amsi, Persian-cum-Islamic solar calendar

Transliteration Table

ء	’	ز	z	ق	q	Long vowels			
ب	b	س	s	ك	k			ا	ā
ت	t	ش	sh	ل	l			و	ū
ث	th	ص	ṣ	م	m			ي	ī
ج	j	ض	ḍ	ن	n	Short vowels			
ح	ḥ	ط	ṭ	ه	h			ـَ	a
خ	kh	ظ	ẓ	و	w			ـُ	u
د	d	ع	‘	ي	y			ـِ	i
ذ	dh	غ	gh	ة	ah				
ر	r	ف	f	ال	al-				

About the Author

The late Ayatollah Muḥammad-Sadiq Najmi was born in the village of Haris around Shabestar, Azerbaijan, Iran, in 1315 Sh/ 1936. His father, Ḥajj Mirza Ahmad Aqa Harisi, was a cleric in the same region. His mother was a cousin of the late Grand Ayatollah Sayyid Hujjat Kuhkamari.

The late Ayatollah Najmi started his education when he was at the age of eight. After about seven years of studying at the local schools of his hometown, his father took him to Tabriz where he continued his education at Talebiyeh Madrasa. In the end of the summer of 1332 Sh/ 1953, he left Tabriz for Qom to pursue his higher education. His education was not limited to his study in Qom; whenever he found any opportunity, mainly in the summer holidays, he visited Mashhad to perform ziyāra (pilgrimage) of Imām 'Ali al-Riḍa's Sacred Sanctuary and to benefit from the lessons offered at the madrasas there. In Mashhad, he made close relations with the late Ayatollah Ḥajj Sayyid Hadi Milani.

During his studentship, he had several mentors and professors. Some of them include: Sheikh Ali-Akbar Ahari, Sheikh Abulfazl Ulamayi-Sarabi, Sheikh Abdullah Nurani, Sheikh Sa'ini-Zanjani, Ayatollah Dr. Muḥammad Mufatteh, Ayatollah Mortaza Mutahhari, Ayatollah Meshkini, Ayatollah Sobhani, Ayatollah Mūsawi-Ardabili, Ayatollah Soltani, Ayatollah Mujahedi, Ayatollah Zahedi-Qomi, Ayatollah Allama Sayyid Muḥammad-Husayn Tabatabaie, Ayatollah Khazali, Ayatollah Hasanzade-Amoli, Ayatollah Milani, Ayatollah

Morteza Haeri, Ayatollah Golpayegani, Ayatollah Mohaqeq-Damad, and the late Imām Khomeini, the founder of the Islamic Republic of Iran.

The late Ayatollah Najmi was both a prolific scholar and a social activist. His meeting with the late Ayatollah Allama 'Abd al-Husayn Amini, the author of *al-Ghadir*, in the village of Sharafkhaneh near the lake Urumiyeh, northwest Iran in the summer of 1350 Sh/ 1971, proved very insightful and full of inspiration. The late Ayatollah Najmi authored several books, mainly concerning Islamic history as well as the Qur'ān and *hadith*. He established the Islamic Azad University in Khoy in the 1364 Sh/ 1985 and was its rector for 16 years until 1380/ 2001. He received a letter from Imām Khomeini in 1360 Sh/ 1981 on the basis of which he was nominated as the leader of the Friday Prayer in the city of Khoy, West Azerbaijan.

The late Ayatollah Najmi visited other countries for research purposes. He visited great libraries in Damascus, Syria; Istanbul, Turkey; and Mumbai, Lucknow, and Benares, India.

In 1380 Sh/ 2002, the late Ayatollah Najmi decided to leave his posts and responsibilities to come back to Qom. In Qom he continued his scholastic pursuit for over ten years. During these years, he saw some of his works, including the present book, translated into several languages.

The late Ayatollah Najmi had a heart attack in the late summer of 1390 Sh/ 2011. He breathed his last on 25 Shahrivar 1390/ 16 September 2011 and was buried at Qom. May his soul rest in peace! Amen!

Acknowledgements

I would like to express my gratitude to the Creator of the Pen, Allāh the Almighty, for the unique opportunity He has granted me to discharge my humblest and most sincere religious and academic duty toward Imām al-Ḥusayn so as to internationalise his epoch-making discourses. I am also thankful to Imām al-Ḥusayn for providing me with this opportunity to acquire the grace and honour of translating his brilliant ideas and ideals into English. No doubt, it was his special attention to select me, albeit with all my shortcomings, to undertake such a sacred and monumental task.

I am grateful to my parents whose sincere prayers took me to this sacred and promising line of scholarship. My father's clerical knowledge, expertise, and advice as well as his rich private library proved really invaluable.

My thanks go to Hujjatoleslam Muḥammad-Reza Nourollahiyan-Mohajer, the late Ayatollah Muḥammad-Sadiq Najmi, Ahmad Najmi, Afsaneh Namazi, Hashem Qavidel, Dr. Muḥammad-Hadi Khaleqi, Abd al-Husayn Taleie, Mostafa Nezamabadi, Sayyid Abbas Muḥammad-Hoseyni Siahnouri, Dr. Gholam-Reza Sami-Gorganroudi, Muḥammad-Baqer Pour-Amini, Dr. Muḥammad-Saeed Bahmanpour, Sayyid Morteza Haerizadeh, Ayatollah Muḥammad-Javad Tabasi, Ayatollah Najm al-Din Tabasi, Sayyid Ali-Reza Nasser-Sheikholeslami, Sayyid Muḥammad-Reza Nasser Sheikholeslami, Shahin Eftekhary Targhi, Dr. Hyder Reza Zabeth, Ali-Akbar Ahmadlou, and Dr. Sayyid Khalil Tousi.

I also benefited from the help of a number of friends and scholars in other countries: Dr. Muḥammad-Reza Kazimi, and Prof. Dr. Sayyid

Hosain M. Jafri (Pakistan); Sheikh Ali al-Fatlawi, Husayn al-Salami, Haydar al-Mankoushi, Prof. Dr. Sayyid Hasan Isa al-Hakim, Ayatollah Sheikh Abd al-Mahdi al-Karbalāyi, Ayatollah Sayyid Muḥammad-Mahdi al-Mūsawi al-Khirsan, Ayatollah Dr. Sayyid Sami al-Badri, Dr. Sayyid Salman Hadi Āl Tu'mah, and the late Ayatollah Sheikh Baqir Sharif al-Qarashi (Iraq); Dr. Anton Bara (Kuwait); Mareike Beez, Dr. Sebastian Guenther, and Dr. Werner Ende (Germany); Dr. David Cook, Dr. David Greetham, Nuncy Mulvany and the Rev. Dr. F. Peter Ford (USA); Dr. Torsten Hylen (Sweden); Prof. Syed Sadiq Naqvi, Prof. Dr. Syed Muḥammad Azizuddin Hosain Hamadani, and Mr. Aejaz Ali al-Husaini Bhujwala (India). I ought to express my gratitude to Tehseen Fatema Merali (UK) of Sun Behind the Cloud Publications from whom I learned a lot; as well as Zainab Merali and Zainab Ali whose help with editing and proofreading proved invaluable.

Last but not least, I am indebted to my family. My wife provided me with a fitting environment at home. Her patience and convincing my children not to distract my concentration remains far beyond answering her help by ordinary thanks. I hope she will receive much more spiritual reward (than I might deserve) for her sacrifice for this translation.

Translator's Introduction

To begin with, the present work could not have been prepared save by the grace of the Almighty Allāh to whom is directed our most sincere and ardent gratitude.

This translation seeks to serve several purposes. Firstly, it is a complete collection of Imām al-Ḥusayn's discourse, both oral and written, from the moment he received the ultimatum to recognise Yazīd b. Mu'āwīya as a ruler up until his tragic, but certainly triumphant, martyrdom on the plains of Karbalā on Ashurā, the 10th of Muharram, 61 AH/ 680. Although a complete translation of all of Imām al-Ḥusayn's discourse has not been available in English, some parts of them have appeared in other works. No doubt, the present translation can provide a background for those who seek to find the truth of Imām al-Ḥusayn's mission on the basis of his own words. This will be a humble service both to Imām al-Ḥusayn and to those who aspire to find out more about his life and character.

Secondly, it is a humble contribution to research literature that pertains to Imām al-Ḥusayn — provisionally referred to as Ḥusaynī literature. I would like to apply the term 'Ḥusaynī literature' to whatever research and religious materials that pertain to Imām al-Ḥusayn. Ḥusaynī literature can then be divided roughly into educational, celebratory, and mourning literature, with the last category mainly known as *maqtal* or *maqātil* literature that focuses on the martyrdom accounts of Imām al-Ḥusayn. While maqtal or maqātil literature focuses on the tragic scenes, with a heavy emphasis on the events of the Ashurā tragedy, historical accounts seek to cover the lifetime of Imām al-Ḥusayn from his graceful birth to his triumphant martyrdom.

There has long been a need for such a treasure of Imām al-Ḥusayn's discourses in English. In contrast to such languages as Arabic, Persian, and Urdu in which Ḥusaynī literature can be relatively easy to find, in English it has long been neglected. Due to the international importance of the English language, the present book can, and is expected to, make an impact on those who feel that having access to Imām al-Ḥusayn's own words is a prerequisite to understanding and appreciating Shī'ī Islam in general and specifically Imām al-Ḥusayn's movement. It will benefit researchers and preachers, as well as elegizers and eulogizers of Imām al-Ḥusayn and his matchless companions. This is because each and every word uttered by Imām al-Ḥusayn contains several lifelong lessons so far undiscovered or unnoticed by mankind.

The process of translating this work has been an honour and a great lesson. It has been my lifelong grace to be able to humbly serve Imām al-Ḥusayn and the other Ashurā personalities. Although the original work was written for a Persian-speaking audience, producing an English translation was certainly a labor of love. Not all fragments of the text were necessary for translation; some fragments needed details in translation. To cite but a few examples, sections dealing with the Iranian Islamic Revolution of 1979 did not seem necessary for translation, especially the sections concerning a specific page in the history of a certain town in Iran. Certainly, the international audience, particularly those from some remote parts of the world, cannot be expected to be aware of a local history of another country far away from them. Elsewhere, it was necessary to add some sentences for clarification where some background religious and cultural knowledge was presupposed or regarded as prerequisite. Fortunately, the author, the late Ayatollah Muḥammad-Sadiq Najmi, had granted me permission to incorporate such modifications in the translation at the outset of this translation project. While the present translation was in progress, I learned a lot about some deficiencies in some of the research literature available on Imām al-Ḥusayn and the Ashurā tragedy, particularly about those works which are available in English as not all passages can be regarded as reliable texts. Some translations are utterly flawed, and in some others, much Islamic religious and historical knowledge was presupposed on the part of typical international audience.

I hope the present work will fill a serious religious and scholarly gap. While the present translation was in its initial stages, I realised that Imām al-Ḥusayn's speeches, conversations, and letters have seldom been translated fully into English. In consequence, it is hoped that the messages of Imām al-Ḥusayn's discourses would be communicated globally through the present English translation.

Throughout the whole project, every effort has been made to ensure that the words of Imām al-Ḥusayn were taken from reliable sources. This practice was warmly appreciated by the late Ayatollah Najmi. Obtaining several reference books, particularly old works and editions was by no means a simple task. This proved very hard and at times frustrating, especially when a title was no longer in print. Hence, I was always on the look-out for the desired volumes both at home and abroad. At times, it proved that a certain, and in some cases the only, English translation of a volume could not be considered a reliable source, although a considerable amount of time had been spent in obtaining that specific book. Nonetheless, such efforts, both educative and often exhausting, were full of invaluable lessons that could not be found anywhere else, except in a project like this.

Arabic proper names have been rendered in precisely the way they are written and produced in Classical Arabic. For this purpose, almost all proper names of places, personalities, and concepts, have been checked in authoritative texts in Arabic. For instance, the name "al-Ḥusayn" has been retained instead of "Ḥusayn", or its several variant spellings. Also, the Arabic definite article "al-" has carefully been retained to abide by Arabic rules of spelling. As for place names, priority has been given to the correct English spelling and the canonical forms have been retained.

Every effort has been made to make the texts and explanations as clear as possible. Typically, Islamic texts in Arabic, and by extension in Persian, refer to a personality in more than one way. This indirect and indeed honourific mode of reference has been replaced by making use of the commonly-used name of the personality. For the purpose of such clarification, several endnotes have been added to each chapter.

Lastly, I pray that this translation will be accepted as a token of religious deposit and capital in the Hereafter and on the Day of Judgment.

Figure 1: Imām al-Ḥusayn's Route From Medina to Karbalā

1. Milal
2. Sīyālah
3. Rūhā
4. Ruwaytha
5. Laḥy Jabal
6. Suqyā
7. Abwā
8. Rī' Harshī
9. Ghadīr Khumm
10. Qudayd
11. 'Asfān
12. Marr al-Zahrān
13. Al-Tan'īm
14. Al-Ṣifāḥ
15. Bustān b. Ma'mar
16. Awtās
17. 'Ufay'īyyah
18. Ma'din Bani Sulaym
19. 'Umaq
20. Al-Salīlah
21. Rabadhah
22. Maghīthah al-Ma'wān
23. Al-Naqirah
24. Al-Hājar/ Baṭn al-Rammah
25. Samīrā'
26. Tūz
27. Fayd
28. Ajfar
29. Al-Khuzaymīyah
30. Zarūd
31. Al-Tha'labīyyah
32. Biṭān
33. Shuqūq
34. Zubālah
35. Al-Qā'
36. 'Aqabah
37. Wāqiṣah
38. Sharāf
39. Dhū Ḥusum
40. Al-Bayḍah
41. 'Adhīb al-Hijānāt
42. Al-Ruhaymah
43. Al-Ququtānah
44. Mālik
45. Qaṣr Banī Muqātil
46. Al-Ṭaff
47. Al-Kūfa

A. Al-Juḥfa
B. Qarn al-Manāzil
C. Dhāt 'Īrq
D. Ghamrah
E. Maslaḥ

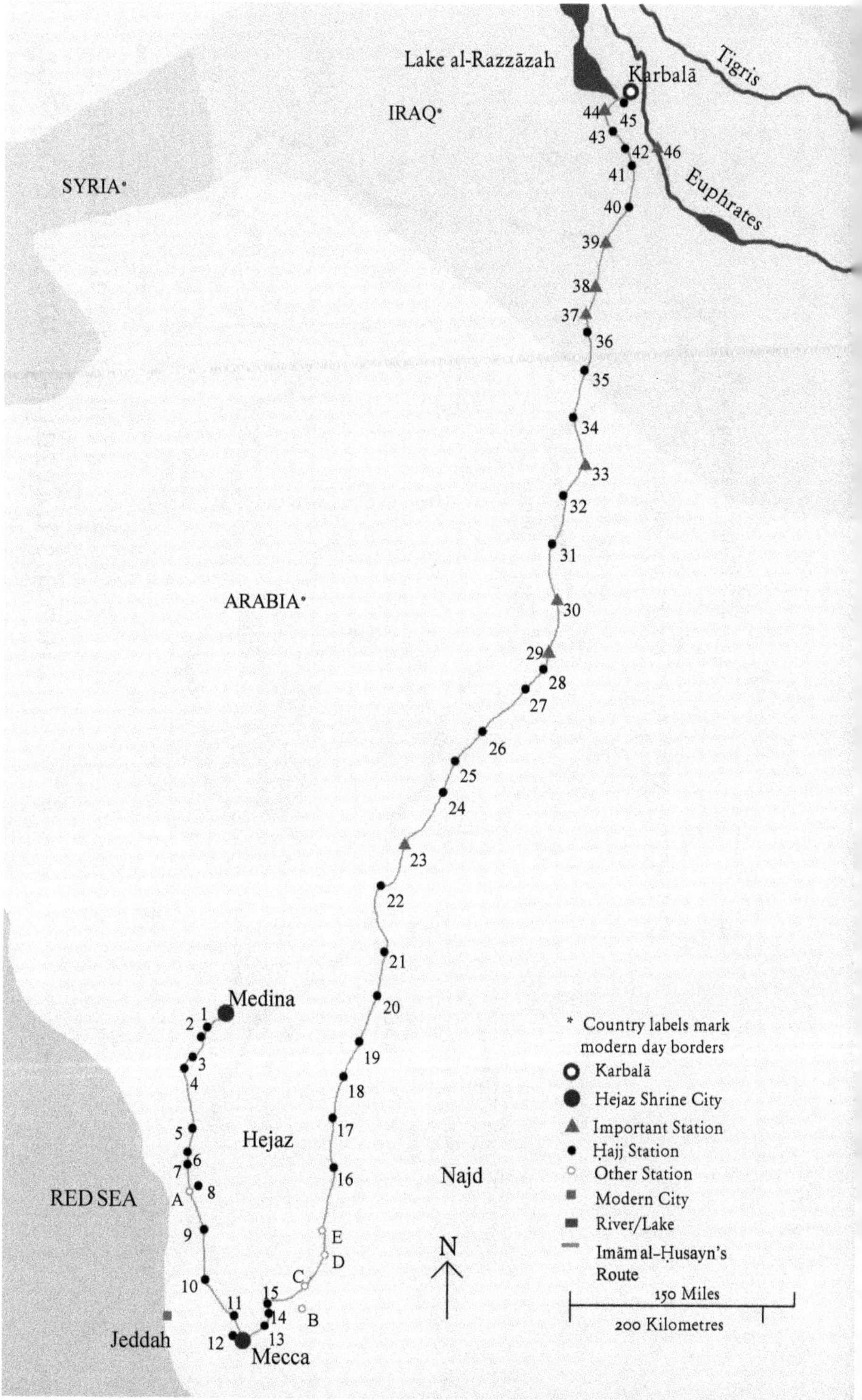

Lake al-Razzāzah
Karbalā
Tigris
IRAQ*
SYRIA*
Euphrates
ARABIA*
Medina
Hejaz
Najd
RED SEA
Jeddah
Mecca
N
* Country labels mark modern day borders
Karbalā
Hejaz Shrine City
Important Station
Ḥajj Station
Other Station
Modern City
River/Lake
Imām al-Ḥusayn's Route
150 Miles
200 Kilometres

Figure 2: Imām al-Ḥusayn's Route in the region of Mecca

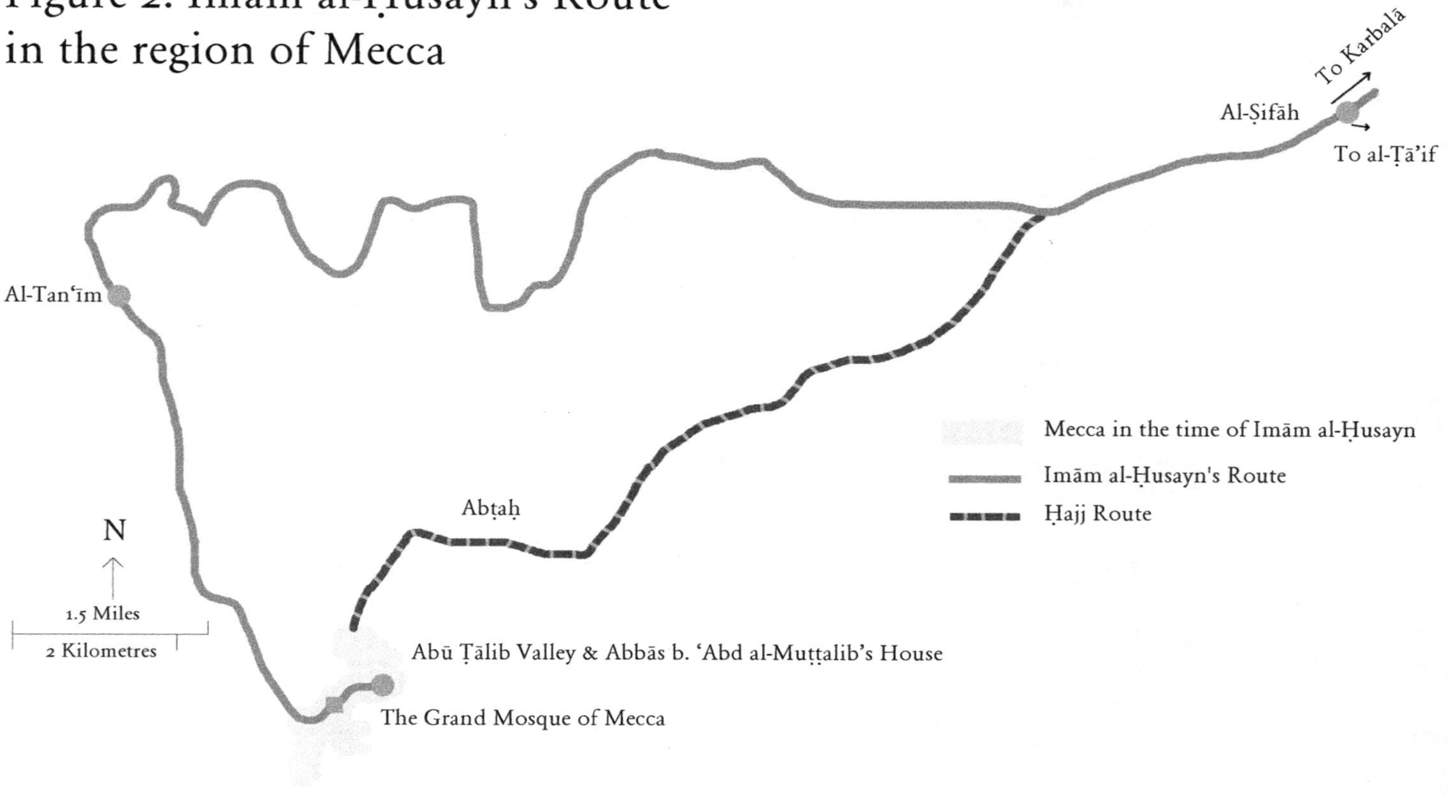

Figure 3: The Region of Karbalā at the Time of Imām al-Ḥusayn's Movement

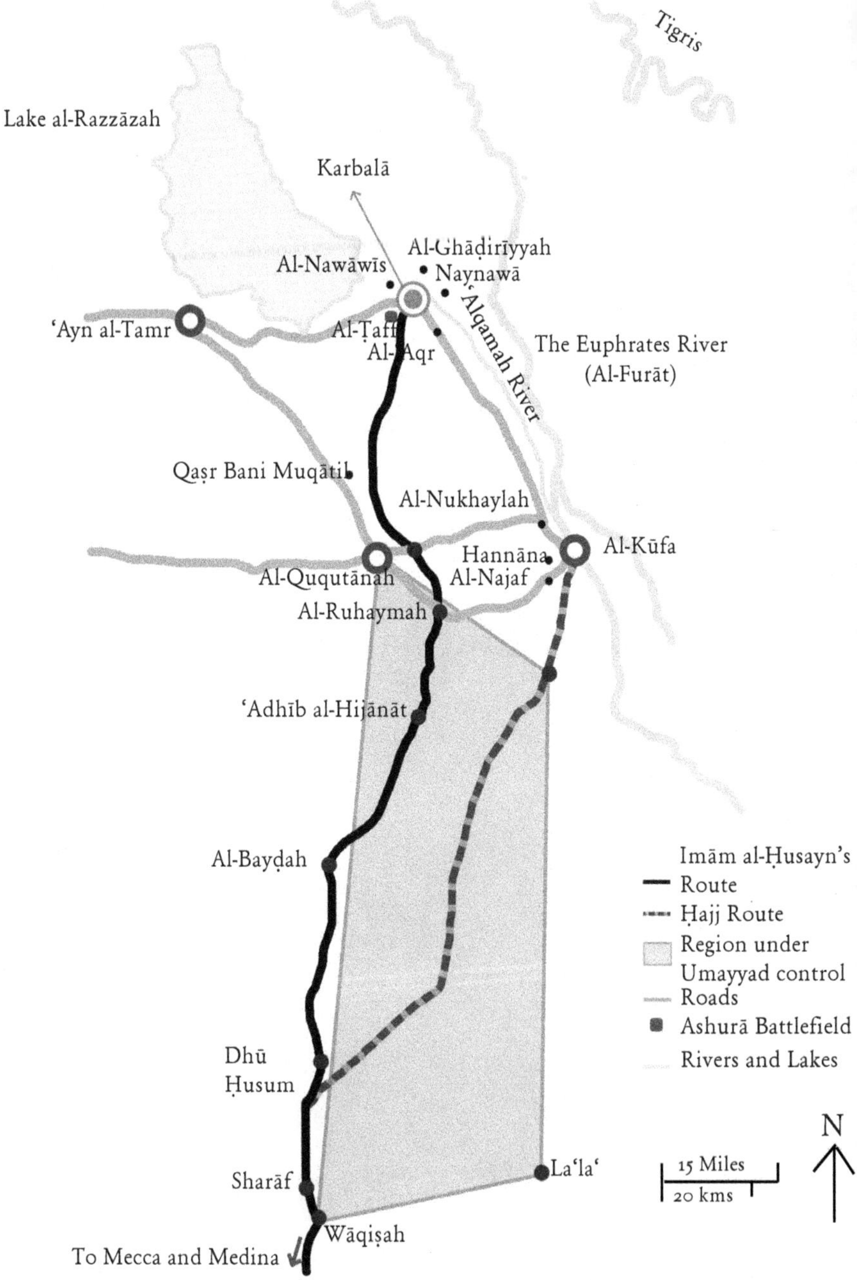

Part 1

From Medina to Mecca

1

Addressing the Governor of Medina

ايّها الامير! انّا اهلبيت النّبوّة ومعدن الرّسالة ومختلف الملائكة ومهبط الرّحمة! بنا فتح اللّه وبنا يختم! ويزيد رجل شارب الخمر وقاتل النّفس المحترمة معلن بالفسق ومثلی لايبايع مثله ولكن نصبح وتصبحون وننظر وتنظرون ايّنا احقّ بالخلافة والبيعة.

- ارى انّ طاغيتهم قد هلك؛
- يابن الزّرقاء! انت تقتلنی ام هو؟ كذبت واثمت.

"O Amir! We are the *Ahl al-Bayt* of the [post of] prophethood, and the source of the Divine mission; [our house] is the frequenting place of angels, and the landing site of the Divine grace. Allāh started [Islam] with us [our family] and will continue it to the end with us. [Moreover,] Yazīd [with whom you expect me to take the oath of allegiance] is a man accustomed to drinking wine [1] and has slain [lots of] innocent people, a person who infringes the Divine laws, and openly commits all sorts of lewdness and impiety. Is it fair that such a person like me– with those outstanding background and high family nobility – takes an oath of allegiance with such a profligate? However, you and I must consider the future, and you will realise which of us is more appropriate for assuming the caliphate and leadership of the Muslim ummah, and more fitting for receiving the people's allegiance." [2]

Context

After the death of Mu'āwīya [3] in the middle of Rajab 60 AH/ March 680, his son Yazīd [4] ascended to the post of caliphate. Soon after, he wrote letters to the Umayyad agents in various territories and informed them of his father's death and his succession and ascention to caliphate. [5] Maintaining them in their posts, he ordered them to obtain people's renewed oath of allegiance in his favour. He also wrote a letter in the same way to al-Walīd b. 'Utba, who had been appointed by Mu'āwīya as the governor of Medina. With this letter, Yazīd attached a short note to him in which he emphasised the need to obtain the *bay'a* (oath of allegiance) of three important personalities who had not succumbed to take an oath of allegiance in favour of Yazīd in the time of Mu'āwīya. The three persons were: Imām al-Ḥusayn, 'Abd Allāh b. 'Umar [6], and 'Abd Allāh b. al-Zubayr [7]; he expilictly said: "Exert utmost pressure on al-Ḥusayn, 'Abd Allāh b. 'Umar, and 'Abd Allāh b. al-Zubayr, without any respite until they yield an oath of allegiance. And that's all."

The letter reached al-Walīd b. 'Utba in the evening. He then called on Marwān b. al-Ḥakam [8], Mu'āwīya's former governor of Medina, for consultation on Yazīd's letter and directive. The latter suggested that he summon the three persons concerned as soon as possible so that while the news of Mu'āwīya's death had not reached the general public, al-Walīd b. 'Utba could obtain their pledge of allegiance. Thereupon, al-Walīd dispatched a person to call on them to come to him and discuss a significant and critical subject.

When al-Walīd's courier, 'Abd Allāh b. 'Amr b. 'Uthmān, [9] conveyed his message to Imām al-Ḥusayn and 'Abd Allāh b. al-Zubayr, they were sitting together in the Prophet's Mosque. 'Abd Allāh b. al-Zubayr got scared at such an untimely invitation at night time; however, Imām al-Ḥusayn explained the case to him, just prior to meeting al-Walīd. Imām al-Ḥusayn remarked: "I believe their tyrant [Mu'āwīya b. Abī Sufyān] has died". On the authority of Ibn Namā al-Ḥillī in *Muthīr al-Aḥzān*, Imām al-Ḥusayn added, in support of his view, that he had dreamt the night before that Mu'āwīya's house was on the blaze and his minbar toppled.

Then Imām al-Ḥusayn ordered thirty of his companions and close relatives to take arms and accompany him there. He told them to wait outside the building and defend Imām al-Ḥusayn, if necessary.

As Imām al-Ḥusayn anticipated, al-Walīd informed him of Mu'āwīya's death; he also asked Imām al-Ḥusayn's to take an oath of allegiance in favour of Yazīd. In response to this proposal, Imām al-Ḥusayn replied: "Such a personality like me should not take the oath of allegiance in private, and you should not consider it. And, as you will invite all inhabitants of Medina to renew their allegiance, we would, if considered right, participate and may take an oath of allegiance together with other Muslims. In other words, this allegiance would not be for the sake of Allāh, but for the people's attention, hence it must be made in public, not in private." Al-Walīd then accepted Imām al-Ḥusayn's argument, and no longer insisted on the allegiance at that time of night.

As Imām al-Ḥusayn intended to leave, Marwān b. al-Ḥakam said to al-Walīd "By God, if he departs from here without pledging the oath of allegiance, you will never get a similar opportunity without shedding much bloodshed between you and him. Seize him and do not let him leave without pledging allegiance, or execute him as instructed by Yazīd."

Upon this gesture of Marwān, Imām al-Ḥusayn turned to him and addressed him: "O son of al-Zarqā'! [10] Do you, or does he, [intend to] kill me? You have told a lie and committed a sin".

After that Imām al-Ḥusayn addressed al-Walīd in the way indicated in the beginning of this chapter.

Due to the heated debate which took place at al-Walīd's assembly and the harsh words of Imām al-Ḥusayn to Marwān, Imām al-Ḥusayn's companions realised the danger, and some of them joined him in the room. After this futile debate, which weakened al-Walīd's hope that Imām al-Ḥusayn's would pay allegiance, Imām al-Ḥusayn left the gathering.

Conclusion

In this dialogue Imām al-Ḥusayn explicitly stated his standpoint on the issue of pledging allegiance with Yazīd and not recognizing his rule. After stating some of the defining characteristics of his family merits and his own status, all proving his own and his family's qualification for the office of Imāmate and leadership of the *ummah*, he mentioned Yazīd's disqualification and vices which count for his inappropriateness for claiming leadership.

Imām al-Ḥusayn also indicated his incentive for uprising as well as his future strategy. He stated his strategy when he had not even received any letters of invitation from the people of al-Kūfa or their pledge of allegiance with him. This was because al-Walīd was given the directive to obtain Imām al-Ḥusayn's oath of allegiance either before or at the same time as when the inhabitants of al-Kūfa got informed of Mu'āwīya's death. As soon as the inhabitants of al-Kūfa were informed of Imām al-Ḥusayn's brave disownment, initiated by his leaving Medina for Mecca, they dispatched letters of invitation to him.

In conclusion, although it seemed that there were multiple factors and motivations for Imām al-Ḥusayn's uprising, the major reason was to stand against the leadership of tyranny and corruption, which was leading the Muslim *ummah* into an abyss of immorality. Moreover, if there had not been any obstacle, Yazīd intended to introduce and practice, quite hypocritically, the objectives of the house of Abū Sufyān which were previously defeated in the way of defeating Islam and the Holy Qur'ān, all in the guise of a seemingly Islamic caliphate. It is the demolishment of this Yazīd-oriented power that is mentioned as enjoining good and forbidding evil in the discourses of Imām al-Ḥusayn.

Not only did Imām al-Ḥusayn allude to this in his meeting with al-Walīd; he also emphasised it quite clearly on a second occassion when he met Marwān b. al-Ḥakam, who was Mu'āwīya's former governor in Medina and an enemy of Prophet Muḥammad's family. Imām al-Ḥusayn's conversation is presented in the following chapter.

Notes to Chapter 1
Addressing the Governor of Medina

1. Drinking wine and intoxicant liquids is regarded unlawful, *ḥarām*, hence strictly forbidden in Islam.

2. Al-Khaṭīb al-Khwārazmī, *Maqtal al-Ḥusayn*, vol. 1, p. 184; Ibn Ṭāwūs, *al-Luhūf*, p. 19; al-Majlisī, ed., *Biḥār al-Anwār*, vol. 44, p. 325; and 'Abd Allāh b. Nūr al-Dīn al-Baḥrānī, *Maqtal al-'Awālim*, p. 174.

3. Mu'āwīya b. Abī Sufyān (r. 661-680).

4. Yazīd b. Mu'āwīya (r. 680-683).

5. Mu'āwīya's act of taking allegiance by force in favour of his son, Yazīd, against the conditions of the peace treaty was one of the most tragic occurances in early Islamic history. For a detailed account in this regard, see al-Amīnī, *al-Ghadir*, vol. 10.

6. 'Abd Allāh b. 'Umar, the eldest son of 'Umar b. al-Khaṭṭāb, was born in the 3rd year after the advent of Islam. His mother was Zaynab bt. Maẓ'ūn. He did not pay the oath of allegiance to Imām 'Alī; however, later on he rushed to take an oath of allegiance with al-Ḥajjāj b. Yūsuf, the Marwānid tyrant and ruthless ruler. He died at the age of 87 at Mecca in the year 73 AH/693.

7. 'Abd Allāh b. al-Zubayr was born in the 20th month, that is, the second year, after the *hijra* (exodus) of Prophet Muḥammad from Mecca to Medina. His mother was Asmā' bt. Abī Bakr. His father, al-Zubayr, was a companion of Prophet Muḥammad and Imām 'Alī. 'Abd Allāh b. al-Zubayr was an opportunist and regarded himself as suitable for leadership. His insistence on Imām al-Ḥusayn's leaving Mecca for Iraq was because he did not like Imām al-Ḥusayn as a rival. After the Battle of Karbalā, 'Abd Allāh b. al-Zubayr migrated to Mecca and initiated a movement apparently to take revenge for the martyrdom of Imām al-Ḥusayn; however, he was in fact seeking his own benefits. He took refuge by the Ka'bah, and the Umayyad forces surrounded him and his men there. 'Abd Allāh b. al-Zubayr

was an opponent of the *Ahl al-Bayt*; in consequence, they never trusted him. He died at Mecca in 73 AH/692.

8. Marwān b. al-Ḥakam was born ca. 623, r. 684-5. He was the first of the Marwānid offshoot of the Umayyad dynasty. He was an opponent of the *Ahl al-Bayt* and took side with whoever had the slightest leaning towards the enemies of the *Ahl al-Bayt.* He openly and publicly abused the Shi'i Infallible Imāms. A former Umayyad ruler of Medina, he tried to force al-Walīd b. 'Utba to obtain Imām al-Ḥusayn's oath of allegiance in favour of Yazīd. He was known for his suppression of the Shi'is and the devotees of Imām 'Alī. His short reign was the first step in establishing the Marwānid dynasty.

9. The name is taken from Bāqir Sharīf al-Qarashī, *Ḥayāt al-Imām al-Ḥusayn* (10th ed., 3 vols., Qom, 1427 AH/2006), vol. 2, p. 264.

10. Al-Zarqā' was Marwān's grandmother, a lady of ill fame, sometimes translated as "Son of a blue-eyed woman".

2

In Response to Marwān b. al-Ḥakam

انا لله و انّا اليه راجعون! وعلى الاسلام السلام اذا بليت الامّة براع مثل يزيد ولقد سمعت جدّى رسول الله صلّى الله عليه و اله يقول: الخلافة محرّمة على ال ابى سفيان! فاذا رايتم معاوية على منبرى فابقروا بطنه وقد راه اهل المدينة على المنبر فلم يبقروا، فابتلاهم الله بيزيد الفاسق.

"'Surely we belong to Allāh, and to Him we shall return'. [1] The world of Islam will disappear as soon as the *ummah* is afflicted with such a supporter like Yazīd. And, I have heard from my grandfather, the Messenger of Allāh, [Prophet Muḥammad] who used to remark: 'Caliphate is forbidden to the descendants of Abī Sufyān, so when you notice Mu'āwīya [having ascended] on my minbar, tear his abdomen [i.e. kill him].' However, the inhabitants of Medina have noticed him on the minbar but they never killed him; in consequence, Allāh has afflicted them with Yazīd the Profligate [worse than Mu'āwīya]." [2]

Context

According to Ibn Ṭāwūs, the author of *al-Luhūf*, and other authorities, on the following morning of the night when Imām al-Ḥusayn met Marwān b. al-Ḥakam outside the governor's office, Marwān said: "O Abā 'Abd Allāh! [3] I am your well-wisher and would like to suggest you something which will prove beneficial for you if you accept it."

"Come on with your suggestion," Imām al-Ḥusayn replied.

"As discussed last night in the office of al-Walīd b. 'Utba, you had better take an oath of allegiance with Yazīd; it will be beneficial for both your faith and your worldly life." Marwān remarked.

In response, Imām al-Ḥusayn commented as above.

Two Distinct Functions in the Infallible Imām's Struggles

Once again, this discourse of Imām al-Ḥusayn shows the clarity and candor of his standpoint, it was an open struggle which he persued until the end of his life.

All the Imāms had very distinct and diverse roles in confronting and battling against oppressors and tyrants. It was not only Imām al-Ḥusayn who stood against oppression and struggled against the unjust rulers. Rather all the Infallible Imāms, as supporters of Islam, led such a struggle and resistance in their own times and in their own way. However, the Imāms led two kinds of struggles: covert and overt.

The Covert Struggle

The Imāms chose to avoid open opposition when the current climate overwhelmingly favoured the corrupt leaders. Confronting and fighting the well-organised forces of the enemy under such conditions would result in certain defeat and not bring about any benefit for true Islam in the long run. Rather, it would have resulted in strengthening and maintaining the power of the enemy.

In such conditions, the Infallible Imāms resorted to covert struggle and resistance. That is, while they abstained from resorting to revolutionary actions and armed struggles, they quietly kept true Islam alive, while still being in constant conflict with the tyranical system. The struggles resulted in the Infallible Imāms' being imprisoned, subjected to restrictions, being poisoned, and finally achieving martyrdom.

There were several instances of the Imāms' covert struggle. Among them, there was a strict ban against any relation, inclination, or cooperation with the caliphate orders. Even seeking one's right through them was forbidden. A dialogue between the seventh Imām

Mūsā b. Ja'far [4] and Ṣafwān al-Jammāl [5] is an illustrative example: Ṣafwān had leased his camels out to the courtiers of Hārūn al-Rashīd, the Abbasid ruler, [6] to use for travel to Mecca for the Ḥajj pilgrimage. Imām Mūsā b. Ja'far strongly prohibited Ṣafwān from doing so; Ṣafwān obeyed Imām Mūsā b. Ja'far's command to the degree that he immediately sold all his camels before the courtiers arrived. When the whole affair was reported to Hārūn al-Rashīd, he summoned Ṣafwān and threatened his life for doing so. [7]

Covert struggling had several functions. In addition to weakening the ruling body, some officials learned to abstain from cooperating with the caliphal order, and this method served as an indication for their struggle against the regime in power and the unlawfulness of the administration. In fact, the Infallible Imāms' strategy in resorting to covert struggle informed people of the real face and character of the tyrant caliphs and served as a step toward future resistance as well as overt struggle.

The Overt Struggle

The Imāms always acted in the best interests of Islam and Muslims, so when an overt struggle would render positive and influential results, even if in the distant future, the Imāms entered the arena of overt struggle. In such cases, ignoring the command of the Imām and resorting to covert struggle against the tyrant rulers were regarded as the gravest sin, or even as "Denying and neglecting what Allāh has revealed," as expressed by Imām 'Alī.

The life of Imām al-Ḥusayn displayed both types of struggles manifestly. In the ten-year period from the martyrdom of the second Imām, al-Ḥasan al-Mujtabā, in the year 50 AH/ 669 to the death of Mu'āwīya in 60 AH/ 680, Imām al-Ḥusayn practised a covert struggle. However, the event of Mu'āwīya's death precipitated the conditions for overt struggle. Imām al-Ḥusayn initiated his overt struggle against Yazīd without any hesitation and delay, although some of his relatives and companions had been against this strategy. Despite his limited number of companions and people's disloyalty, unsteadiness, and fear – of which Imām al-Ḥusayn was well aware, he was determined in a way that resulted in his martyrdom. In this way, his body was hit by arrows, spears, and swords. However, the conditions of the time were such that the effects of this sacred blood could not be neglected or ignored, nor could the Umayyad propaganda nullify its effects, despite their attempts.

One might question why Imām al-Ḥusayn had not waged an overt struggle against the leadership at the time of Mu'āwīya's reign. However, the conditions were not appropriate and so his treatment of Mu'āwīya was similar to that of his brother Imām al-Ḥasan al-Mujtabā.

Notes to Chapter 2
In Response to Marwān b. al-Ḥakam

1. The Holy Qur'ān, Sūrah al-Baqara [2]: 156.
2. Ibn Ṭāwūs, *al-Luhūf*, p. 20; Ibn Namā al-Ḥillī, *Muthīr al-Aḥzān*, p. 25; 'Abd Allāh al-Baḥrānī, *Maqtal al-'Awālim*, p. 125; al-Khwārazmī, *Maqtal al-Ḥusayn*, vol. 1, p. 184; and al-Majlisī, ed., *Biḥār al-Anwār*, vol. 44, p. 326.
3. "Abā 'Abd Allāh" is his *kunya*, a filial byname and honourific designation, of Imām al-Ḥusayn,
4. The seventh Imām Mūsā b. Ja'far, known as Imām Mūsā al-Kāẓim (128-183 AH/ 744-799).
5. Ṣafwān b. Mihrān al-Jammāl was a companion of the seventh Imām Mūsā al-Kāẓim.
6. Hārūn al-Rashīd (r. 786-809), the Abbasid ruler who imprisoned Imām Mūsā al-Kāẓim for about seven or fourteen years until the latter was martyred in the Baghdad prison in 183 AH/ 799.
7. Murtaḍā al-Anṣārī, *al-Makāsib*, the chapter on the unlawfulness of cooperating with the tyrants.

3

By the Shrine of His Grandfather (1)

السّلام عليك يا رسول اللهّ! انا الحسين بن فاطمة! فرخك وابن فرختك وسبطك الّذى خلّفتنى فى امّتك فاشهد يا نبىّ اللهّ! انّهم خذلونى ولم يحفظونى وهذه شكواى اليك حتّى القاك ...

"May peace (salām) be bestowed unto you, O Prophet of Allāh. I am al-Ḥusayn, son of Fāṭima; [I am] your grandson and son of your daughter; [I am] your grandson whom you have appointed as your successor [for leadership] of your *ummah*. Bear witness, O Prophet of Allāh, that they [the Umayyads] have indeed weakened me and never considered me [i.e. my spiritual status]. This is my complaint to you until I will come to your presence." [1]

Context

After leaving al-Walīd's office, Imām al-Ḥusayn decided to leave Medina and embark on his everlasting and epic movement.

According to historical records, Imām al-Ḥusayn had the opportunity of paying several ziyārats (pilgrimages) to the shrine of his grandfather, Prophet Muḥammad, before setting out on his journey. Of course, not all of his supplications and communications have been recorded in the accounts; only two of them have been recorded, yet they are clearly indicative of the intent behind his journey. An analysis will be rendered in the next chapter, following Imām al-Ḥusayn's second prayer.

According to al-Khaṭīb al-Khwārazmī, Imām al-Ḥusayn went to the shrine of Prophet Muḥammad soon after he left al-Walīd's office. There he performed his ziyāra as indicated above.

Note to Chapter 3
By the Shrine of His Grandfather (1)

1. Al-Khwārazmī, *Maqtal al-Ḥusayn*, vol. 1, p. 186; ʻAbd Allāh b. Nūr al-Dīn al-Baḥrānī, *Maqtal al-ʻAwālim*, p. 177.

4

By the Shrine of His Grandfather (2)

اللّهمّ! انّ هذا قبر نبيّك محمّد صلّى اللّه عليه و اله وانا ابن بنت نبيّك وقد حضرنى من الا مر ما قد علمت اللّهمّ! انّى احبّ المعروف وانكر المنكر واسالك ياذا الجلال والاكرام! بحقّ القبر ومن فيه الا اخترت لى ما هو لك رضى ولرسولك رضى.

"O Allāh! Indeed this is the tomb of Your Prophet, Muḥammad, (may peace and blessings be upon him and his family), and I am the son of Your Prophet's daughter and, as You know, something has happened to me.

"O Allāh! Indeed I love the good and hate the forbidden. I beseech You, O Lord of Majesty and Honour! By [the honour of] this tomb and the one [buried] herein, provide me with a cause with which You and Your Prophet are delighted."

Context

Before leaving Medina, Imām al-Ḥusayn visited the tomb of his grandfather, Prophet Muḥammad. He performed the ziyāra as cited above.

According to Al-Khwārazmī, Imām al-Ḥusayn spent that night worshiping Allāh and performing prayers by the tomb of Prophet Muḥammad. He was so deeply engrossed in the prayer that the sound of his tears being shed could be heard.

Conclusion

In these ziyāra and supplications, Imām al-Ḥusayn outlined his future cause and the significance of his movement. In his first ziyāra, he expressed his readiness for martyrdom, while stressing on his complaint against the Umayyad rulers, all in a single and short sentence: "This is my complaint to you until I come to your presence."

In the second ziyāra, his discourse is indicative of a significant and critical incident, which he was able to view due to his disposition which was an established part of the Imām's character. Imām al-Ḥusayn had ardent love for goodness and truth, and utter hatred toward evil and injustice taking place at the time. This ardent love and profound resentment – endorsed by Allāh and His Prophet – necessitated his eagerness to give everything he had to establish truth and justice and demolish the basis of evil and inequity, even at the cost of his life.

Note to Chapter 4: By the Shrine of His Grandfather (2)

1. al-Khwārazmī, *Maqtal al-Ḥusayn*, vol. 1, p. 186.

5

In Response to ʿUmar al-Aṭraf

حدّثني ابي انّ رسول الله صلى الله عليه و اله اخبره بقتله وقتلي وانّ تربته تكون بالقرب من تربتي. اتظنّ انّك علمت مالم اعلمه؟ والله! لا اعطي الدّنيّة من نفسي ابدا ولتلقينّ فاطمة اباها شاكية ما لقيت ذرّيّتها من امّته ولا يدخل الجنّة احد اذاها في ذرّيّتها.

"On the authority of Prophet Muḥammad, my father informed me of his martyrdom as well as my own, and that my tomb will be near his. Do you think that I am unaware of what you are informed? Nevertheless, I will never shoulder denigration, and on the Day of Judgment, my mother Fāṭima al-Zahrā will take her complaint to her father concerning the tortures and pressures her children received from the *ummah* of her father. And, whoever has annoyed her by disturbing her descendants, they will never be let into Paradise." [1]

Context

Soon after Imām al-Ḥusayn refused to make an oath of allegiance to Yazīd b. Muʿāwīya and resolutely decided to challenge them and to leave Medina, news spread among the noblemen of his relatives. Some of them, who were uninformed about the duties and responsibilities of Imāmate and leadership, realised that the Imām's life was in danger and out of love went to Imām al-Ḥusayn and suggested that he should compromise with Yazīd. One of such people who met Imām al-Ḥusayn was 'Umar al-Aṭraf, a son of [2]. According to Ibn Ṭāwūs in *al-Luhūf*, he advised Imām al-Ḥusayn in this way:

"O Brother! My brother [Imām] al-Ḥasan al-Mūjtabā related some news from my father 'Alī: 'That the enemies will slay you'. And I suppose your opposition against Yazīd b. Mu'āwīya will result in their killing you, and that piece of news will come true. Nonetheless, if you take the oath of allegiance with Yazīd, this danger will be removed, and you will escape being killed."

In response to his suggestion, Imām al-Ḥusayn's answer was as indicated above.

Conclusion

In this short dialogue, Imām al-Ḥusayn disclosed the knowledge of the certainty of his martrydom, as fortold by their father. He also informed 'Umar al-Aṭraf of the details of his burial site.

Notes to Chapter 5
In Response to 'Umar al-Aṭraf

1. Ibn Ṭāwūs, *al-Luhūf*, p. 23.
2. 'Umar b. 'Alī, commonly known as 'Umar al-Aṭraf, was a son of Imām 'Alī, hence, a step-brother of Imām al-Ḥusayn; his mother's name was Ṣahbā'. Some authorities believe that 'Umar al-Aṭraf refused to help Imām al-Ḥusayn in the Battle of Karbalā, without any excuse. He died at the age of 77.

6

In Response to Lady Umm Salamah

يا امّاه! و انا اعلم انّى مقتول مذبوح ظلما وعدوانا وقد شاء عزّ و جلّ ان يرى حرمى ورهطى مشرّدين واطفالى مذبوحين ماسورين مقيّدين وهم يستغيثون فلا يجدون ناصرا...

"O dear mother! I am aware that I shall be slain out of animosity, and the Almighty [Allāh] has wanted to see my family members dispersed and my children slain and captivated, bound by chains, while they are crying and appealing for help but they do not find any helper." [1]

Context

According to the late Quṭb al-Dīn al-Rāwandī, al-Baḥrānī, and other *hadith* scholars, when Lady Umm Salamah [2] was informed of Imām al-Ḥusayn's departure, she went to him, and said: "Please do not make me gloomy by your departure to Iraq, for I heard from your grandfather, Prophet Muḥammad, who had remarked 'My grandson, al-Ḥusayn, shall be slain in Iraq at a place called Karbalā.'" In response to Lady Umm Salamah, Imām al-Ḥusayn's reply is recorded above.

Imām al-Ḥusayn's Awareness of Future Incidents

According to Imām al-Ḥusayn's replies to 'Umar al-Aṭraf and Lady Umm Salamah as well as other discourses mentioned in this book, Imām al-Ḥusayn was well aware of the afflictions which he and his family and companions would face including his family's captivity and the site of his own tomb.

Imām al-Ḥusayn's knowledge was not only due to his foresight as an Infallible Imām (a doctrinal issue in its own right) but through other channels such as the conversations and reports from his esteemed father and grandfather. Furthermore, some wives and companions of the Prophet were also aware. It was in view of reaching his lofty objective and fulfilling his divine mission, liberating Islam and the Qur'ān, and challenging oppression and cruelty that Imām al-Ḥusayn left Medina and faced all these afflictions knowingly.

As mentioned earlier, Imām al-Ḥusayn's reply to Lady Umm Salamah, related elsewhere with some minor variations, has been quoted in several books of *hadith* and history. [3] It might be the case that all these books have quoted this point from one and the same source which might be subject to some suspicion concerning its authenticity. On the other hand, there is no insistence on the authority of this report, nor can Imām al-Ḥusayn's knowledge of the future incidents be attributed only to this report. This is because the contexts of tens of *hadiths* reported the distressing details of the day of Ashurā from previous prophets as well as Prophet Muḥammad and Imām 'Alī, through Shi'i sources [4] and Sunnite books [5].

Hence the argument that Imām al-Ḥusayn was aware of his martyrdom and the details of the events in Karbalā is not soley based on the above conversation. The inclusion of this conversation is due to the content of the Imām's reply and that they were his exact words.

It is strange to see that an author went to great lengths to show that Imām al-Ḥusayn's conversation with Lady Umm Salamah was invalid and unreliable. He tried hard to regard the text unauthoritative on the basis of the chain of authorities. However, what would be his argument in view of so many other *hadiths*? It is yet uncertain how he could ignore so many other *hadiths*.

The reasons why Imām al-Ḥusayn initiated his movement while he was already informed of his certain martyrdom will be discussed in the following chapters. Also, the meaning of his statement "Allāh wishes to see me slain" will be clarified.

Notes to Chapter 6
In Response to Lady Umm Salamah

1. Quṭb al-Dīn al-Rāwandī, *al-Kharā'ij wa al-Jarā'iḥ*, p. 26; and Sayyid Hāshim al-Baḥrānī, *Madīna al-Ma'ājiz*, p. 244.
2. Lady Umm Salamah, whose name was Hind bt. Abī Umayya, was one of the ladies who migrated to Abyssinia with her first husband, who was injured and then martyred owing to receiving wounds in the Battle of Uḥud (625). Afterwards, she married Prophet Muḥammad and remained loyal to him and his descendants. She was credited with taking care of Imām al-Ḥusayn, too.
3. Al-Rāwandī, *al-Kharā'ij wa al-Jarā'iḥ*, p. 26; al-Baḥrānī, *Madīna al-Ma'ājiz*, p. 244; al-Mas'ūdī, *Ithbāt al-Waṣīyya*, p. 162; and al-Majlisī, ed., *Biḥār al-Anwār*, vol. 44, p. 331.
4. The late al-Majlisī quotes 71 *hadiths* in this regard in his *hadith* compendium *Biḥār al-Anwār*, vol. 44.
5. Al-Amīnī quotes in his *Sīratanā wa Sunnatanā* about 20 *hadiths* from Sunni sources, with ample discussions about their relators and chains of authorities as well as the authenticity of those *hadiths*.

7

In Response to Muḥammad b. al-Ḥanafīyyah

a) يا اخى! لولم يكن فى الدّنيا ملجا ولا ماوى لما بايعت يزيدبن معاوية ...

b) يا اخى! جزاك الله خيرا! لقد نصحت واشرت بالصّواب وانا عازم على الخروج الى مكّة وقد تهيّات لذلك انا و اخوتى وبنو اخى وشيعتى وامرهم امرى ورايهم رايى و امّا انت، فلا، عليك ان تقيم بالمدينة فتكون لى عينا عليهم لا تخفى عنّى شيئا من امورهم.

c)

لا ذعرت السّوام فى فلق الصّبح مغيرا ولا دعيت يزيدا

يوم اعطى مخافة الموت كفّا والمنايا يرصدننى ان احيدا

a) "O Brother! If there would not be any shelter or place of refuge in the world, I would never make the oath of allegiance to Yazīd b. Mu'āwīya." [1]

(b) "O brother! May Allāh reward you abundantly! You have indeed expressed your advice and pointed to the right choice, but I am determined to set out to Mecca, and for this purpose, my followers, nephews, brothers, and I have got ready, their decision is mine, and their opinion is mine. However, you are not like them [in this regard]: you are supposed to stay in Medina so as to remain my eye and/ or reporter over them [the Umayyad agents]: you should not hide any one of their activities from me [you should constantly keep me informed]." [2]

(c) *"I do not care about the shepherds who may attack me in the morning,*
Then I should not be called Yazīd if,
I pledge allegiance lest death,
And keep myself away from the probable dangers." [3]

Context

One of those who was worried about Imām al-Ḥusayn's decision and expressed his anxiety in this regard was Muḥammad b. al-Ḥanafīyyah, a son of Imām 'Alī. [4] According to al-Ṭabarī and other historians, he met Imām al-Ḥusayn and expressed his concern as follows:

"O Brother! You are the most beloved and dearest of people. I ought to convey to you what might prove beneficial for you. I believe you had better, so far as possible, not live at a certain city, rather you and your family must lodge at a place far from Yazīd and these cities. It would be better for you to dispatch from your place of residence some envoys to people and seek their support such that if they have taken oath of allegiance with you, then you would thank Allāh, and if they had taken oath of allegiance with someone else, you would not have received any harm. However, if you come over to these cities, I fear it would result in dispersion amongst people: some people will support you, and some will fight against you, and the whole affair will result in a massacre, meanwhile you will be slain: in that case, the blood of the best person will be wasted in vain and your family will be utterly denigrated."

Upon this statement, Imām al-Ḥusayn enquired which territory would be better for moving to. Muḥammad b. al-Ḥanafīyyah stated: "In my opinion, enter the city of Mecca, and in case there was not security therein, go from one city to another via desert routes so as to observe people and their future situation. With the profound understanding I see in you, I hope you will always come up with the right decision and solve the problems one after another with prudence."

In response to Muḥammad b. al-Ḥanafīyyah, Imām al-Ḥusayn remarked as indicated in (a) above. Thereupon, while Muḥammad b. al-Ḥanafīyyah was shedding tears, Imām al-Ḥusayn continued as indicated in (b) above.

After this conversation with Muḥammad b. al-Ḥanafīyyah, Imām al-Ḥusayn again went to the Prophetic Mosque. Walking toward the Mosque, he recited the lines of the Arab poet Yazīd b. Mufarrigh [5] composed in respect of maintaining his dignity regardless of any danger which may threaten him. This is quoted in (c) above. [6]

Abū Sa'īd al-Muqbirī said that upon hearing Imām al-Ḥusayn's reciting the above verses, Muḥammad b. al-Ḥanafīyyah realised that Imām al-Ḥusayn must be pursuing a sublime aim and a brilliant plan.

Conclusion

In his conversation with Muḥammad b. al-Ḥanafīyyah as well as through the poem of Yazīd b. Mufarrigh, Imām al-Ḥusayn expressed the motive for his uprising, that is, opposing Yazīd b. Mu'āwīya. In the same way, he declared his resolute decision that if there would not be any shelter or refuge for him over the globe, he would never pledge allegiance with Yazīd; in consequence, he would steadfastly resist against any danger in favour of his objective. Such was Imām al-Ḥusayn's sublime aim and eloquent discource recorded in the forms of the conversation and the poems.

Notes to Chapter 7 In Response to Muḥammad b. al-Ḥanafīyyah

1. 'Abd Allāh b. Nūr al-Dīn al-Baḥrānī, *Maqtal al-'Awālim*, p. 54; and al-Khwārazmī, *Maqtal al-Ḥusayn*, vol. 1, p. 188.
2. 'Abd Allāh b. Nūr al-Dīn al-Baḥrānī, *Maqtal al-'Awālim*, p. 54; and al-Khwārazmī, *Maqtal al-Ḥusayn*, vol. 1, p. 188.
3. Al-Ṭabarī, *Ta'rīkh*, Events of the Year 61 AH; and Ibn al-Athīr, *al-Kāmil fī al-Ta'rīkh*, vol. 3, p. 265; and al-Mufīd, *Kitāb al-Irshād*, p. 202.
4. Muḥammad b. al-Ḥanafīyyah was a younger step-brother of Imām al-Ḥusayn. His mother was Khawla bt. Ja'far b. Qays.

Muḥammad b. al-Ḥanafīyyah was a brave man, and participated in the Battles of the Camel and Nahrawān. He passed away during the reign of 'Abd al-Malik the Marwānid in Medina in 81 AH/ 700.

5. Yazīd b. Mufarrigh al-Ḥimyarī (d. *ca.* 69 AH/ 688) was a Shi'i Arab poet who satirized the Umayyad ruler 'Ubayd Allāh b. Zīyād for playing a role in slaying Imām al-Ḥusayn, Hānī b. 'Urwa, and the sons of 'Aqīl b. Abī Ṭālib. It is said that the renowned Shi'i poet Abū Hāshim Ismā'īl b. Muḥammad, better known as al-Sayyid al-Ḥimyarī (105-173 AH/ 694-788) was his decendant.

6. al-Ṭabarī, *Ta'rīkh*, Events of the Year 61 AH; Ibn al-Athīr, *Al-Kāmil fī al-Ta'rīkh*, vol. 3, p. 265. According to Ibn Abī al-Ḥadīd, *Sharḥ Nahj al-Balāgha*, vol. 1, p. 375, these verses were originally composed by Yazīd b. Mufarrigh al-Ḥimyarī.

8

Imām al-Ḥusayn's Last Will and Testament

بسم الله الرّحمن الرّحيم، هذا ما اوصى به الحسين بن علي الى اخيه محمّد بن الحنفيّة انّ الحسين يشهد ان لا اله الا الله وحده لا شريك له وانّ محمّدا عبده ورسوله جاء بالحقّ من عنده وانّ الجنّة حقّ والنّار حق والسّاعة اتيةً لاريب فيها وانّ الله يبعث من فى القبور و انّى لم اخرج اشرا ولا بطرا ولا مفسدا ولا ظالما و انّما خرجت لطلب الاصلاح فى امّة جدّى صلى الله عليه و اله اريد ان امر بالمعروف وانهى عن المنكر واسير بسيرة جدّى وابى على بن ابى طالب فمن قبلنى بقبول الحقّ فالله اولى بالحقّ ومن ردّ علىّ هذا اصبر حتّى يقضي الله بينى وبين القوم وهو خيرالحاكمين وهذه وصيّتى اليك يا اخى وما توفيقى الا بالله عليه توكّلت واليه انيب.

"In the Name of Allāh, the Most Compassionate, the Most Merciful. This is what al-Ḥusayn b. 'Alī has commended to his brother Muḥammad b. al-Ḥanafīyyah [1], that al-Ḥusayn bears witness that there is no deity except Allāh, Who is Unique, with no partner for Him; and that Muḥammad is His servant and messenger, rightly came from His side; and that Paradise is a fact, and Hell is a fact; that the Hour [2] will come, there is no doubt thereof; and because Allāh shall raise those who are in the graves. [3] And, indeed, I have not revolted boisterously, insolently, corruptingly, or oppressively; rather, I have risen up seeking to rectify (the affairs of) the *ummah* of my grandfather [4]: I intend to call for the good and to prohibit committing the undesirable, and to act in accordance with the conduct of my grandfather and father, 'Alī b. Abī Ṭālib. Hence, anybody who accepts this from me, they have already accepted the cause of Allāh; and if nobody answers me in this regard, I shall remain steadfast until Allāh judges between me and the people [5], 'for He is the best of all judges' [6]. And this is my last will and testament to you, my brother. 'And my success is from Allāh alone, in Him I have placed my trust and to Him I turn (repentant)." [7, 8]

Context

Imām al-Ḥusayn wrote the above testamentary bequest at the time of leaving Medina for Mecca, put his seal on it, and gave it to his step-brother Muḥammad b. al-Ḥanafīyyah .

Imām al-Ḥusayn's Motivation for Uprising

In the meeting with al-Walīd b. 'Utba and Marwān b. al-Ḥakam, Imām al-Ḥusayn explained that he would not give allegiance to Yazīd, by saying "Is it fair that such a person like me – with those outstanding background and high family nobility – takes an oath of allegiance with such a profligate?"

Now, at the time of leaving Medina, he indicated another reason for his uprising: calling for the enjoining good and prohibiting the undesirable, that is, challenging against the widespread corruption as well as the anti-Islamic and inhumane characteristics of Yazīd and the Umayyad rulership.

Even if the Umayyads had not tried to force Imām al-Ḥusayn to pay allegiance, he would not have remained silent, for his disagreement with the ruling caliphate was not solely concerned with pledging allegiance to Yazīd as an individual. Rather, Imām al-Ḥusayn objected to the spread of corruption by Yazīd and his dynasty, and deterioration in the Islamic rules away from the Islam of his grandfather, Prophet Muḥammad. Therefore, it was Imām al-Ḥusayn's duty to correct those corruptions and rise up to establish the good and prohibit the undesirable. In this way, he would rise up to enliven justice and to eradicate the root of all of these aberrations, that is, the Umayyad dynasty. He proclaimed that he had never been an opportunist, mercenary, boisterous, tyrant, or ruffian person; this has been the case since the beginning and it lasted conspicuously until the last moment of life in the soul of Imām al-Ḥusayn.

One might question whether commending people to do the good and prohibiting them from evil is required if doing so endangers one's life. The reality is that Imām al-Ḥusayn bravely put this cause above his own safety and the safety of his family and companions. This issue is further explained in Part Two, Chapter 35, of this book.

Notes to Chapter 8 Imām al-Ḥusayn's Last Will and Testament

1. Muḥammad b. al-Ḥanafīyyah was Imām al-Ḥusayn's younger step-brother. For further information, see chapter 7, note 4.
2. "The Hour" means the "Resurrection"
3. The Holy Qur'an, Sūrah al-Ḥajj [22]: 7.
4. "My grandfather" means "Prophet Muḥammad".
5. "The people means" "the Umayyads".
6. This fragment is mentioned in several places in the Holy Qur'ān, e.g., Sūrah al-A'rāf [7]: 87; Sūrah Yūnūs [10]: 109; and Sūrah Yūsuf [12]: 80.
7. The Holy Qur'ān, Sūrah Hūd [11]: 88.
8. al-Khwārazmī, *Maqtal al-Ḥusayn*, vol. 1, p. 188; and 'Abd Allāh b. Nūr al-Dīn al-Baḥrānī, *Maqtal al-'Awālim*, p. 179.

9

Imām al-Ḥusayn's Remark while Departing Medina

a) فخرج منها خائفا يترقّب قال ربّ نجّنى من القوم الظّالمين.

b) لا واللّه! لا افارقه حتّى يقضي الله ما هو قاض

a) "So he went forth from thence, looking fearfully about him, and prayed: 'O my Sustainer! Save me from all evil-doing folk.' "[1]

b) "No, by Allāh! I will not deviate from it [the main route] until Allāh shall determine what He judges." [2]

Context

Unlike Imām al-Ḥusayn who met al-Walīd b. 'Utba when he was summoned and expressed his views openly and frankly, 'Abd Allāh b. al-Zubayr refused to meet al-Walīd and left Medina secretly at nighttime and made a detour to Mecca.

However, Imām al-Ḥusayn set out with his children and family members for Mecca on Sunday, two days before the end of Rajab. While leaving the city of Medina, he recited the above Qur'ānic verse. This verse was revealed in reference to Prophet Mūsa and his readiness to oppose the followers of Pharaoh, indicating that he had left Egypt in a state of fear and agitation.

Unlike 'Abd Allāh b. al-Zubayr, Imām al-Ḥusayn took the same common route which the rest of travelers and caravans took. One of the companions of Imām al-Ḥusayn suggested that he should take a mountainous byway, as 'Abd Allāh b. al-Zubayr did; therefore, there would not be any probable harm to him on the side of Yazīd's agents. In response to this suggestion, Imām al-Ḥusayn's remark was mentioned in (b) above.

In conclusion, it is understood from Imām al-Ḥusayn's reply that he did not leave Medina out of fear, nor to escape. Had it been for this purpose, he could have taken a mountainous byway instead of the normal route, as 'Abd Allāh b. al-Zubayr did. Rather, Imām al-Ḥusayn took the way whereon everybody could see him. He intended to accomplish the Divine mission, that is, embarking on a *jihad* against the Umayyads in a state of freedom and quite peacefully until Allāh would decide on the whole affair.

Notes to Chapter 9
Imām al-Ḥusayn's Remark while Departing Medina

1. The Holy Qur'ān, Sūrah al-Qiṣaṣṣ [28]: 21.
2. Al-Ṭabarī, *Ta'rīkh*, The Events of the Year 61 AH; Ibn al-Athīr, *al-Kāmil,* vol. 3, p. 265; al-Mufīd, *Kitāb al-Irshād,* p. 202; and Al-Khwārazmī, *Maqtal al-Ḥusayn*, vol. 1, p. 189.

10

While Entering Mecca

ولمّا توجّه تلقاء مدين قال عسى ربّى ان يهدينى سواء السّبيل

"And as he turned his face toward Midian, he said [to himself]: 'It may well be that my Sustainer will [thus] guide me unto the Right Path.'" [1]

Context

Having traveled the distance between Medina and Mecca within five days, Imām al-Ḥusayn reached Mecca on the eve of Friday, 3rd Sha'ban 60 AH/680 AD. While entering the city of Mecca, he recited the above Qur'ānic verse. In the same way as when Prophet Mūsa left the followers of Pharaoh and took refuge at the city of Midian [2], he said he wished Allāh would direct him to the Right Path and to the good. [3]

The Significance of the Two Qur'ānic Verses

By reciting these two successive verses [4] within a time span of five days, Imām al-Ḥusayn implied that just as Prophet Mūsa had left his hometown and sought refuge in a strange city for an important aim, he was also pursuing a sublime aim at the time of leaving Medina. In the same way, at the time of entering Mecca, he was in pursuit of a high and noble aim which could not be attained save by the special grace and direction of Allāh. Just as Prophet Mūsa saved the Israelites, Imām al-Ḥusayn would save the Muslim ummah and humanity.

Notes to Chapter 10
While Entering Mecca

1. The Holy Qur'ān, Sūrah al-Qiṣaṣ [28]:22.

2. The Arabic name of Midian is Madyan. "The region of Madyan – the Midian of the Bible – extended from the present-day Gulf of Aqaba westwards deep into the Sinai peninsula and to the mountains of Moab east of the Dead Sea; its inhabitants were Arabs of the Amorite group of tribes." Muḥammad Asad, tr., *The Message of the Qur'an* (1980; Bitton, UK, 2003), p. 246, note 67, under Sūrah al-A'rāf [7]: 85. Another piece of information about Midian reads as follows: "Ancient region of NW Arabian penin[sula], E. of the Gulf of Aqaba and bordered by Edom on the NW; the Midianites of Old Testament times were frequently at war with the Israelites." *Merriam-Webster's Geographical Dictionary*, 3rd ed. (Springfield, MA, 2001) s.v. Midian.

3. Al-Ṭabarī, *Ta'rīkh*, The Events of the Year 61 AH; Ibn al-Athīr, *al-Kāmil fī al-Ta'rīkh*, vol. 3, p. 265; al-Mufīd, *Kitāb al-Irshād*, p. 200; al-Khwārazmī, *Maqtal al-Ḥusayn*, vol. 1, p. 189.

4. The two Qur'ānic verses refer to Sūrah al-Qiṣaṣ [28]: 21-22.

11

In Response to 'Abd Allāh b. 'Umar

يا ابا عبدالرّحمن! اما علمت انّ من هوان الدّنيا على الله انّ راس يحيى بن زكريّا اهدى الى بغي من بغايا بنى اسرائيل؟ اما تعلم ان بنى اسرائيل كانوا يقتلون ما بين طلوع الفجر الى طلوع الشّمس سبعين نبيّا ثمّ يجلسون فى اسواقهم يبيعون ويشترون كان لم يصنعوا شيئا فلم يعجّل الله عليهم بل امهلهم واخذهم بعد ذلك اخذ عزيز ذى انتقام. اتّق الله يا ابا عبدالرّحمن! ولا تدعنّ نصرتى.

"O Abā 'Abd al-Raḥmān, have you not realised that a trait of the despicableness of the world before Allāh is that the head of Yayḥā, son of Zakariyyā, was given as a gift to one of the adulteresses of the Israelites? Do you not know that the Israelites killed seventy prophets at the time between the dawn and sunrise, and then went to their markets and [started] buying and selling [goods] as if they had not committed anything? Allāh never made haste against them, rather He gave them some respite and then got hold of them after that; the grip of a resolute retributive one. Fear Allāh, O Abā 'Abd al-Raḥmān [1], and never deny me your help." [2]

Context

'Abd Allāh b. 'Umar had gone to Mecca on personal business as well as for performing 'Umrah. A few days after Imām al-Ḥusayn's arrival in Mecca, 'Abd Allāh b. 'Umar decided to return to Medina. Upon this decision, he went to Imām al-Ḥusayn and suggested that he come to a compromise and pledge allegiance to Yazīd; he also warned Imām al-Ḥusayn of the risky and critical consequence of opposing the tyrant Yazīd, and initiating any war.

According to al-Khwārazmī, 'Abd Allāh b. 'Umar said: "O Abā 'Abd Allāh! As the people have already pledged allegiance with this fellow [Yazīd], and he has got hold of all the financial resources and power, they will be naturally inclined to him. And, as his family – the Umayyads – have a long hostility against you, I fear that you will be martyred upon opposing him, hence a group of Muslims will be slain too. I did hear Prophet Muḥammad saying, 'Al-Ḥusayn will be slain, and if people leave him alone, they will be receiving denigration and humiliation.' Therefore, my suggestion to you, the same as all other people's, is to pledge allegiance [to Yazīd] and be scared of causing the blood of Muslims to be shed!" [3]

As Imām al-Ḥusayn was considerate towards the capacity of understanding of the person he was speaking with, he formulated his response according to their level of understanding and appreciation. Hence, in response to 'Abd Allāh b. 'Umar, he gave the response cited above in the beginning of the chapter.

According Sheikh al-Ṣadūq [4], when 'Abd Allāh b. 'Umar found out that his suggestion to Imām al-Ḥusayn had proved futile, he said: "O Abā 'Abd Allāh! At this time of separation I wish to kiss that part of your body which Prophet Muḥammad used to kiss a lot." Upon such a request, Imām al-Ḥusayn pulled up his garment and 'Abd Allāh b. 'Umar kissed three times a spot just under his chest. Having done this and while shedding tears, he said: "I leave you in Allāh's care and bid farewell to you, for you shall be slain in this journey."[5]

The Profile of 'Abd Allāh b. 'Umar

It is timely to get to know more about the real face and profile of 'Abd Allāh b. 'Umar. He was such a person that suggested Imām al-Ḥusayn should reach a compromise and agreement with Yazīd b. Mu'āwīya, quite hypocritically kissed Imām al-Ḥusayn's chest, shed tears for him, and left him alone. It is certain that he had heard from Prophet Muḥammad that Imām al-Ḥusayn would be slain in the cause of the Qur'ān and anybody who abandons helping him, they would certainly be denigrated and humiliated. Despite Imām al-Ḥusayn's open remark: "Fear Allāh, O Abā 'Abd al-Raḥmān, and never deny me your help!", he not only refused to help him but set out for Medina and announced his loyalty to Yazīd.

It is appropriate at this point to discuss the real character of 'Abd Allāh b. 'Umar. Such knowledge helps us identify other people similar to him who, instead of helping Imām al-Ḥusayn, hypocritically shed tears and moan and perhaps, quite secretly, signed treaties of cooperation with Yazīd and other unjust rulers.

'Abd Allāh b. 'Umar's Opposition against Imām 'Alī

After 'Uthmān was murdered, all the Muslims in Medina rushed willingly to Imām 'Alī to pledge allegiance to him, except for seven people who refused to do so. 'Abd Allāh b. 'Umar was one of them. He stressed that he wished to be the last Muslim pledging allegiance to Imām 'Alī.

Mālik b. al-Ḥārith al-Ashtar al-Nakha'ī approached Imām 'Alī and said: "Since he – 'Abd Allāh b. 'Umar – is not scared of your whip and sword, he brings this excuse; shall we force him to pledge allegiance?" Thereupon, Imām 'Alī replied that he would not force anybody to pledge allegiance, and let 'Abd Allāh b. 'Umar make his own choice.

'Abd Allāh b. 'Umar took action. The next day Imām 'Alī was informed that 'Abd Allāh b. 'Umar had gone to Mecca to plot against him to overthrow his administration. Upon this news, Imām 'Alī dispatched a person to stop his anti-governmental activities. At last, 'Abd Allāh b. 'Umar returned to Medina without any gain, and never recognised Imām 'Alī's administration, nor pledged allegiance to him. [6] However, after Imām 'Alī's martyrdom, he pledged allegiance with Mu'āwīya and recognised his ruling. Such was 'Abd Allāh b. 'Umar's treatment and behaviour with such a noble personality like Imām 'Alī as well as his administration and at the same time his allegiance to Mu'āwīya and his recognition of Mu'āwīya's ruling.

'Abd Allāh b. 'Umar and his Allegiance to Yazīd

When Mu'āwīya was seeking people's allegiance in favour of Yazīd, 'Abd Allāh b. 'Umar joined the opponents and dissidents. However, neither Mu'āwīya nor Yazīd cared about his opposition. Once while talking about the opponents, Mu'āwīya expressed thus: "As for 'Abd Allāh b. 'Umar, although he has refused to pledge allegiance, he is still on your [Yazīd's] side, hence value him, and never detract him."

According to Mu'āwīya's anticipation, 'Abd Allāh b. 'Umar's opposition regarding pledging allegiance to Yazīd never harmed him. Rather, he later on showed yet the greatest and most significant support toward Yazīd: Just when he was expected to join the ranks of Imām al-Ḥusayn's movement, he suggested Imām al-Ḥusayn reach a compromise with Yazīd to strengthen the foundations of Yazīd's rulership. And, when his attempts resulted in vain, he bid farewell to Imām al-Ḥusayn, went back to Medina, and wrote a letter to Yazīd b. Mu'āwīya in which he declared his loyalty with sincerity. [7] He was very staunch in his allegiance to Yazīd. When the inhabitants of Medina reacted against Yazīd b. Mu'āwīya's rulership after the tragic martyrdom of Imām al-Ḥusayn and expelled the governor, 'Uthmān b. Muḥammad, from Medina, 'Abd Allāh b. 'Umar gathered his closest friends and children and said: "I heard the Prophet saying, 'A flag will be fixed for every betrayer on the Day of Resurrection', we have given the oath of allegiance to this person (Yazīd) in accordance with the conditions enjoined by Allāh and His Apostle. I do not know of anything more faithless than fighting a person who has been given the oath of allegiance in accordance with the conditions enjoined by Allāh and His Apostle, and if ever I get informed that any person among you has agreed to dethrone Yazīd, by giving the oath of allegiance (to somebody else), then there will be separation between him and me.' " [8]

'Abd Allāh b. 'Umar and al-Ḥajjāj b. Yūsuf

After Yazīd b. Mu'āwīya, 'Abd al-Malik b. al-Marwān became the caliph. He dispatched al-Ḥajjāj b. Yūsuf to Mecca to suppress 'Abd Allāh b. al-Zubayr who had initiated a revolt in Medina. On the way to Mecca, al-Ḥajjāj b. Yūsuf entered Medina. Thereupon, 'Abd Allāh b. 'Umar rushed to al-Ḥajjāj at night time to pledge allegiance to him, and said: "O Amir! Give me your hand to pledge allegiance in favour of the caliph."

Upon this urgent hurry, al-Ḥajjāj enquired of the reason for 'Abd Allāh b. 'Umar's restless rush, while he could postpone it to the following day. 'Abd Allāh b. 'Umar replied: "Because I heard Prophet Muḥammad saying 'Anybody who dies without having chosen an imām and/or a leader, they have indeed died like the people in the Jāhiliyya period'.[9] Hence I have been anxious that I might die at night time and because of not having had an imām (a leader), I might be one of those described so by the Prophet; therefore, I would be regarded as a dead person in the Jāhiliyya period."

Upon hearing this, al-Ḥajjāj stretched his leg out of the blanket and said: "Kiss my foot instead of my hand." (It implied that you recount this *hadith* of Prophet Muḥammad, while you were so oblivious of it in the time of Imām 'Alī and Imām al-Ḥusayn.) [10]

This is the significance of the sentence Imām al-Ḥusayn quoted from Prophet Muḥammad, that is, abstention from helping Imām al-Ḥusayn would lead to denigration and humiliation.

Conclusion

History gives us a clear example in 'Abd Allāh b. 'Umar . He did not give allegiance to a noble leader like Imām 'Alī, but pledged his allegiance to Mu'āwīya and Yazīd. Furthermore, his arrogance did not allow him to help Imām al-Ḥusayn, resulting in his going to al-Ḥajjāj in humiliating circumstances.

Those that turn away from the Imāms despite knowing that they are the rightful leaders must realise that they will certainly receive their punishments. The covert conspiracies of the Umayyads to achieve their goals were effective only by means of portraying 'Abd Allāh b. 'Umar as a *hadith* copyist and an expert in the realm of *hadith* scholarship in Islam. [11]

Two Noteworthy Points in the Conversation Between Imām al-Ḥusayn and 'Abd Allāh b. 'Umar.

There are two points worth highlighting in the conversation between Imām al-Ḥusayn and 'Abd Allāh b. 'Umar. First, Imām al-Ḥusayn made reference to Prophet Yaḥyā being slain and that his severed head was sent as a gift to a criminal. This is frequently cited in the literature, the Imām had also made several references to his grave and bitter crime throughout his journey. No doubt, it was no accident that Imām al-Ḥusayn mentioned the case of the Prophet Yaḥyā: there was some similarity between Imām al-Ḥusayn's movement and struggle on the one hand, and Prophet Yaḥyā's struggles, on the other hand, so that Imām al-Ḥusayn referred to that bitter tragedy.

The second point concerns 'Abd Allāh b. 'Umar's expression. When he was leaving Imām al-Ḥusayn, he said, "O Abā 'Abd Allāh! May Allāh protect you; you will be slain in this way." There are a few questions related to this case, namely, how did 'Abd Allāh b. 'Umar know that the Imām would be slain? Is it possible that he would know this without Imām al-Ḥusayn knowing this and being aware of all the details?

This reinforces the argument put forward in the previous pages, that in addition to his divine knowledge through Imāmate [12], Imām al-Ḥusayn was well-informed of the details of his death and the suffering of his family and companions in advance through ordinary channels and the reports he received, both directly and indirectly, from Prophet Muḥammad.

Notes to Chapter 11
In Response to 'Abd Allāh b. 'Umar

1. Abā 'Abd al-Raḥhmān was a *kunya*, a respectful filial byname, of 'Abd Allāh b. 'Umar (d. 77 AH/ 696). 'Abd Allāh b. 'Umar who was born in the third year after the Prophethood of Prophet Muḥammad. He died at the age of 87 at Mecca. (M.-B. Pour-Amini, *Chehreha dar Ḥemāseh-ye Karbalā* [Qom, 1382 Sh/ 2002], pp. 245-249.)

2. Ibn Ṭāwūs, *al-Luhūf*, p. 26; and Ibn Namā al-Ḥillī, *Muthīr al-Aḥzān*, p. 20.

3. Al-Khwārazmī, *Maqtal al-Ḥusayn*, vol. 1, p. 190.

4. Sheikh al-Ṣadūq = Muḥammad b. 'Alī b. al-Ḥusayn b. Mūsā b. Bābawayh al-Qummī, known as Sheikh al-Ṣadūq (d. 381 AH/991), was a distinguished Shi'i scholar. Al-Ṣadūq authored

around 300 books most of which have long been extinct. His works are regarded as the most trustworthy writings. For a detailed biography of al-Ṣadūq, see his volume, *Kitīb al-Hidāya* (2nd ed.; [Qom, 1384 Sh/ 1426AH/ 2005], pp. 34-230).

5. Sheikh al-Ṣadūq, *al-Amālī,* Session 20.

6. Ibn Abī al-Ḥadīd, *Sharḥ Nahj al-Balāgha*, vol. 4, pp. 9-11.

7. *Fatḥ al-Bārī'*, vol. 13, p. 60.

8. Muḥammad b. Ismā'īl al-Bukhārī, *Ṣaḥīḥ al-Bukhārī,* vol. 9, Kitāb al-Fitan, *hadith* No. 6,694. This English translation was taken from *The Translation of the Meanings of Ṣaḥīḥ al-Bukhārī, Arabic- English*, 4th ed., tr. Muḥammad Muhsin Khan, vol. 9 (Beirut: 1405 AH/ 1985), pp. 175- 176, *hadith* No. 227.

9. The Arabic word *jāhiliyya* 'Ignorance' refers to the pre-Islamic Arabia, characterised by public ignorance, tribal wars, false values, beliefs, and paganism. The word *jāhiliyya* appears four times in the Holy Qur'ān, 3:154; 5:50; 33:33; and 48:26. The *jāhiliyya* period ended with the advent of Islam; however, some Arabs, especially the opponents of Prophet Muḥammad and the Infallibles, were still loyal to its beliefs and customs. Although the *jāhiliyya* period was largely characterised by tribal wars, bloodshedding, and other types of individual and social corruption, there existed some admirable and positive practices, e.g., fulfilling one's promises and stopping wars in honourable 'ḥarām' months.

10. Ibn Abī al-Ḥadīd, *Sharḥ Nahj al-Balāgha,* vol. 13, p. 242.

11. It is because of this phenomenon that in the *Musnad* of Aḥmad b. Ḥanbal, the greatest Sunni *hadith* collection, there are over 1,700 *hadiths* related from 'Abd Allāh b. 'Umar, while there are only six *hadiths* related from the two beloved grandsons of Prophet Muḥammad, viz., Imām al-Ḥasan and Imām al-Ḥusayn.

12. Knowledge through Imāmate refers to the knowledge an Infallible Imām has such that his anticipation is always correct on the basis of very sound piece of knowledge.

12

A Letter to the Hāshimids

بسم الله الرّحمن الرّحيم من الحسين بن علىّ الى محمّد بن علي ومن قبله من بنى هاشم،امّا بعد: فانّ من لحق بي استشهد ومن تخلّف لم يدرك الفتح، والسّلام.

"In the Name of Allāh, the All-Compassionate, the All-Merciful. (This is a letter) from al-Ḥusayn b. 'Alī to Muḥammad b. 'Alī [1] and through him to the Hāshimids [who are with him] [2]. Any of you who joins me will be martyred, and those who turned away have not attained the victory. Peace be with you." [3, 4]

Context

There are some interesting points in this short letter. Ibn Ṭāwūs quoted it from al-Kulaynī that Imām al-Ḥusayn issued this letter when he had set out from Mecca [5]. Ibn 'Asākir and al-Dhahabī confirm the views of Ibn Qūlawayh and add that after this letter reached Medina, some descendants of 'Abd al-Muṭṭalib (the Hāshimids) set out to Mecca to join Imām al-Ḥusayn. Muḥammad b. al-Ḥanafīyyah joined them in Mecca, too. [6])

Conclusion

Imām al-Ḥusayn was certain of his own martrydom as well as those who would join him. Furthermore, he was not aiming for any overt victory for himself, the circumstances showed no sign of resulting in an apparent victory or taking over the power for any of the Hāshimids or his family members, dethroning the Umayyad dynasty, or making a radical change. At the same time, he was confident that the ultimate triumph, with everlasting effects was dependent on his as well as his companions' martyrdom and the captivity of his family members.

Notes to Chapter 12
A Letter to the Hāshimids

1. Muḥammad b. al-Ḥanafīyyah was a step-brother of Imām al-Ḥusayn; his father was Imām 'Alī, and his mother was Khawla, daughter of Ja'far b. al-Qays of al-Ḥanafīyyah clan, hence referred to as Muḥammad b. al-Ḥanafīyyah.
2. The Arabic text contains the phrase *ammā ba'd*, which literally means "but then" and is a "phrase of transition from the beginning of a letter, and so on, to the chief matter." It has no equivalent in English.
3. The Arabic phrase *wa al-salām* marks the end of a letter or any written discourse. It has no equivalent in English.
4. Ibn Qūlawayh al-Qummī, ed., *Kāmil al-Zīyārāt*, p. 76.
5. Ibn Ṭāwūs, *al-Luhūf*, p.25. Also, in the text of the letter, as indicated in *al-Luhūf*, *Lam yablugh al-fatḥ* (has not achieved the victory) appears instead of *Lam yudrik al-fathḥ* (has not attained the victory).
6. See the section "al-Ḥusayn b. 'Alī", in Ibn 'Asākir's *al-Ta'rīkh*, and al-Dhahabī's *Ta'rīkh al-Islam*, vol. 2, p. 343.

13

Imām al-Ḥusayn b. ʻAlī's Letter to the Inhabitants of Baṣrah

امّا بعد: فانّ اللّه اصطفى محمّدا صلّى اللّه عليه و اله من خلقه واكرمه بنبوّته واختاره لرسالته ثمّ قبضه اليه وقد نصح لعباده وبلّغ ما ارسل به وكنّا اهله واولياءه واوصياءه وورثته واحقّ الناس بمقامه فى النّاس فاستاثر علينا قومنا بذلك فرضينا وكرهنا الفرقة واحببنا العافية ونحن نعلم انّا احقّ بذلك الحقّ المستحقّ علينا ممّن تولاه وقد بعثت رسولى اليكم بهذا الكتاب وانا ادعوكم الى كتاب اللّه وسنّة نبيّه فانّ السّنّة قد اميتت والبدعة قد احييت فان تسمعوا قولى اهدكم الى سبيل الرّشاد والسّلام عليكم ورحمةاللّه وبركاته.

"Now, Allāh selected [the Prophet] Muḥammad – May Allāh bestow His grace unto him and his progeny – from among the people and honoured him with His prophethood and appointed him for His apostleship. And after he had done his prophetic duty well and directed the people to Allāh, He took him to Himself (made him pass away). And, we have been his family members, associates, vicegerents, and heirs. And we have been the most rightful of the people to attain his [the Prophet's] post."

"However, some people usurped this right from us, but we gave consent, for we disliked division and favored public welfare. And, we know that we are indeed more deserving over this right than those who have gained it. I have already dispatched my envoy to you with this letter and invite you to the Book of Allāh and His Prophet's way (*sunnah*); for the *sunnah* has diminished and heresy has been restored.

Hence, if you listen to me, I shall direct you to the Path of Felicity. And, may salām be unto you and the Mercy and Grace of Allāh be with you all." [1]

Context

According to al-Ṭabarī's *Ta'rīkh*, Imām al-Ḥusayn issued the above letter to the heads of the tribes of Baṣrah, namely, Mālik b. Musmā' al-Bakrī, Mas'ūd b. 'Amr, al-Mundhir b. al-Jārūd, and others. Imām al-Ḥusayn gave the above letter to Sulaymān [2] to deliver it to the people of Baṣrah. Having accomplished his mission and delivered the letter to its recipients, Sulaymān was arrested. He was hung on the order of 'Ubayd Allāh b. Zīyād just one day before he departed for al-Kūfa.

Two Important Observations

In this letter, Imām al-Ḥusayn addressed a number of issues: he asked the people of Baṣrah to cooperate with him to oppose the anti-Islamic and anti-Qur'ānic atmosphere, he affirmed the status of the *Ahl al-Bayt*, and explained the divergence of the case of caliphate with regard to the ongoing struggle.

He also explained the reason for the *Ahl al-Bayt*'s silence in one period by saying "we gave consent, for we disliked division", but that in this situation maintaining that stance would not prove effective, as the enemies, hypocrites, and opportunists would benefit from his silence for their own purposes.

The situation at the time of the previous caliphs was so delicate that the *Ahl al-Bayt* had to oppose the leadership covertly to prevent a lot of hazardous plots and riots from taking place. In this way, they guided the Muslims to intellectual growth and progression through disseminating knowledge amongst them. However, at the time of Imām al-Ḥusayn's revolution another situation emerged, which was that Islam was not only on the wrong track, but it was heading for deterioration, hence Imām al-Ḥusayn's statement: "the *sunnah* has diminished and heresy has been restored."

The laws levied by Prophet Muḥammad had already diminished, and heresy and egocentrism had taken their place. Thus, the condition were ripe for fighting corruption. In other words, it would take the heinous murder of the grandson of the Prophet and his noble companions for the people to realise the extent of corruption the ummah had decended to. The enemy could not take advantage of the situation for its own ends and so the revolution could commence.

Notes to Chapter 13
Imām al-Ḥusayn b. 'Alī's
Letter to the Inhabitants of Baṣrah

1. Al-Ṭabarī, *Ta'rīkh*, The Events of the Year 61 AH.

2. Sulaymān b. Razīn, or Sulaymān whose *kunya* was Abā Razīn, was a servant of Imām al-Ḥusayn. When he arrived at Baṣrah, and passed on Imām al-Ḥusayn's letter to the great men of Baṣrah, the addressees of the letter concealed it from 'Ubayd Allāh b. Zīyād, then the governor of Baṣrah, except al-Mundhir b. al-Jārūd al-'Abdī who was 'Ubayd Allāh b. Zīyād's father-in-law and reported this event to him. Although 'Ubayd Allāh b. Zīyād had just been appointed to his new post, as the governor of al-Kūfa, he ordered Sulaymān b. al-'Awf al-Ḥaḍramī to behead Imām al-Ḥusayn's envoy Sulaymān.

14

Imām al-Ḥusayn's Letter in Response to the Letters of the Kūfans

بسم اللّٰه الرّحمن الرّحيم ، من الحسين بن علي الى الملا من المؤمنين والمسلمين،
امّا بعد؛ فانّ هانيا وسعيدا قدما علىّ بكتبكم وكانا اخر من قدم علىّ من رسلكم
وقد فهمت كلّ الّذى قصصتم و ذكرتم و مقالة جلّكم انّه ليس علينا امام فاقبل.
لعل اللّٰه يجمعنا بك على الهدى و الحقّ. و قد بعثت اليكم اخى وابن عمىّ و
ثقتى من اهل بيتى وامرته ان يكتب الىّ بحالكم وامركم ورايكم فان كتب انه
قد اجتمع راي ملاءكم وذوى الفضل والحجى منكم على مثل ما قدم علىّ به
رسلكم وقرات فى كتبكم اقدم عليكم وشيكا ان شاء اللّٰه. فلعمرى ما الامام الا
العامل بالكتاب والا خذ بالقسط والدّائن بالحقّ والحابس نفسه على ذات اللّٰه
والسّلام.

"In the Name of Allāh, the All-Compassionate, the All-Merciful [This is a letter] from al-Ḥusayn b. 'Alī to the noblemen of the believers and Muslims. With regard to our subject matter: indeed Hānī [1] and Sa'īd [2] have come to me with your letters, and have been the last people who have come to me with your letters. I understand that all of you have indicated and mentioned in your remark that 'There is no imām for us, so hurry up, perhaps Allāh may direct us to the direct path and the right because of you.' Hence, I have dispatched to you my brother [in faith], cousin, and the reliable person from my family members [3]; I have ordered him to write to me about your situation, affairs, and point of view. Hence, if he reports to me the same view that your noblemen, learned, and intellectual people have written to me that I read in your letters, then I will rush to you Insh'Allāh as soon as possible. By my life, [4] the Imām cannot be but one who puts the Book [of Allāh] [5] into practice [6], is passionate about social justice [7], is devoted to the right, and has devoted everything for the sake of Allāh. Peace be with you."

Context

As soon as the inhabitants of al-Kūfa were informed about Imām al-Ḥusayn's opposition to pledging allegiance [to Yazīd], his readiness to confront corruption, and his decision to enter al-Kūfa, they started dispatching several envoys to him, together with many letters and scrolls whose content were as follows:

"Now that Mu'āwīya has perished, and the Muslims have got rid of him, we find ourselves in need of an imām and a leader who would rescue us from agitation and anxiety and to lead our wrecked ship to the shore of survival. We have now opposed al-Nu'mān b. Bashīr, Yazīd's governor, and have cut any relation with him; we have not recently been attending his Friday prayer [8]. We are now eagerly waiting for your arrival and shall devote our utmost to support your strategy to attain your aims. We shall not fall short of devoting our properties and lives to your cause. "[9]

In response to such requests as the one just mentioned above, Imām al-Ḥusayn issued the above letter. According to al-Ṭabarī [10] and al-Dīnawarī [11], Imām al-Ḥusayn dispatched his letter to them by Hānī [12] and Sa'īd [13], two couriers who were from al-Kūfa. However, al-Khwārazmī maintains that Imām al-Ḥusayn entrusted Muslim b. 'Aqīl to take the letter there. Furthermore, Imām al-Ḥusayn addressed him thus: "I dispatch you to al-Kūfa, and may Allāh make you successful in accomplishing whatever He pleases. Set out and may Allāh support you! I hope you and I will achieve the status of the martyrs." [14]

Conclusion

In this letter, Imām al-Ḥusayn positively answered the request of the inhabitants of al-Kūfa and dispatched his delegate there as his own brother [in faith] and trustee. Additionally, Imām al-Ḥusayn explained, quite expressly, the characteristics of the imām and the fair leader whom every Muslim must obey, as a person whose concern must be acting in accordance with the Book of Allāh – the Holy Qur'ān – and his aim must be practicing justice and he must be determined to devote himself to the cause of Allāh.

Notes to Chapter 14 Imām al-Ḥusayn's Letter in Response to the Letters of the Kūfans

1. Hānī b. Abī Hānī al-Subay'ī was a prominent figure who later joined the Tawwābūn [Penitents'] Movement.
2. Sa'īd b. 'Abd Allāh al-Ḥanafī was an Ashurā martyr who carried Imām al-Ḥusayn's letter to al-Kūfa.
3. Muslim b. 'Aqīl
4. A mode of expressing a swear or an oath in Arabic.
5. The Holy Qur'ān.
6. He practices the percepts indicated in the Holy Qur'ān.
7. The Arabic term used is *qisṭ*, a Qur'ānic concept.
8. Friday prayers have a religious and political significance in Islam.
9. Al-Ṭabarī, *al-Ta'rīkh*, The Events of the Year 61 AH; Ibn al-Athīr, *al-Kāmil*, vol. 3, p. 267; al-Mufīd, *Kitāb al-Irshād*, p. 204; al-Khwārazmī, *al-Maqtal*, vol. 1, p. 195.
10. Al-Ṭabarī, *al-Ta'rīkh*, The Events of the Year 61 AH.
11. Al-Dīnawarī, *al-Akhbār al-Ṭuwāl*, p. 238.
12. Op. cit., note 1.
13. Op. cit., note 2.
14. Al-Khwārazmī, *Maqtal al-Ḥusayn*, vol. 1, p. 196.

15

A Letter to Muslim b. 'Aqīl

امّا بعد: فقد خشيت ان لا يكون حملك على الكتاب الىّ فى الاءستعفاء من الوجه الّذى وجّهتك له الا الجبن فامض بوجهك الّذى وجّهتك فيه والسّلام.

"Now to our subject matter: I wonder if feeling scared was the reason [for you] to resign from the mission I have appointed you to accomplish, so go for the mission I entrusted you for. Peace be with you." [1]

Context

In the middle of the month of Ramadan 60 AH/680, [2] Muslim b. 'Aqīl left Mecca for al-Kūfa at the behest of Imām al-Ḥusayn. On the way to al-Kūfa, he entered Medina and had a short stay there. Having visited the tomb of Prophet Muḥammad as well as his relatives, he set out to al-Kūfa together with two guides from the al-Qays tribe. Having left Medina, they lost their way and knew no way to cross the large and sand-covered desert of Hejaz.

After the two guides lost their lives because of sweltering heat and intense thirst, Muslim b. 'Aqīl was lucky to reach a place called al-Maḍīq where some Arab nomads were residing. In this way, he survived.

Having reached al-Maḍīq, Muslim wrote a letter to Imām al-Ḥusayn and sent it through the agency of a man from the same tribe. In the letter Muslim gave an account of the accident, the two guides' death, and his survival. Additionally, he enquired Imām al-Ḥusayn to reconsider dispatching him to al-Kūfa and, if he would regard it suitable, to dispatch someone else to carry out the same task, for he then regarded it as an unauspicious event as well as an unfortunate one. At the end of his letter, Muslim indicated that he would stay there until he receives Imām al-Ḥusayn's reply. [3] Upon receiving the letter, Imām al-Ḥusayn issued the above letter.

Fear and Feeling Scared

It is understood from this encouraging discourse of Imām al-Ḥusayn that not only must such a leader like Imām al-Ḥusayn – who intended to make a radical and profound change to the Muslim community – not feel fearful of anything, but his associates and delegates must also have courage. Otherwise, such a leader's movement will collapse and its mission would not be accomplished.

Imām al-Ḥusayn was not scared of the enemy's forces or weapons, rather he was concerned with any probable weakness which might occur from *his* envoy and delegate.

Notes to Chapter 15
A Letter to Muslim b. 'Aqīl

1. Al-Ṭabarī, *al-Ta'rīkh*, The Events of the Year 61 AH; al-Mufīd, *Kitāb al-Irshād*, p. 204; and al-Khwārazmī, *Maqtal al-Ḥusayn*, vol. 1, p. 196.
2. Al-Mas'ūdī, *Murūj al-Dhahab*, vol. 2, p. 86.
3. Al-Ṭabarī, *al-Ta'rīkh*, The Events of the Year 61 AH.

16

Imām al-Ḥusayn's Sermon in Mecca

الحمدللّه وماشاءاللّه ولا قوّة الا باللّه وصلّى اللّه على رسوله، خطّ الموت على ولد ادم مخطّ القلادة على جيد الفتاة وما اولهنى الى اسلافى اشتياق يعقوب الى يوسف وخيّر لى مصرعا انا لاقيه كانّى باوصالى تتقطّعها عسلان الفلوات بين النّواويس وكربلا فيملانّ منّى اكراشا جوفا واجربة سغبا لامحيص عن يوم خطّ بالقلم. رضا اللّه رضانا اهل البيت نصبر على بلائه ويوفّينا اجورالصّابرين. لن تشذّ عن رسول اللّه لحمته بل هى مجموعة له فى حظيرة القدس تقرّبهم عينه وينجزبهم وعده. الا ومن كان فينا باذلا مهجته موطّنا على لقاء اللّه نفسه فليرحل معنا فانّى راحل مصبحا ءانشاء اللّه .

"All Praise is due to Allāh, and [there is nothing] except what Allāh wishes, and there is no Power except through Allāh, and may Allāh bestow grace on His Apostle [Prophet Muḥammad].

Death has been destined for the descendants of Adam like a necklace on the neck of young girls. My passion to be reunited with my ancestors is like that of Ya'qūb for Yūsuf. And, there has been a battlefield [determined for me] whereto I am moving as if my body organs are being severed by desert wolves between Nawāwīs [1] and Karbalā so that they will fill their empty bellies with my flesh; there is no escape from a day destined. Whatever pleases Allāh also pleases us, the *Ahl al-Bayt*. We are patient over His tests and He shall grant us the rewards of those who are patient. The Prophet's relatives will not get separated from him, rather they shall be gathered before his presence in Paradise; they are his hopes and his promises will be fulfilled by them. Beware that whoever is willing to sacrifice his blood for us in the cause of Allāh, they must accompany us, for I will set off tomorrow morning, Insh'Allāh." [2]

Context

As the Ḥajj days were approaching, the pilgrims of the sacred House of Allāh were entering Mecca. Around the beginning of Dhu al-Ḥijja, Imām al-Ḥusayn was informed that 'Amr b. Sa'īd b. al-'Āṣ [3] had already entered Mecca to accomplish an abhorrent mission. He was ordered by Yazīd to assassinate Imām al-Ḥusayn wherever he found him. Consequently, Imām al-Ḥusayn decided to leave Mecca so that the sanctity and divine security of Mecca would not be compromised. In doing so, his decision was to change his Ḥajj intention and rituals to that of an individual 'Umrah and to leave Mecca on Tuesday 8th Dhu al-Hijja. However, before setting out, Imām al-Ḥusayn delivered the above sermon.

Conclusion

In this sermon, Imām al-Ḥusayn informed his companions expressly of his own martyrdom to ensure that they were ready for such a mission to sacrifice their blood in the cause of the Qur'ān and to attain meeting Allāh.

Why Accept Martyrdom Knowingly?

A question that is often asked in connection to Imām al-Ḥusayn's struggle concerns his awareness of his own martyrdom: What does accepting martyrdom with awareness mean? Is it not obligatory to save one's own life, particularly that of an Infallible Imām?

The answers to the above questions are as follows: *Jihad* is one of the most significant commandments of Islam, and martyrdom is an honour for any Muslim. There are tens of verses in the Holy Qur'ān about *jihad* and martyrdom, [4] none of which make it dependent on some knowledge gained in advance. Nevertheless, battling and sacrificing one's life against the enemies of Islam has been credited with being a trait of the believers. The Holy Qur'ān is explicit: "Indeed Allāh has bought the souls and possessions of the faithful in exchange for a promise of Paradise. They fight in the cause of Allāh, and kill and are killed. This is a promise incumbent on Him, as indicated in the Torah, so in the Gospel and in the Qur'ān. And who is more true to one's promise than Allāh? So rejoice at the bargain you have made with Him; for this will be a triumph supreme." [5]

The above verse describes the sacrificing believers with nine qualities: "To those who repent and pay homage, give praise and are devout, who kneel in prayer and bow in supplication, who enjoin good deeds and prohibit the undesirable, and keep to the limits set by Allāh, announce the news of rejoicing to the faithful." [6] Such faithful people are indeed guardians of the rules and regulations devised by Allāh; the nature of this guardianship is in such a way that it leads them to the level of sacrificing their lives. As before, in this very verse, just like other verses about *jihad*, there is no stipulation about gaining wordly victory.

The life of Prophet Muḥammad serves as a good example. He participated in brutal battles and fought very strong and mighty enemies. He sometimes lost some of his dearest relatives. Hence, *jihad* and martyrdom would have lost their significance if victory was a condition of the battle.

Defending Islam is the duty of all Muslims. Since *jihad* in the cause of Allāh is the responsibility of each and every Muslim, it is more critical for the Infallible Imām in the post of safeguarding Islam and the Holy Qur'an. He is the restoring force of Islam. Hence, if the Imām would not defend Islam, who else could shoulder this responsibility? If the Imām would not protect the Divine rules and regulations, who else could protect them?

Imām al-Ḥusayn considered the situation suitable for this overt struggle. He regarded the victory to be rescuing Islam, the Muslims, the Qur'an, the *sunnah* from the domination of the disbeliever, and making a radical change and revolution in the history of Islam. Which victory could stand higher than this? As a result, he took the decision to sacrifice his life in favour of Islam.

Notes to Chapter 16
Imām al-Ḥusayn's Sermon in Mecca

1. Nawāwīs, pl. of *Nāwūs*, means 'Christian cemeteries'; however, it refers to a ruined Christian village which was located near Karbalā. The above stands in harmony with the definitions provided in such monolingual Arabic dictionaries as Ibn Manẓūr's *Lisān al-'Arab* and L. Malouf's *al-Munjid* (33rd ed., Beirut, 2000). In contrast to this, F. Steingass regards the word *Nāwūs* as a loanword, derived from the Greek origin *Naòs*, meaning "A cemetery of the Magi; a fire-temple" (*A Comprehensive Persian-English Dictionary* [London, 1892]) and "fire-temple; burial-place of the Parsees; sepulchre, tomb; sarcophagus, coffin" (idem, *A Learner's Arabic-English Dictionary* [London, 1884]).

2. Ibn Ṭāwūs, *al-Luhūf*, p. 53; Ibn Namā al-Ḥillī, *Muthīr al-Aḥzān*, p. 21; al-Khwārazmī, *Maqtal al-Ḥusayn*, vol. 2, p. 5.

3. 'Amr b. Sa'īd b. al-'Āṣ was Yazīd's governor of Medina. When Imām al-Ḥusayn was at Mecca, Yazīd ordered 'Amr to move to Mecca, together with an army, in the guise of the Ḥājjis' chief, viz., *amīr al-ḥājj*; however, his real mission was to assassinate Imām al-Ḥusayn wherever and whenever he found an opportunity to do so.

4. At a glance, there are about one hundred verses in the Holy Qur'ān which pertain to *jihad* and martyrdom.

5. The Holy Qur'ān, Sūrah al-Tawba [9]: 111.

6. The Holy Qur'ān, Sūrah al-Tawba [9]: 112.

17

In Response to Ibn 'Abbās

a) يا ابن عم! ءانّى واللّٰه لاعلم انك ناصح مشفق وقد ازمعت على المسير ...

b) يا ابن عم! ما ارى ءالا الخروج بالاهل والولد

(a) "O Cousin! By Allāh I am aware that you are a kind advisor and [that] I am resolute on the movement..."

(b) "O Cousin! I do not consider any way other than uprising together with [my] family and children." [1]

Context

When Imām al-Ḥusayn announced his movement to Iraq, some people expressed opposition and suggested that he took a different path. The main reason for this caution was concern over the loyalty of the majority of the Kūfans.

Everybody believed that the Kūfans would warmly welcome the Imām in the beginning and they would leave him with a bitter farewell in the end. Hence, they anticipated that the journey would result in killing Imām al-Ḥusayn and captivity of his family members. The reality is that although their expectation proved correct, they only foresaw one aspect of the case. They were trying to prevent Imām al-Ḥusayn from being killed, since this would be tantamount to the fall of Islam and the Muslims' front; however, Imām al-Ḥusayn was considering another aspect.

Imām al-Ḥusayn referred to several Qur'ānic verses concerning *jihad*. He used to recite the verses: "Enjoined on you is fighting, and this you abhor." [2] and "You should fight the allies of Satan" [3]. He evaluated the reality of the situation, and decided that it was the right time to battle against Satan and its allies. Who else could make a better ally and successor than Yazīd for Satan? Hence the Qur'ānic verdict for *jihad* and fighting him was primarily addressed to the one who was the Imām of the *ummah* and the chief guardian of Islam. As a result, Imām al-Ḥusayn declared in his speech that anybody who was ready to sacrifice his life should be prepared for martyrdom and for heightening and strengthening the Right Word, they should join him and get ready for the departure the following day. Those who were prepared in that capacity and did not have any high regard for the materialistic life in this world answered Imām al-Ḥusayn's call and joined him. Nonetheless, like in any other significant movement, some renowned Muslims distanced themselves from the Imām and never answered positively to his call (thereby missing this supreme blessing), and others started expressing their opposition as soon as they learned about the reality of Imām al-Ḥusayn's movement.

Some openly opposed the Imām's actions both in Mecca and on the way from Mecca to Karbalā, either because they feared for Imām al-Ḥusayn's life or because they wanted to force him to pay allegiance. This range of people included almost everybody, from Imām al-Ḥusayn's relatives to ordinary people and to his opponents. However, the relatives of Imām al-Ḥusayn intended to rescue his life while his opponents wanted to serve Yazīd. At any rate, the suggestion of Imām al-Ḥusayn's relatives would satisfy the aim of Yazīd's supporters.

These suggestions began the moment Imām al-Ḥusayn declared that he would not pay allegiance to Yazīd in Medina and continued throughout his journey. The conversations in Medina were discussed in previous chapters; this chapter is devoted to similar proposals by Ibn 'Abbās to which Imām al-Ḥusayn gave a definitive reply.

The Suggestion of 'Abd Allāh b. 'Abbās

One of those who contacted Imām al-Ḥusayn, soon after he declared his intention to leave Mecca, was 'Abd Allāh b. 'Abbās.

His suggestion was as follows: "O Cousin! Although I pretend to be patient, I cannot remain still and endure it, for I fear that you would be slain and your family get captured simply because the people of Iraq are utterly disloyal and cannot be relied on." He then continued in the following way: "As you are the chief of the people of Hejaz, and respectable before the inhabitants of Mecca and Medina, I think you had better reside in Mecca. In case the people of Iraq want you and are against Yazīd's administration, as they have been so, they must first expel Yazīd's governor and their own enemy from their city, and then you can go there." The final remark of 'Abd Allāh b. 'Abbās was in this manner: "Should you insist on leaving Mecca, you had better to go to Yemen, for there are not only a lot of followers – Shi'i – of your father there, there are very strong and fortified castles, as well as high and remote mountains over there where you can carry out your activities quite away from the reach of the Umayyad government. From there, you can call people to yourself by letters and envoys. I hope you would achieve your aims in this way, without any trouble."

Imām al-Ḥusayn's Reply to 'Abd Allāh b. 'Abbās

In response to 'Abd Allāh b. 'Abbās, Imām al-Ḥusayn, replied as mentioned in (a) at the beginning of this chapter.

Upon receiving the reply, 'Abd Allāh b. 'Abbās realised that Imām al-Ḥusayn had already made his firm decision, he made no further attempt to change his mind. Instead, he remarked as follows: "Now that you have decided to depart, please do not take the women and children with you, for I fear the Kūfans would kill you before them."

In response to this suggestion, Imām al-Ḥusayn remarked as mentioned in (b) above, signifying that his decision was to take them with him.

Conclusion

The above discourses signify Imām al-Ḥusayn's firm conviction in his way and his resoluteness in leading his movement. Although he was confident about the good intentions of 'Abd Allāh b. 'Abbās's sincere suggestion and that he was right about the obstacles and hardships he would face, Imām al-Ḥusayn was still determined to pursue his own way. Similarly, when ʻAbd Allāh b. ʻAbbās tried to warn him not to take his wives and children, Imām al-Ḥusayn's repeated his decision. This is the significance of Imāmate and leadership which remains resolute on the Right Path and is courageous in the face of danger.

Notes to Chapter 17
In Response to Ibn ʻAbbās

1. Al-Dīnawarī, *al-Akhbār al-Ṭuwāl*, p. 361; al-Ṭabarī, *al-Ta'rīkh*, Events of the Year 61 AH; Ibn al-Athīr, *al-Kāmil fī al-Ta'rīkh*, vol. 3, p. 276.
2. The Holy Qur'ān, Sūrah al-Baqara [2]: 216.
3. The Holy Qur'ān, Sūrah al-Nisā' [4]: 76.

18

In Response to 'Abd Allāh b. al-Zubayr

a) انّ ابى حدّثنى انّ بمكّة كبشا به تستحلّ حرمتها فما احبّ ان اكون ذلك الكبش ولئن اقتل خارجا منها بشبر احبّ الىّ من ان اقتل فيها ولئن اقتل خارجا منها بشبرين احبّ الىّ من ان اقتل خارجا منها بشبر وايم الله لو كنت فى جحر هامّة من هذه الهوامّ يستخرجونى حتّى يقضوا بى حاجتهم.

b) والله! ليعتدنّ علىّ كما اعتدت اليهود فى السّبت.

... يا ابن الزّبير! لئن ادفن بشاطئ الفرات احبّ الىّ من ان ادفن بفنا الكعبة.

c) ا نّ هذا يقول لى كن حماما من حمام الحرم ولئن اقتل وبينى وبين الحرم باع احبّ الىّ من ان اقتل وبينى وبينه شبر ولئن اقتل بالطّفّ احبّ الىّ من ان اقتل بالحرم .

d) انّ هذا ليس شىء من الدّنيا احبّ اليه من ان اخرج من الحجاز وقد علم انّ النّاس لا يعدلونه بى فودّ انّى خرجت حتّى يخلو له.

(a) "My father reported that there would be a ram at Mecca whose honour would be desecrated. Hence, I never liked to be that ram. And, if I get slain out of it [Mecca] by a span, it is more desirable for me to get slain inside it. And, if I get slain out of it by two spans, it is more desirable to me than getting slain in it by a span. By Allāh, had I been in the burrow of a small animal like these animals, they would draw me out until they do with me their job (to kill me). By Allāh! They will assault me as the Jews did on Saturday, O Ibn al-Zubayr! If I am buried on the river bank of the Euphrates, [1] it will be more desirable to me than being buried within the precinct of the Ka'bah."

(b) "This person – 'Abd Allāh b. al-Zubayr – has been suggesting to me: 'Be one of the doves of the *ḥaram*' [2], and if I get slain while the distance between me and the *ḥaram* is by a fathom, it would be more desirable to me than getting slain and the distance between me and it – the *ḥaram* – is by a span, and if I get slain at al-Ṭaff [3], it would be more desirable to me than getting slain within the *ḥaram*."

(c) "There is nothing in the world more desirable to him – 'Abd Allāh b. al-Zubayr – than that I leave Hejaz, and he has realised that people would not regard him equal with me; therefore, he wishes for me to depart here until they get around him." [4]

Context

'Abd Allāh b. al-Zubayr was one of those who suggested that Imām al-Ḥusayn change his mind and not to go to Iraq. As a purported opponent of Yazīd, 'Abd Allāh b. al-Zubayr, left Medina secretly after refusing to give allegiance, and sought refuge in Mecca. After Imām al-Ḥusayn's arrival in Mecca, he used to visit the Imām's house either every day or every other day, just as the rest of the Muslims did. He also used to participate in Imām al-Ḥusayn's meetings. When he learned of Imām al-Ḥusayn's decision to leave Mecca for Iraq, he went to him and seemingly suggested to the Imām to change his mind and not go to Iraq.

According to al-Balādhurī and al-Ṭabarī, 'Abd Allāh b. al-Zubayr proposed a twofold suggestion: "O Grandson of the Prophet! Had I had some staunch followers like your men, I would have preferred there to anywhere else."

To escape any future blame, 'Abd Allāh b. al-Zubayr continued thus: "However, you may stay at Mecca and, in case you may desire to continue the Imāmate and leadership of the Muslims in this city, we will also pledge allegiance to you as well and will not deny you our support."

In response to the above suggestion, Imām al-Ḥusayn remarked as quoted in (a) above, that his father – Imām 'Alī – had informed him that the city of Mecca would be dishonoured through the killing of a ram [a person being innocently sacrified], and that he never wanted to be an excuse for such disrespect to the holy precinct.

Following this discourse, Imām al-Ḥusayn maintained, as indicated in (b) above, that if he had sought refuge in the burrow of a small creature, the Umayyads would drag him out to disrespect him, just in the same way as the Jews disrespected Saturday – as their symbol of unity and proximity to Allāh. Finally, he emphasised that he would prefer to be on the banks of the river Euphrates than within the precinct of the Ka'bah.

According to Ibn Qūlawayh, [6] after 'Abd Allāh b. al-Zubayr left Imām al-Ḥusayn's meeting, the Imām remarked as indicated in (c) above. He stated that Ibn al-Zubayr had suggested him to be one of the doves of the *ḥaram*, and reside in the safe region of Mecca. In response to this suggestion, Imām al-Ḥusayn emphasised that it would be more desirable for him to be slain a cubit away from the *ḥaram* than by a span; it would be more desirable for him to get slain on the plains of al-Ṭaff – Karbalā – than within the *ḥaram* region.

According to al-Ṭabarī and Ibn al-Athīr, when 'Abd Allāh b. al-Zubayr left the session, Imām al-Ḥusayn told the audience that although 'Abd Allāh b. al-Zubayr pretended to be interested in Imām al-Ḥusayn's stay at Mecca, the reality was that he favored his departure, for as long as Imām al-Ḥusayn was at Mecca, nobody would pay attention to him. This is indicated in (d) above.

Conclusion

In this discourse, Imām al-Ḥusayn did not make reference to the past deeds and profile of 'Abd Allāh b. al-Zubayr and the standpoint he had adopted against Imām 'Alī and in the Battle of Baṣrah. 'Abd Allāh b. al-Zubayr was a central figure in organizing the Battle of Baṣrah in opposition to Imām 'Alī. However, in a short statement, Imām al-Ḥusayn portrayed the future of himself as well as that of 'Abd Allāh b. al-Zubayr.

As for himself, Imām al-Ḥusayn remarked that the ruling power would never leave him alone, that they would never stop harassing him, for Imām al-Ḥusayn's would never compromise the truth. Nor would Imām al-Ḥusayn yield to their whim.

In his discourse, Imām al-Ḥusayn referred to the "banks of the Euphrates" and "al-Ṭaff". This is most striking and significant. Furthermore, Imām al-Ḥusayn had alerted 'Abd Allāh b. al-Zubayr that Imām 'Alī's remark was that the Ka'bah and the secure Divine Sanctuary (i.e. the *ḥaram*) will be dishonoured. Hence, he decided not to be in place of that ram, and to prevent any disrespect to be done to the Ka'bah, he decided to leave Mecca. On the basis of this view, Imām al-Ḥusayn's being slain a span away from the Ka'bah is preferred to than being slain within the precinct of the Ka'bah.

Finally, Imām al-Ḥusayn warned 'Abd Allāh b. al-Zubayr that he must not, in the future, take refuge by the *ḥaram* and become a dove of the *ḥaram*, and to take it as his shelter, lest he may disrespect the Ka'bah.

The Truth of Imām al-Ḥusayn's Prediction

Despite Imām al-Ḥusayn's continued warning, 'Abd Allāh b. al-Zubayr never realised the truth. Within thirteen years, 'Abd Allāh b. al-Zubayr took refuge within the holy sanctuary and caused the Ka'bah to be catapulted with stones twice. The Ka'bah was then set ablaze and destroyed. In this way, the predictions of Imām 'Alī and Imām al-Ḥusayn came true. The two incidents of catapulting the Ka'bah were as follows.

The first attack took place three years after the martyrdom of Imām al-Ḥusayn. On the 3rd of Rabi I 64 AH/ 684 AD. Yazīd's troops turned to Mecca, after having committed the massacre at the Battle of Ḥarra near Medina. The troops surrounded the city of Mecca and, as 'Abd Allāh b. al-Zubayr sought refuge at the Ka'bah, they surrounded Mecca, and catapulted the Grand Mosque and the Ka'bah from above the Abū Qubays Mountain. In consequence, the *kiswa* – clothes covering the Ka'bah – caught fire and the Ka'bah was damaged. The horns of the ram, which had been sent down from Paradise as a sacrifice in place of Ishmael, caught fire. In the heat of this battle, the troops received the news of Yazīd's death and they dispersed. Then 'Abd Allāh b. al-Zubayr reconstructed the Ka'bah.

The second attack took place when 'Abd Allāh b. al-Zubayr called people to rally under his leadership at the time of 'Abd al-Malik b. Marwān. Upon his call, some people followed him. It was in the year 73 AH/ 692 AD that 'Abd al-Malik b. Marwān appointed al-Ḥajjāj b. Yūsuf al-Thaqafī to combat 'Abd Allāh b. al-Zubayr, and surrounded Mecca with thousands of troops. This operation took several months. Again 'Abd Allāh b. al-Zubayr sought refuge by the Ka'bah and, in consequence, at the command of al-Ḥajjāj b. Yūsuf, the Ka'bah was attacked by catapult. The Ka'bah was damaged, and it was reportedly ruined. Finally, 'Abd Allāh b. al-Zubayr was killed, and al-Ḥajjāj b. Yūsuf rebuilt the Ka'bah. [7]

Notes to Chapter 18
In Response to 'Abd Allāh b. al-Zubayr

1. In Arabic, al-Furāt, the Euphrates, is a river to the west of which the region and city of Karbalā are situated.
2. By '*ḥaram*', it is meant a greater zone around Mecca wherein killing or annihilating a living thing, mankind, fona, or flora, is strictly forbidden, all due to the sanctity of the Ka'bah.
3. Al-Ṭaff is one of the several titles of the land of Karbalā.
4. Al-Balādhurī, *Anṣāb al-Ashrāf*, vol. 3, p. 164; al-Ṭabarī, *al-Ta'rīkh*, The Events of the Year 61 AH; Ibn al-Athīr, *al-Kāmil fī al-Ta'rīkh*, vol. 3, p. 276; and Ibn Qūlawayh al-Qummī, *Kāmil al-Zīyārāt*, p. 72.
5. Ja'far b. Muḥammad b. al-Qūlawayh al-Qummī, (d. 368 AH/978) was a renowned and authoritative *hadith* scholar, whose famous work is *Kāmil al-Zīyārāt*, a collection of ziyāra-texts.
6. The accounts given are summarised from those provided in Ibn al-Athīr, *al-Kāmil fī al-Ta'rīkh*; Ibn Kathīr al-Dimashqī, *Al-Bidāya wa al-Nihāya*; and Jalāl al-Dīn al-Suyūṭī, *Ta'rīkh al-Khulafā'*.

Part 2

From Mecca to Karbala

19

In Response to Muḥammad b. al-Ḥanafīyyah

بلی! ولکن بعدما فارقتك اتانی رسول اللّٰه صلّی اللّٰه علیه و اله وقال یا حسین اخرج فانّ اللّٰه تعالی شاء ان یراك قتیلا ... وقد شااللّٰه ان یراهنّ سبایا.

"Yes, but after I got separated from you, the Prophet of Allāh – May Allāh bestow His blessings upon him and his progeny – came to my dream and said: 'O Ḥusayn! Get out, [1] for Allāh the Almighty wishes to see you slain ... and Allāh wishes to see them [2] as captives.'"[3]

Context

Imām al-Ḥusayn received the third suggestion from his step-brother Muḥammad b. al-Ḥanafīyyah advising him not to set out to Iraq. The account is as follows: Muḥammad b. al-Ḥanafīyyah had arrived in Mecca to perform the Ḥajj rituals as well as meet Imām al-Ḥusayn. According to the late Allama al-Ḥillī, Muḥammad b. al-Ḥanafīyyah was severely ill; [4] however, he reached Imām al-Ḥusayn at night and said: "O Brother! You have noticed the infidelity and perfidity of the Kūfans in respect of your father [Imām] 'Alī and your brother [Imām] al-Ḥasan. I fear that they would prove disloyal to you as well. Hence, you had better not to set out to Iraq and reside here in Mecca, for in this city and in the vicinity of the sanctum (*ḥaram*) of Allāh, [5] you are more beloved and respectable than anybody else."

Then Imām al-Ḥusayn responded: "It is plausible that Yazīd may kill me within the sanctum of Allāh out of conspiracy, hence the due respect of the House and sanctum (*ḥaram*) of Allāh would be violated."

Upon hearing this, Muḥammad b. al-Ḥanafīyyah suggested Imām al-Ḥusayn go to Yemen or to a safer place. In response to this well-wishing suggestion, Imām al-Ḥusayn assured him he would consider his suggestion.

However, early next morning, Imām al-Ḥusayn started his journey toward Iraq. When this news reached Muḥammad b. al-Ḥanafīyyah, he swiftly rushed to Imām al-Ḥusayn in a little while, took hold of the bridle of his camel, and enquired if he had not promised the night before to think over his suggestion and request.

Imām al-Ḥusayn confirmed he had, but expressed, as indicated in the beginning of this chapter, that he had a revelatory dream in which the Holy Prophet told him to set out to Iraq because it was the Divine Will to find him slain.

Muḥammad b. al-Ḥanafīyyah then recited the Qur'ānic verse "We are from Allāh to Him we shall return." [6] He then enquired of Imām al-Ḥusayn's reason to take the women and children when they would certainly be held captive. Imām al-Ḥusayn indicated that this was Allāh's wish.

Was Imām al-Ḥusayn Forced to Choose Martyrdom?

Whether Imām al-Ḥusayn was forced to choose martyrdom or not is a crucial question. The response of Imām al-Ḥusayn to the concerns raised by Muḥammad b. al-Ḥanafīyyah indicate that it was the Divine Will of Allāh to see him slain. Furthermore, his answers to Lady Umm Salamah and Lady Zaynab might lead to the view that Imām al-Ḥusayn's movement, his martyrdom, and the captivity of his family members were but merely a Divine Will, some event which Allāh desired to take place. Accordingly, his martyrdom was inevitable.

It is understandable to question the role that Divine Will as opposed to Free Will had to play in Imām al-Ḥusayn's martyrdom, as even learned people debate this. When talking about Imām al-Ḥusayn's martyrdom, some scholars may tend to regard him as a unique case based on the authority of the expression "Indeed Allāh has wished to see you slain."

There are two main issues regarding the Divine Will view. Firstly, on the basis of the view that Imām al-Ḥusayn's martyrdom was inevitable, his martyrdom would seem less valuable and praiseworthy than any ordinary person's martyrdom who accepts martyrdom willingly. As an ordinary person would choose martyrdom out of his free will, while Imām al-Ḥusayn seemed to have no other choice and could not do anything other than what Allāh had determined for him. Nevertheless, the reality is that the inhabitants of the Earth and the sky praise Imām al-Ḥusayn's decision.

Secondly, on the basis of this argument, the killers of Imām al-Ḥusayn cannot be reproached or blamed, as it was the Will of Allāh for Imām al-Ḥusayn to be martyred, and any martyr must by necessity have a killer, hence there is no blame on the killers of Imām al-Ḥusayn.

In response, firstly, the origin of the above argument stems from a misunderstanding of "the Divine Will", "fate", and "destiny". Allāh's Will may sometimes be evolutive and sometimes dutitive. The evolute Divine Will is not subject to man's control, they must submit to it. For example the birth and death of mankind, and the creation of the earth and heavens.

However, the dutitive Divine Will consists of Allāh's commands concerning actions over which man has a choice. Examples of dutitive Divine Will include mandatory ritual duties such as fasting, performing the ritual *salat*, Ḥajj, and *jihad* all of which had been prescribed for mankind according to Divine Will. Furthermore, it is out of Divine Will that all unlawful and *ḥarām* deeds be abandoned; otherwise, He would not prohibit them. This type of Divine Will does not emcompass the deeds directly, the actual implementation of such deeds has been left to the will of people.

An example of dutitive Divine Will is mentioned in the Qur'ān: "Indeed Allāh has enjoined justice, the doing of good, and the giving of gifts to your relatives; and forbidden indecency, impropriety and oppression. He warns you so that you may remember." [7] According to this verse, Allāh wills the implementation of justice, doing good to everybody and the relatives, and the removal of any type of abominable act and oppression of the Muslim community. However, Allāh has left its implementation to the will of the people; hence, there is no imposition. In other words, it is the people – the servants of

Allāh – that must accept the Divine Will and act freely according to it. While commending people to do good and preventing them from committing evil, Allāh invites people to the Right Path only through giving advice; hence "He warns you so that you may remember." [8]

With this clarification in mind, it is time to return to the main topic. Imām al-Ḥusayn envisaged the situation to be very critical and acute. He found himself to be the addressee of the Divine commandment that "Fighting is prescribed upon you ...". [9] Accordingly, he realised that he had to step into the battlefield, for he had announced that Islam and the way of his grandfather had been dishonoured since the time Yazīd came into power. Now, he had to sacrifice whatever belonged to him: his own self, children, and companions. It had to be fulfilled so that it would give the dying Islam a new life and restore the life of the Qur'ān. This is exactly what he expressed so succinctly in his statement: "Allāh wishes to see me slain and them as captives."

This was the Will of Allāh, and Imām al-Ḥusayn was on the mission to carry it out as confirmed by the revelatory dream of his grandfather the Holy Prophet.

Imām al-Ḥusayn Chose Martyrdom Willfully

The value of Imām al-Ḥusayn's endeavor lies in his willful decision. He was not evolutively forced to take up the martyrdom journey, but he was free at any stage – right up to the moment of martyrdom – to change his decision. In fact, at each point in the journey he offered his companions a chance to leave as the end was certainly martyrdom. Furthermore, he could have avoided his journey to Iraq on the basis of several religious and rational reasons. Despite knowing all the details of his future, he was firm in his conviction that he would sacrifice everything he had for the pleasure of Allāh and to follow His Divine Will.

As anticipated, the battle ended with the apparent defeat, which everybody anticipated. However, the main result of Imām al-Ḥusayn's movement was what he indicated in his letter and testament on leaving Medina; that he rose up to reform (the affairs of) the *ummah* of his grandfather, Prophet Muḥammad.

In summary, Imām al-Ḥusayn was free in his movement. He was capable of abandoning his way at any moment, and to put an end to his revolution. However, he did not, for he was the leader and Imām, hence he was a role model for the entire world.

The Value of an Anticipated Martyrdom

One might ask whether there was any value in Imām al-Ḥusayn's martyrdom as it had been foretold so far in advance.

Allāh knew that Imām al-Ḥusayn would certainly and willingly obey the Divine commandment and would sacrifice whatever he had for the cause of Allāh: He would not make any mistake regarding the Divine commitment. Hence, Allāh had informed Prophet Muḥammad of this certain news. Nevertheless, this Divine knowledge and pre-announcement of the tragedy of Karbalā played no role in forcing Imām al-Ḥusayn to make, or not to make, his choice. Similarly, just as we perform our Divinely-determined rituals voluntarily, such as the ritual prayer (salaṭ), and Allāh informs Prophet Muḥammad of our religious deeds, His informing the Prophet does not affect our will, decision, or deed.

Conclusion

Divine Knowledge and anticipation does not prevent any incident from taking place. Rather, it informs of a reality dependent on the expression of the free will of a person in the future.

This Divine Knowledge, together with a prior announcement, regarding performing one's duty is not unique to Imām al-Ḥusayn. Rather, Divine Knowledge encompasses the cases of all prophets and holy people who would voluntarily perform their duties and would of course be capable of undertaking such tasks. Hence, it is an appreciative remark to inform all or part of their sacrifice to other prophets.

Notes to Chapter 19
In Response to Muḥammad b. al-Ḥanafīyyah

1. Alternatively, the imperative mood '*ukhruj*' also means 'revolt' [against Yazīd and the Umayyads].
2. The plural feminine pronoun *hunn[a]* refers to the women who were accompanying Imām al-Ḥusayn.
3. Ibn Ṭāwūs, *al-Luhūf*, p. 65.
4. Al-Qummī, *Safīna al-Biḥār*, vol. 1, p. 322. It was due to a serious physical defection that he could not accompany Imām al-Ḥusayn to Iraq.
5. The Grand Mosque where the Ka'bah is situated, the whole city of Mecca, and a certain radius around the city of Mecca have been regarded as the security zone.
6. The Holy Qur'ān, 2:156.
7. The Holy Qur'ān, 16: 90.
8. Ibid.
9. The Holy Qur'ān, Sūrah al-Baqara [2]: 216.

20

In Reply to ‘Abd Allāh b. Ja‘far and ‘Amr b. Sa‘īd

a) انّى رايت رؤيا فيها رسول اللّه صلّى اللّه عليه و اله وامرت فيها بامر انا ماض له علىّ كان اولى.

b) ... ما حدّثت احدا بها وما انا محدّث بها حتّى القى ربّى.

c) ... امّا بعد، فانّه لم يشاقق اللّه ورسوله من دعا الى اللّه عزّوجلّ وعمل صالحا وقال انّنى من المسلمين وقد دعوت الى الايمان والبرّ والصّلة فخير الامان امان اللّه ولن يؤ من اللّه يوم القيامة من لم يخفه فى الدّنيا فنسال اللّه مخافة فى الدّنيا توجب لنا امانه يوم القيامة فان نويت بالكتاب صلتى و برّى فجزيت خيرا فى الدّنيا والا خرة؛ والسّلام.

(a) “I dreamt of the Holy Prophet, and in the dream, I was ordered to accomplish a task which I have to fulfill, whether it would be in my favour or against me.”

(b) ... “I have not talked about it [the dream] with anybody, nor will I talk about it until I meet my Lord [Allāh].” [1]

(c) “Surely God and His Messenger (peace be upon him) do not separate [from themselves] one who calls to God, the Mighty and Majestic, does righteous works, and says: “Surely I am of the Muslims.” I have called to faith, righteousness and kinship, so the best safety is the safety of God and none will be safe from God on the Day of Resurrection. If you intended by your letter my kinship and righteousness to me, then you have been rewarded in this world and the next. Peace be to you.” [2]

Context

On the authority of al-Ṭabarī, the fourth Imām 'Alī al-Sajjād reported that 'Abd Allāh b. Ja'far was the fourth person to suggest that Imām al-Ḥusayn change his mind from going to Iraq and insisted on his suggestion. After Imām al-Ḥusayn left Mecca, 'Abd Allāh b. Ja'far wrote a letter to Imām al-Ḥusayn and gave it to two of his sons, namely, 'Awn and Muḥammad, to deliver it to him.

The letter of 'Abd Allāh b. Ja'far was as follows: "I swear by Allāh to change your mind from taking this journey and return to Mecca as soon as this letter reaches you. This is because I feel apprehensive about your being slain and your family members and children will become helpless; I fear that by slaying you, as the guiding flag and the hopes of the Muslims, the light of Allāh's guidance will be extinguished. Please do not proceed in a hurry, for I will join you." [3] Soon after dispatching the above letter, 'Abd Allāh b. Ja'far met 'Amr b. Sa'īd who had been appointed as the governor of Medina. The latter was present in Mecca apparently as the chief of the Hajjis, while his real mission was to assassinate Imām al-Ḥusayn in Mecca. 'Abd Allāh b. Ja'far requested 'Amr b. Sa'īd to issue a pledge of safe conduct in favour of Imām al-Ḥusayn which would prove effective on his return to Mecca. Moreover, he obtained 'Amr b. Sa'īd's consent to dispatch his brother Yaḥyā b. Sa'īd to submit the pledge of safe conduct to Imām al-Ḥusayn.

When 'Abd Allāh b. Ja'far and Yaḥyā b. Sa'īd reached Imām al-Ḥusayn's caravan outside Mecca, he renewed the pledge to Imām al-Ḥusayn and expressed his request in addition to the demand of Yaḥyā b. Sa'īd, and asked the Imām to change his mind and not go to Iraq.

In response, Imām al-Ḥusayn replied, as mentioned in (a) above, that he had dreamt of Prophet Muḥammad and received a mission which he would pursue at any cost.

Upon 'Abd Allāh b. Ja'far's insistence to know more about the dream and Imām al-Ḥusayn's new mission, the Imām replied that he would not reveal it to anybody, as quoted in (b) above. Following the above conversation, Imām al-Ḥusayn wrote the letter quoted in (c).

According to al-Balādhurī, al-Ṭabarī, and Ibn al-Athīr, ʻAbd Allāh b. Jaʻfar and Yaḥyā b. Saʻīd returned to Mecca, for Imām al-Ḥusayn was resolute in his decision. Consequently, ʻAmr b. Saʻīd ordered his brother Yaḥyā to gather an armed group to approach Imām al-Ḥusayn and force him to return to Mecca. When this group reached Imām al-Ḥusayn's caravan, they quarreled amongst themselves and attacked each other with whips. Thereupon, Yaḥyā b. Saʻīd could not tolerate the situation and went to Mecca.

Remarks on the Discourse of Imām al-Ḥusayn

There are several important indications in Imām al-Ḥusayn's reply to ʻAbd Allāh b. Jaʻfar as well as in his reply to ʻAmr b. Saʻīd's pledge of safe conduct. Firstly, in response to ʻAbd Allāh b. Jaʻfar, Imām al-Ḥusayn spoke of a mission entrusted to him from Prophet Muḥammad in a revelatory dream, and that he was supposed to carry it out even if it proved dangerous. Moreover, Imām al-Ḥusayn maintained that he would not reveal the nature of his dream to anybody.

There remain some questions about the mission mentioned in his dream. What was the mission? Was it about *jihad*, the martyrdom of Imām al-Ḥusayn, or the captivity of his family members and children? However, he had already spoken of these points with Muḥammad b. al-Ḥanafīyyah before leaving Mecca. Moreover, from Medina to the moment of his martyrdom, he used to refer to these events, explicitly and implicitly. The question remains: What was the new mission revealed to Imām al-Ḥusayn by the Holy Prophet? And, why did Imām al-Ḥusayn vow to never speak of it to anyone? We do not know anything in this regard, and it is a secret between Allāh, His Prophet and Imām al-Ḥusayn.

Secondly, with regard to the pledge of safe conduct, Imām al-Ḥusayn remarked, first implicitly, about his plan to invite everybody to Allāh, and then he advised ʻAmr b. Saʻīd, that on the Day of Resurrection those who had accomplished their jobs out of fearing Allāh, they shall certainly be entitled to benefit from the Divine security. Secondly, by using the Arabic conditional word "*'in* (if)", he exposed ʻAmr b. Saʻīd's real purpose. This is because in the tone of supplication, use of this conditional word would be subject to question and implies rebuke.

Notes to Chapter 20
In Reply to 'Abd Allāh b. Ja'far and 'Amr b. Sa'īd

1. Al-Mufīd, *Kitāb al-Irshād*, p. 214; Ibn Kathīr al-Dimashqī, *al-Bidāya wa al-Nihāya*, vol. 8, p. 167; Ibn 'Asākir, *al-Ta'rīkh*, p. 202. Markworthy is that Ibn 'Asākir mentions the first part as the text of a letter in response to 'Abd Allāh b. Ja'far's letter.
2. Al-Balādhurī, *Anṣāb al-Ashrāf*, vol. 3, p. 164; al-Ṭabarī, *al-Ta'rīkh*, The Events of the Year 61 AH; Ibn al-Athīr, *al-Kāmil fī al-Ta'rīkh*, vol. 3, p. 277.
3. Al-Ṭabarī, *al-Ta'rīkh*, The Events of the Year 61 AH; and Ibn al-Athīr, *al-Kāmil fī al-Ta'rīkh*, vol. 3, p. 277.

21

With al-Farazdaq

... صدقت للّه الامرو كل يوم هو فى شان ان نزل القضاء بما نحبّ ونرضى فنحمداللّه على نعمائه وهو المستعان على اداء الشّكر وان حال القضاء دون الرّجا فلم يتعدّ من كان الحقّ نيّته والتّقوى سريرته.

"You have said the truth for the sake of Allāh, and 'Everyday He manifests Himself in yet another (wonderous way)' [1]. If destiny goes with what we favour and desire, we will praise Allāh for His bounties and He is the helper [for us] to discharge this gratitude. And, if destiny denied the hope, such a person whose intention was right and piety had been their inward disposition, they have not gone astray." [2]

Context

The fifth suggestion to Imām al-Ḥusayn to abandon his journey to Iraq came from al-Farazdaq, a famous Arab poet.[3] Imām al-Ḥusayn was on the way from Mecca to Iraq, and al-Farazdaq was heading for Mecca to perform Ḥajj. Al-Farazdaq met Imām al-Ḥusayn outside Mecca and enquired about the reasons for his decision to leave Mecca. A report of this meeting and conversation is narrated below on the authority of the late Sheikh al-Mufīd.[4] Al-Farazdaq reported: In the year 60 AH/ 680 AD, I was on the way to Mecca together with my mother to perform Ḥajj. When I entered the Holy Sanctum area, while I was holding the bridle of my mother's camel and was pulling it from behind, I came across Imām al-Ḥusayn's caravan. I hurried toward him, greeted him, and asked him why he was rushing to leave Mecca prior to the commencement of the Ḥajj ceremonies.

Upon this, Imām al-Ḥusayn remarked: "If I did not hurry up, I would be arrested." Thereupon, Imām al-Ḥusayn enquired of al-Farazdaq's identity, and he introduced himself simply as an Arab. Al-Farazdaq mentions that Imām al-Ḥusayn had not asked any further question regarding his identity. Then Imām al-Ḥusayn asked him of the Iraqis' public opinion and the prevailing political atmosphere.

In response to Imām al-Ḥusayn's enquiry, al-Farazdaq replied: "You have sought the news from its expert. The people's hearts are with you but their swords are against you, and the destiny is in the hand of Allāh and He will direct them as He wishes."

In reply, Imām al-Ḥusayn made the statement quoted in the beginning of this chapter. Al-Farazdaq said, "That is right. Allāh be with you."

After this, al-Farazdaq's continued asking questions about the rituals of the Ḥajj and other subjects. Then they went their separate ways.

Two Noteworthy Points

Imām al-Ḥusayn's above discourse alludes to two important issues. Firstly, this discourse is another example of how the Imām was aware of the situation in Iraq and the forthcoming events from ordinary channels of gaining information, other than his special knowledge as the Infallible Imām. Hence, he continued on his mission with full knowledge. This was evident for such ordinary people like al-Farazdaq.

Secondly, Imām al-Ḥusayn's reliance on Allāh was integral to his success. His movement was to accomplish a purpose; fulfilling his Divine mission, and attaining a sublime spiritual aim, not necessarily an apparent victory. It was on the basis of this philosophy that Imām al-Ḥusayn commenced his movement, maintaining that if destiny is against one's hope, the righteous, pious person would not be the loser.

Notes to Chapter 21
With al-Farazdaq

1. The Holy Qur'ān, Sūrah al-Raḥmān[55]: 29.
2. Al-Balādhurī, *Anṣāb al-Ashrāf*, vol. 3, p. 164; al-Ṭabarī, *al-*
3. , vol. 6, p. 218, Ibn al-Athīr, *al-Kāmil*, vol. 3, p. 276; al-Mufīd, *Kitāb al-Irshād*, p. 218; Al-Khwārazmī, *Maqtal al-Ḥusayn*, vol. 1, p. 223; Ibn Kathīr al-Dimashqī, *al-Bidāyah wa al-Niḥyāh*, vol. 8, p. 166.
4. Al-Farazdaq, the by-name of Hammām b. Ghālib (*ca.* 38-110 AH/ *ca.* 641- 729) whose *kunya* (filial byname) was Abū Firās. He composed a eulogy about Imām 'Alī al-Sajjād for which he was imprisoned for a while. He used to frequent at the house of Sakīnah, Imām al-Ḥusayn's daughter out of ardent devotion and veneration for the descendants of Imām al-Ḥusayn. He passed away at the age of 100 in Baṣrah, southern Iraq.
5. Al-Ṭabarī mentions al-Ṣifāḥ (a station to the north of Mecca, situated somewhere between Ḥunayn and the northern border of the *ḥaram* [the larger sanctum of Mecca]) as the place where the meeting took place. However, al-Dhahabī in *Tadhkira al-Ḥuffaẓ*, vol. 1, p. 338, records it as Dhāt 'Irq (a station between Mecca and Iraq at a distance of two stations away from Mecca to the east, a meeting place where those who wish to perform Ḥajj must put on their *iḥrām* [Ḥajj garments] there). These sources also report al-Farazdaq's question differently, yet they quote Imām al-Ḥusayn's reply in exactly the same way as indicated here. As the account provided by the late Sheikh al-Mufīd seems more sound and reliable, this account was quoted from al-Mufīd's *Kitāb al-Irshād.*

22

A Suggestion to the Cameleers

من احبّ منكم ان ينصرف معنا الى العراق اوفينا كراه و احسنّا صحبته و من احبّ المفارقة اعطيناه من الكراء على ما قطع من الارض.

"Any of you who may wish to change his way (and join us in the journey) to Iraq, we shall pay off his travel fare, and he will receive our best treatment; and whoever favors leaving us, we shall pay their travel fare for the distance they have travelled [up to here]." [1]

Context

Outside Mecca, at al-Tanʿīm [2], Imām al-Ḥusayn met a camel-train, en-route from Yemen to Damascus that was carrying fine cloaks and other goods sent as gifts by Buḥayr b. Yasār al-Ḥīmyarī, the Umayyad governor of Yemen, for Yazīd. Imām al-Ḥusayn confiscated the goods from the cameleers and addressed them as quoted above.

In response to Imām al-Ḥusayn's suggestion, some of the cameleers took their fares and returned to Yemen, but some expressed willingness to join him in his journey to Iraq.

The Secret of the Gesture

The secret of this gesture of Imām al-Ḥusayn and his revolutionary act lies in his support for the oppressed and challenge to the oppressors. It is a model and lesson for all true leaders of movements and revolutions that every single opportunity to challenge and weaken the tyrants must be seized.

Imām al-Ḥusayn repossesed the wealth and goods which were usurped from the poor Yemenite people by the Umayyads and Mu'āwīya's appointed governor of Yemen. This gesture of Imām al-Ḥusayn aimed to exert an economic and political pressure on the Umayyad rulership, and to gain back part of what was the right of the Shi'is and the *Ahl al-Bayt*, according to the peace treaty signed earlier by Imām al-Ḥasan and Mu'āwīya [3].

Imām al-Ḥusayn used the released goods for the benefit of the *ummah* and the poor people he encountered all the way from Hejaz to Iraq. However, the cameleers – all from the poor and needy classes of their community – had come and accompanied the camel-train in expectation of receiving their wages. In consequence, Imām al-Ḥusayn paid their wages and travel fares, treated them graciously, and set them free either to return home or to join him on his journey to Iraq. Moreover, he promised them his good treatment. Needless to say, the promise of good treatment from the grandson of Prophet Muḥammad in a journey to Iraq and in his company brings about eternal felicity, grandeur, and Paradise; this is indeed the wish of any faithful and good-doer.

Notes to Chapter 22
A Suggestion to the Cameleers

1. Al-Balādhurī, *Anṣāb al-Ashrāf*, vol. 2, p. 164; al-Ṭabarī, *Ta'rīkh*, vol. 7, p. 277; Ibn al-Athīr, *al-Kāmil fī al-Ta'rīkh*, vol. 3, p. 276; al-Mufīd, *Kitāb al-Irshād*, p. 219; Ibn Ṭāwūs, *al-Luhūf*, p. 60; Al-Khwārazmī, *Maqtal*, vol. 1, p. 220.
2. Al-Tan'īm is a place where those who wish to perform Ḥajj must put on the *iḥrām*, the Ḥajj garment, there. It is located at some 12 kms to the north of Mecca.
3. According to the late Shi'i scholar al-Majlisī one of the articles of the peace treaty was that Mu'āwīya had to pay 50,000 dirhams a year to Imām al-Ḥasan al-Mujtabā, all out of the taxes the former received from the inhabitants of Dārābjird, a city near Ahwaz in ancient Persia (see Muḥammad-Bāqīr al-Majlisī, *Jalā' al-'Uyūn*, 2nd imp. [Tehran, 1390 Sh/ 2011]). Yet

the late Shi'i scholar Sheikh Rāḍī Āl-i Yāsīn holds that the fourth article of the treaty was that of Mu'āwīyah had to pay two million dirhams each year to Imām al-Ḥusayn (see Rāḍī Āl-i Yāsīn, *Sulh-e Imām Ḥasan 'Alayh al-Salām*, tr. Ayatollah Sayyid 'Alī Khāmenei, 8th ed. [Tehran, 1388 Sh/ 2009], p. 305). The Arabic original is available in the author's volume, *Ṣulhḥal-Ḥasan* (1372 AH/ 1952; repr. Beirut, 1412 AH/ 1992), p. 260. Dārābjird, or Dārābgerd (the former is the Arabicised variant), is city located in the Fars Province to the south of the lake of Neyrīz. In Persian, the suffix *-gerd* (or in Arabic variant *-jird*) signifies a place name; this suffix means 'a city'. See F. Steingass, *A Comprehensive Persian-English Dictionary* (London, 1892), sv *gerd.*

23

The Second Letter to the Inhabitants of al-Kūfa

امّا بعد: فقد ورد علىّ كتاب مسلم بن عقيل يخبرنى باجتماعكم على نصرنا والطّلب بحقّنا فسالت الله ان يحسن لنا الصّنع ويثيبكم على ذلك اعظم الاجر وقد شخصت اليكم من مكّة يوم الثّلاثاء لثمان مضين من ذى الحجّة فاذا قدم عليكم رسولى فانكمشوا فى امركم فانّى قادم فى ايّامى هذه.

"Now then, the letter of Muslim b. 'Aqīl has reached me, indicative of your companionship and pledge to help us gain our right; so I have prayed to Allāh to make it a good arrangement for us and to grant you the highest reward in return of this. I have departed from Mecca to you on Tuesday, 8th of Dhū al-Hijja. Hence, when my envoy [1] reaches you, hurry up in your affair, [and] I will arrive within some days." [2]

Context

On the way to al-Kūfa, Imām al-Ḥusayn reached a station called al-Ḥājir, where he received a letter from Muslim b. 'Aqīl. Imām al-Ḥusayn replied with the letter above, addressing the inhabitants of al-Kūfa, and dispatched it to them via Qays b. Mūsahhir al-Ṣaydāwī.

Why al-Kūfa?

There have been some misconceptions regarding Imām al-Ḥusayn's movement and the invitations of the people of al-Kūfa. Sometimes the invitations of the Kūfans, their expression of support, and building the Islamic state are regarded as the main reason for Imām al-Ḥusayn's movement. This is not actually the case according to historical sources. Moreover, this devalues and denigrates the significance of this movement, such that any ordinary Muslim politician without a Divine mission could carry it out. However, upon a closer, step-by-step scrutiny, it is evident that the case of the Kūfans' invitations and establishment of the Islamic state did not have any central role in Imām al-Ḥusayn's intention and movement. This is because he had refused to pledge allegiance to Yazīd, and his defiant departure from Medina to Mecca followed his careful agenda. It was in this line of struggle that he replied to Ibn 'Abbās that the Umayyads would follow him until they would shed his blood. Likewise, he told 'Abd Allāh b. al-Zubayr that the enemy would take him out and kill him even if he had taken refuge inside a bird's nest.

The Kūfans' invitations were just a marginal issue as the letters were written long after the Imām's refusal to pledge allegiance and his arrival at Mecca, hence it could not be a major cause for his movement. Nevertheless, this could have been part of the lofty agenda of Imām al-Ḥusayn.

The situation in Mecca made it an unsafe place for Imām al-Ḥusayn to stay. Having started the struggle against Yazīd, he would continue it to the end. Nonetheless, remaining in Mecca was tantamount to his assassination which would have resulted in insulting the sanctity of the Ka'bah and that would be to the benefit of Yazīd b. Mu'āwīya. As observed before, 'Amr b. Sa'īd b. al-'Āṣ, who was given the responsibility of assassinating Imām al-Ḥusayn, first tried to draw Imām al-Ḥusayn to a compromise through suggesting a pledge of safe conduct. He then resorted to applying force to return Imām al-Ḥusayn to Mecca in order to put an end to all the turmoil in Mecca and cut short the Imām's revolution.

The question arises, where could Imām al-Ḥusayn have gone to escape this conspiracy? In the vast Muslim empire at that time, the largest region that was susceptible to uprisings was al-Kūfa in Iraq. Al-Kūfa was one of the largest provinces, that contained army barracks, was a rival for Damascus, the Levant [3], and even militarily more important than Mecca and Medina. From the point of public awareness, it is important to mention the large number invitation letters sent to Imām al-Ḥusayn from Mecca, indicative of their willingness to host him. In consequence, if all this public and general readiness and knowledge were suppressed by force, this suppressed revolutionary energy would erupt in a forthcoming revolution and the future revolutions would break out in the same place.

This throws up more questions: did Imām al-Ḥusayn have any choice other than setting out to al-Kūfa? In light of the factors mentioned, what might ask whether there was any other way for Imām al-Ḥusayn, other than moving to Iraq, after receiving so many letters of invitation? Was there any excuse for him to neglect going to al-Kūfa? Could it be acceptable for Imām al-Ḥusayn not to go to al-Kūfa on the basis of a conjecture that they *might* betray him, while they expressed their willingness and readiness to sacrifice their lives and property in the hope of his accepting their leadership? Had Imām al-Ḥusayn taken such a solution, would the Kūfans not claim that they were staunchly faithful in their invitations?

Imām al-Ḥusayn might seem to have been in a historical dilemma. Had he not given a positive answer to the Kūfans, he would have been condemned and history would have judged that the situation was ripe enough for him, but he was not capable of making the most of it, or he could not benefit from the situation due to cowardice and pressure.

Imām al-Ḥusayn answered the Kūfans in the affirmative. To issue an ultimatum to the people who had appealed to him, he answered their invitations positively. Religiously, it was his duty to challenge and oppose Yazīd's rulership to the last drop of his blood in support of the Right Word.

Outwardly, to answer the public readiness of the Kūfans, he was expected to move towards al-Kūfa to inform them of his agenda, and to give them the right orders to get prepared.

Imām al-Ḥusayn frequently alluded to both aspects of his movement. He referred to his first mission in a different way, as a mission which he received from Prophet Muḥammad in a dream and the Will of Allāh. However, regarding the second mission, he acted according to his outward responsibility, despite his knowledge of the disloyalty of the Kūfans. This is a point earlier touched upon in his answers to such people as ʻAbd Allāh b. al-Zubayr.

In conclusion, Imām al-Ḥusayn, as the rightful leader of Islam, recognised it his own duty to oppose and challenge the tyrant of his time. Like all the Divine prophets, he had to carry out the mission at any cost, precisely, as the incentive for his uprising. Unfortunately, this is rarely discussed in the majority of the books that deal with Imām al-Ḥusayn.

Notes to Chapter 23 The Second Letter to the Inhabitants of al-Kūfa

1. Muslim b. ʻAqīl.
2. Al-Balādhurī, *Anṣāb al-Ashrāf*, vol. 3, p. 167; al-Ṭabarī, *Ta'rīkh*, vol. 7, p. 289; and Ibn Kathīr, *Divineal-Bidāya wa al-Nihāya*, vol. 8, p. 168.
3. The present translator has deliberately chosen "the Levant" for "al-Shām" in the Arabic and/or "Shām" in Persian. This is because "Syria" denotes the present-day country of Syria, while "the Levant" was by far "the eastern Mediterranean, its islands, and the countries on its borders" (J. Everett-Heath, *The Concise Dictionary of World Place-Names* [Oxford, 2005]). It was the Levant and even other regions on its borders that made the greater territories over which the Umayyads were ruling.

24

On the way to al-Kūfa

انّ هؤلا اخافونى وهذه كتب اهل الكوفة وهم قاتلى فاذا فعلوا ذلك ولم يدعو
الله محرّما الا انتهكوه بعث الله اليهم من يذلّهم حتّى يكونوا اذلّ من فرام المراة.

"Indeed they have made it [the whole situation] so insecure for me that these are the letters of the people of al-Kūfa, and they are my killers. When they have committed this and have not feared Allāh for its prohibition but have demolished it, so Allāh shall drive unto them a person who would denigrate them so that they would be more inferior than women's piece of cloth used during the menses [i.e. the most worthless of creatures]." [1]

Context

According to Ibn Kathīral-Dimashqī [2] and Ibn Namā al-Ḥillī [3], a Kūfan gentleman reported the account as follows: "After I performed my Ḥajj rituals, I made a haste to return to al-Kūfa. On the way, I noticed several tents. Upon an enquiry, I realised that they belonged to Imām al-Ḥusayn; I then hastened to meet up with, and pay homage to, the grandson of Prophet Muḥammad at his own tent. I found him a man whose old age had already set in. The Kūfan was reciting some verses of the Holy Qur'ān, with his tears rolling down over his cheeks and beard. He then enquired, 'May my parents be sacrificed for your sake, O son of the Prophet's daughter! What has caused you to come over here to this lifeless and arid desert?'"

In response to this enquiry, Imām al-Ḥusayn gave the reply mentioned above.

Imām al-Ḥusayn's Anticipation

Imām al-Ḥusayn did anticipate the betrayal of the Kūfans. This is a noteworthy point in Imām al-Ḥusayn's reply about the Kūfans that they would certainly kill him and after this crime, Allāh would make someone conquer and massacre them. Such a person would denigrate them to the extent that they would become the most vilified and defamed people.

Imām al-Ḥusayn expressed the same anticipation on several occasions. Earlier when he left Mecca he had expressed the same concern to Ibn al-'Abbās in response to his suggestion at Baṭn al-'Aqaba not to go to al-Kūfa (mentioned in chapter 17). Likewise, on the day of Ashurā, Imām al-Ḥusayn maintained the same thought in his second speech, addressing the Kūfan army in the following way: "By Allāh! After this battle, you will never have a comfortable day, except for a very short while, just like the time span a horseman is riding his horse; however, later on when the mill of the upheavals will make you circle around itself, it will make you agitated and distressed like the pivot of the millstone." (see chapter 55).

The Kūfans' Denigration Realised

When, how, and by whom did this anticipation take place? Who conquered them in such a way that the Kūfans became the most disgraced and vilified people?

As mentioned in Imām al-Ḥusayn's anticipation, the Kūfans were not content and comfortable, except for a very short while. This was because soon after the Ashurā tragedy a group of the Kūfans initiated an uprising as the Penitents (*Tawwābūn*), a movement after which al-Mukhtār b. Abī 'Ubayd al-Thaqafī commenced his movement of revenge through which a number of the war criminals of the Ashurā tragedy were chastised and punished. All of these movements, one after another, involved bloodshed and massacre, and made the people of al-Kūfa feel uneasy and continually agitated and distressed. This unsettling time lasted throughout the reign of the Umayyads and a considerable period of the reign of the Abbasids in Iraq and especially at their seat, al-Kūfa. It was exactly a manifestation of Imām al-Ḥusayn's remark that the rulers would not be content with them at all.

The worst period for the Kūfans was the twenty years of the reign of al-Ḥajjāj b. Yūsuf al-Thaqafī. Al-Ḥajjāj, the despotic and dictator ruler of Iraq and some parts of Persia (Iran), ruled over these territories for twenty years, that is, from 75–95 AH/ 694-714. He suppressed the inhabitants of Iraq and especially those of al-Kūfa to such a great extent that his mere presence meant the rule of terror. He imprisoned, tortured, and killed so many people that it was the darkest period for them, just as Imām al-Ḥusayn foretold.

According to al-Mas'ūdī in *Murūj al-Dhahab* and Ibn al-Athīr in *al-Kamīl*, when al-Ḥajjāj was appointed as the governor of Iraq and arrived at his palace at al-Kūfa, he delivered his first speech in which he threatened people. Starting his speech without uttering 'Bismillah' [4], he showed his cruel face and said: "O People of Iraq! O People of hypocrisy, cruelty, and the worst traits! By Allāh! I see many long necks for which it is time to harvest, and this is what I can do easily. O People of Iraq! By Allāh! I will neither forgive your sins, nor will I accept your excuses!" [5]

Al-Ḥajjāj then ordered that everybody gather outside al-Kūfa and assist Muhallab [6] who was battling with the opponents of the government, and that anybody who abstains, would be beheaded and their house destroyed. On the third day, while al-Ḥajjāj was watching people move toward Baṣrah, an old man by the name of 'Umayr b. Ḍābī, the head of a clan at al-Kūfa, approached al-Ḥajjāj and said that since he was an aged weak man, and several of his children were taking part in the battle, he wanted to inquire if al-Ḥajjāj would exempt him from joining the battle. Al-Ḥajjāj did not let the old man finish his request and instantly ordered him to be beheaded and his properties confiscated. At the sight of this incident, the Kūfans hurried with so much hustle and bustle that some people fell in the river Euphrates and lost their lives. [7]

Historians report that there were about 120,000 people killed at the command of al-Ḥajjāj in his lifetime, excluding those who were killed in the battles. At the time of his death, there were 50,000 men and 30,000 women in prisons; about 16,000 of these women were imprisoned without clothes.

According to al-Mas'ūdī, al-Ḥajjāj imprisoned men and women in the same prisons, places without any roof to guard them against scorching heat and freezing winter winds. [8]

Ibn al-Jawzī mentions in his *al-Ta'rīkh* that the prisoners' food consisted of a mixture of ground barley, salt, and ash. The prisons' situation was so perilous that their skin colour would darken due to the type of food and the strong sunshine. [9]

Ibn Qutayba al-Dīnawarī reported that due to an opposition al-Ḥajjāj noticed in the general behaviour of the people of Baṣrah, he entered the city on a Friday in the month of Ramadan. On the basis of a carefully planned plot, he ordered 70,000 people to be beheaded in the central mosque of Baṣrah. [10]

The contemporary Lebanese scholar Muḥammad Jawād Mughnīya maintains that nobody in history can match al-Ḥajjāj in cruelty and blood-thirstiness. The only possibly comparable person could be the Roman emperor Nero [11] about whom it is quoted that when he set Rome on fire and the flames were soaring high in the sky, he was laughing at hearing the screams and moanings of the children and women who were being burned alive. [12]

'Umar b. 'Abd Allāh b. al-'Azīz [13] used to describe al-Ḥajjāj as the cruelest and most blood-thirsty person in the whole world such that nobody might match him in this regard. [14]

It is here that Imām al-Ḥusayn's remark found expression that Allāh will make someone dominant over them who would make them the most dishonoured and disgraced people, even more worthless than a piece of cloth used by women in their menstruation.

Notes to Chapter 24
On the way to al-Kūfa

1. Ibn 'Asākir, *Ta'rīkh*, p. 211; Ibn Kathīr, *Divineal-Bidāya wa al-Nihāya*, vol. 8, p. 169; Ibn Namā al-Ḥillī, *Muthīr al-Aḥzān*, p. 21. Noteworthy is that the editions of *al-Bidāya wa al-Nihāya* and Ibn 'Asākir's *Ta'rīkh* available to the editor [viz. the late Ayatollah Najmi] do not contain the first sentence of the text. Perhaps the first sentence might have been deleted on purpose.
2. Mentioned in Ibn Kathīr's *al-Bidāya wa al-Nihāya*.
3. Mentioned in Ibn Namā al-Ḥillī's *Muthīr al-Aḥzān*.
4. *Bismillah* is the first sentence in a great majority of Qur'ānic suras. It denotes the merciful character of the Almighty Allāh. Starting a discourse without it implies lack of mercy and a forthcoming harsh and horrible treatment.
5. Al-Mas'ūdī, *Murūj al-Dhahab*, vol. 3, p. 134; and Ibn al-Athīr, *al-Kāmil fī al-Ta'rīkh*, vol. 4, p. 34.
6. Muhallab b. Abī Ṣufra, 632–702, was a pro-Marwānid army commander who was in charge of defeating al-Mukhtar's revolt.
7. Al-Mas'ūdī, *Murūj al-Dhahab*, vol. 3, p. 137.
8. Ibid.
9. Qtd. in Abbās al-Qummī, *Safīna al-Biḥār*, vol. 1, p. 222.
10. Details of this account can be sought in Ibn Qutayba al-Dīnawarī, *al-Imāma wa al-Sīyāsa*, vol. 2, p. 32.
11. Nero (AD 37–68) was a Roman emperor, r. 54–68. His full name was *Nero Claudius Cassar Augustus Germanius.* He was infamous for his cruelty, wanton executions, and a fire that destroyed half of Rome in 64. (Adopted from C. Soanes, and A. Stevenson, eds., *Oxford Dictionary of English*, 2nd ed., rev. [Oxford, 2005]; and M. Parry, ed., *Chambers Biographical Dictionary*, 6th ed. [Edinburgh, UK, 1997].)
12. Muḥammad Jawād Mughnīya, *Shiah and the Despotic Rulers,*

Persian tr. Mustafa Zamani, p. 122.

13. 'Umar b. 'Abd Allāh b. al-'Azīz (61-101 AH/ 681-720) was the eighth Umayyad ruler (r. 99 AH/ 717)

14. Ibn Ḥajar al-'Asqalānī, *Tahdhīb al-Tahdhīb*, vol. 2, p. 211.

25

In Response to Lady Zaynab

يا اختاه! كلّ ما قضي فهو كائن.

"O Dear sister! Whatever has been destined (by Allāh) will take place." [1]

Context

On the way to al-Kūfa, and ultimately Karbalā, Imām al-Ḥusayn reached a station called al-Khuzaymīya. [2] He spent one day there and it was there that his sister Lady Zaynab called on him, [3] reporting that she heard a caller who recited the following lines that made her agitated. The lines were as follows:

O my eyes! Get ready for shedding tears,
for who will weep except me over the martyrs?
Weep over the people whom hazards push ahead to fulfill the promises.

In response to his sister, Imām al-Ḥusayn made only a short statement, as indicated in the beginning of this chapter, that whatever Allāh has determined will certainly take place.

What is Destiny?

On the basis of the aforementioned explanations on the Divine will and the developmental and religious Will of Allāh on the one hand, and in light of the special circumstances in which Imām al-

Ḥusayn was placed on the other hand, it seems that "destiny" has got a clearer meaning in the discourse of Imām al-Ḥusayn. This 'destiny' represents the Divine commandment in that a particular circumstance is connected with fulfilling one's duty on the part of Imām al-Ḥusayn. This is because *qaḍā'* 'destiny' means an ascertained affair and fulfilling the Will of Allāh in accordance with His fate and will.

Notes to Chapter 25
In Response to Lady Zaynab

1. Al-Khwārazmī, *Maqtal al-Ḥusayn*, vol. 1, p. 225.
2. Al-Khuzaymīya was a station on the way from al-Kūfa to Mecca, where Imām al-Ḥusayn stayed for a day. The place is ascribed to Khuzaymīya b. Khāzim.

26

At al-Tha'labīyya

لا خير في العيش بعد هؤلاء.

"There is no more grace in life after them." [1]

Context

The caravan of Imām al-Ḥusayn passed al-Khuzaymīya and Zarūd, and finally reached al-Tha'labīyya. Here, at al-Tha'labīyya, three statements of Imām al-Ḥusayn have been quoted, one on the occasion of Muslim b. 'Aqīl's [2] martyrdom, and the other two statements in reply to two enquirers. These statements are quoted in their original sequence.

The first statement is concerned with the martyrdom of Muslim b. 'Aqīl. Other historians narrated it on the authority of the account rendered by 'Abd Allāh b. Muslim. A synopsis of the account is as follows:

Ibn Sulaym, a Kūfan citizen, reported that soon after finishing their Ḥajj rituals, he and his associate al-Mudhrī rushed to get to Imām al-Ḥusayn's caravan as soon as possible. It was at Zarūd that they reached Imām al-Ḥusayn and at the same station they met a passenger by the name of Bukayr who was coming from al-Kūfa, and they enquired about the latest news of their city, al-Kūfa. Bukayr reported that Muslim b. 'Aqīl and Hānī b. 'Urwa [3] had been killed and that their bodies were dragged in the streets of al-Kūfa.

After receiving this news, 'Abd Allāh b. Muslim joined the caravan of Imām al-Ḥusayn and it was at sunset that they reached the al-Tha'labīyya station where they met Imām al-Ḥusayn and conveyed to him the news of the martyrdom Muslim and Hānī.

According to Ibn Sulaym, when he received this news, Imām al-Ḥusayn recited the Qur'ānic verse *"Innā li-Allāh wa innā ilah[i] rāji'ūn"* Surely we belong to Allāh, and to Him we shall return. [4] Then Imām al-Ḥusayn started shedding tears; in consequence, the rest of Imām al-Ḥusayn's associates, both Hāshimids and non-Hāshimids, started to weep as well. On hearing this, the women began to wail and cry.

When the gathering calmed down, some of the companions addressed Imām al-Ḥusayn in the following way: "O grandson of the Prophet of Allāh! The killing of Muslim and Hānī indicates that you have no supporter in al-Kūfa, so you had better return from here." On the other hand, the descendants of 'Aqīl, Muslim's father, maintained that they were determined to seek revenge for Muslim's blood from his killers, or to be killed like him. [5]

The dialogue continued between 'Abd Allāh and his associate on the one side, and the descendants of 'Aqīl on the other, and each side raised arguments in support of their views. However, everybody looked to Imām al-Ḥusayn's answer for guidance and a decision. Then Imām al-Ḥusayn remarked the above statement indicated in the very beginning of the chapter.

Conclusion

In Imām al-Ḥusayn's opinion, living in such a community is worthless and devoid of any benefit. A community such as al-Kūfa where such personalities like Muslim b. 'Aqīl and Hānī b. 'Urwa were mercilessly killed could no longer serve as a suitable place to take refuge. This is especially the case since al-Kūfa was once the capital of the Islamic empire where Imām 'Alī delivered his speeches, but now, the dead bodies of Muslim b. 'Aqīl and Hānī b. 'Urwa were dragged in its streets. After such crimes and the murder of such pious people, life would be meaningless in this corrupt community. Nonetheless, this mundane and denigrating life tastes so sweet and joyous for those who are devoid of human disposition, although having a human complexion.

Notes to Chapter 26
At al-Tha'labīyya

1. Al-Balādhurī, *Anṣāb al-Ashrāf*, vol. 3, p. 168; al-Ṭabarī, *al-Ta'rīkh*, vol. 7, p. 293; Ibn al-Athīr, *al-Kāmil fī al-Ta'rīkh*, vol. 3, p. 278; Ibn Kathīr, *al-Bidāya wa al-Nihāya*, vol. 8, p. 166; al-Mufīd, *Kitāb al-Irshād*, p. 222; Ibn Ṭāwūs, *al-Luhūf*, p. 41; and al- DhahAbī, *Sīyar A'lām al-Nubalā*, vol. 3, p. 208.
2. Muslim b. 'Aqīl b. Abī Ṭālib was a cousin and a brother-in-law of Imām al-Ḥusayn. His mother's name was 'Alīyah; Muslim married Ruqaya, a daughter of Imām 'Alī. He was a brave man and took part in a number of battles. Upon receiving a large number of the Kūfans' letters of invitation, Imām al-Ḥusayn dispatched him to al-Kūfa to evaluate the situation. When he reached al-Kūfa, a large number of people supported him, but soon after they betrayed and deserted him. He was arrested by the forces of 'Ubayd Allāh b. Zīyād, the Umayyad governor of al-Kūfa. He was beheaded by Bukayr b. Humayran al-Aḥmarī on the roof of the Government Palace at al-Kūfa and his decapitated body was thrown to the ground. Muslim was the first martyr of Imām al-Ḥusayn's movement.
3. Hānī b. 'Urwa was a companion of the Prophet and a helper of Imām 'Alī in the three important battles of al-Jamal, Ṣiffin, and Nahrawān. Hānī was the chief of his clan and had about 12,000 armed forces and swordsmen. When Muslim b. 'Aqīl entered al-Kūfa, Hānī received him at home and assisted him in his cause. However, a spy informed the governor of al-Kūfa 'Ubayd Allāh b. Zīyād of this, and Hānī was soon arrested. Hānī was martyred on 8 Dhū al-Ḥijja 60 AH. When martyred, Hānī was over 90.
4. The Holy Qur'ān, Sūrah al-Baqara [2]: 156.
5. This is an instance of the *thār* (blood) law of the ancient Arab communities.

27

At al-Tha‘labīyya: In Response to a Query

امام دعا الى هدى فاجابوا اليه و امام دعا الى ضلالة فاجابوا اليها هؤلاء فى الجنّة
وهؤلاء فى النّار وهو قوله تعالى : فريق فى الجنّة وفريق فى السّعير.

"An Imām [1] called for a right direction, and some people answered positively toward it [2]; and another imām called for an immorality, and some people answered positively toward it [3]; they (the former group) will be in Paradise, and they (the latter group) will be in the Fire. And, this is His [the Exalted Allāh's] statement: 'A group in Paradise, and a group in the Hell. [4].'" [5]

Context

According to the great Shi‘i *hadith* scholar Sheikh al-Ṣadūq and Khaṭīb Al-Khwārazmī, it was at al-Tha‘labīyya that another person had the honour of meeting Imām al-Ḥusayn and enquired about the interpretation of the following Qur'ānic verse: "*Yawm[a] nad‘ā kull[a] unās[in] bi-imāmihim*" [6] (the day when We will call for the human beings in association with their leaders.) In response to this query, Imām al-Ḥusayn made the above statement.

In the above speech, Imām al-Ḥusayn spoke on the authority of the Holy Qur'ān of two opposite groups and leaderships. Each group is dependent on a leader from whom they follow and take lessons. In reality, there have always been, and will be, such groups of people and leaders. Hence such leaders will be gathered together with their plans and people must follow the leader who invites people to the human and eternal felicity.

Notes to Chapter 27
At al-Tha'labīyya: In Response to a Query

1. In Arabic, the word *Imām* (also an Arabic loanword) in English means 'Leader'.

2. This is in line with the Qur'ānic concept of a similar notion, that is, "*wa ja'alnāhum a'immah[tan] yahdūn[a] bi-amrinā*" [And We made them leaders to guide (the people) by our command] The Holy Qur'ān, Sūrah al-Anbiyā [21]: 73.

3. This stands in line with another Qur'ānic statement, that is, "*wa ja'alnāhum a'immah[tan] yad'ūn[a] ilā al-nār*" [We made them the leaders of those who call to Hell] The Holy Qur'ān, Sūrah al-Qasaṣ [28]: 41.

4. The Holy Qur'ān, Sūrah al-Shūrā [42]: 7.

5. Sheikh al-Ṣadūq, *al-Amālī*, Session 30; and Al-Khwārazmī, *Maqtal al-Ḥusayn*, vol. 1, p. 221.

6. The Holy Qur'ān, Sūrah al-Isrā' [17]: 71.

28

In Response to Another Query

اما واللّٰه! لو لقيتك بالمدينة لاريتك اثر جبرئيل فى دارنا ونزوله بالوحى على جدّى. يا اخا اهل الكوفة! من عندنا مستقى العلم افعلموا وجهلنا؟ هذا ممّا لا يكون.

"By Allāh! Had I met you in Medina, I would have shown to you the impression of Gabriel [1] in our house [2] and his bringing down the revelation unto my grandfather [3]. O Kūfan brother! The treasury of knowledge lies with us; are they [4] learned and we are ignorant? This is impossible." [5]

Context

This is the third speech of Imām al-Ḥusayn at the same station, al-Tha'labīyya. There a Kūfan met with Imām al-Ḥusayn, and during the conversation, Imām al-Ḥusayn enquired about his hometown. He answered that he was from al-Kūfa. Thereupon, Imām al-Ḥusayn delivered the speech quoted above. The context indicates that Imām al-Ḥusayn's speech must have been the answer to question; however, the Kūfan's question seems not to have been recorded in the sources consulted.

Upon a closer scrutiny, there is a negative, rhetorical question embedded in the discourse of Imām al-Ḥusayn which indicates that the Kūfan must have been an unenlightened and shallow person who regarded Imām al-Ḥusayn's movement on a par with those of other dissidents.

We can assume, that to enlighten the Kūfan, Imām al-Ḥusayn informed him of the atrocities of the Umayyads and the deviations they caused in the leadership of the Muslim community after the demise of Prophet Muḥammad. The deviations were so critical and grave that the Umayyads who were the foes of Islam and the Qur'ān regarded themselves as the Muslims' leaders; the Umayyads further committed several crimes in the name of Islam. Nonetheless, the ignorant questioner seemed not to have grasped the truth despite Imām al-Ḥusayn's clear explanations. Like so many superficial and shortsighted Muslims, he regarded the Umayyads' outward practice of Islamic rituals as the basis for their legitimacy and righteousness.

Conclusion

Several conclusions can be drawn from the discourse of Imām al-Ḥusayn. It confirms the perception expressed in the famous Arabic saying, "The members of a house are more knowledgeable than the outsiders about the internal affairs of their house". This standard can help solve and understand the disparity among Muslims after the death of Prophet Muḥammad. To put it differently, these two denominations, that is, Shi'i and Sunni, are similar in respect of a considerable number of doctrinal principles and ritual practices. These include: monotheism, prophethood, resurrection, the Qur'ān, the Qiblah, *salat*, *zakat*, Ḥajj, and so forth. There remain, however, some doctrinal issues such as Imāmate and a few other topics in which they are dissimilar. However, if the past grudges are removed and the controversial issues are dealt with from a purely scholarly and unbiased perspective, re-unity will be possible and these two denominations could form one profound school, as intended by Allāh and Prophet Muḥammad.

Furthermore, there are several general and specific answers to the debate over the successorship of the Prophet. One of the general answers is expressed by the above Arabic saying, implied by Imām al-Ḥusayn's discourse, that the Shi'i denomination has received all of its religious doctrines and rituals from Prophet Muḥammad via his Infallible descendants. In other words, the Shia follow exactly the same school of the Revelation as the Holy Prophet and his household whom Allāh describes as those whom Allāh have kept away from any impurity. [6]

Notes to Chapter 28
In Response to Another Query

1. The Archangel Gabriel.
2. The house of Prophet Muḥammad.
3. Prophet Muḥammad.
4. The Umayyads.
5. Muḥammad b. Ḥasan Saffār, *Baṣā'ir al-Darajāt*, p. 11; al-Kulaynī, *Uṣūl al-Kāfī*, the section on the "Resource of knowledge from the House of the progenies of Muḥammad."
6. The Holy Qur'ān, Sūrah al-Ahāzab [33]: 33.

29

At al-Shuqūq

انّ الا مر لله يفعل مايشاء وربّنا تبارك و تعالى هو كلّ يوم فى شان

فان تكن الدّنيا تعدّ نفيسة فانّ ثواب اللّه اعلا وانبل

وان تكن الاموال للتّرك جمعها فما بال متروك به المرء يبخل

وان تكن الارزاق قسما مقّسما فقلّة حرص المرء فى الكسب اجمل

وان تكن الابدان للموت انشات فقتل امرى ء بالسّيف فى اللّه افضل

عليكم سلام اللّه يا ال احمد فانّى ارانى عنكم سوف ارحل

"The affairs are within the control of Allāh [1]; He does whatever He wishes [2], and Allāh, the Exalted and Sublime, is every day at work [3].
Although life in this world may be invaluable,
Allāh's bounty is indeed superior and most magnificent.
And if the properties collected are to be departed from,
Man should not be stingy regarding them.
And if the sustenance is already portioned,
Man's less greed to obtain is most beautiful.
And if bodies have grown up for death,
Man's being slain by sword in Allāh's cause is most excellent. May Allāh's salām be bestowed upon you, O descendants of Ahmad [4],
I see that I shall be departing you." [5]

Context

As Imām al-Ḥusayn was getting closer to the border of Iraq, he encountered more people from Iraq and especially from al-Kūfa. After the station al-Tha'labīyya, Imām al-Ḥusayn and his entourage reached the station al-Shuqūq. There he encountered a person who was coming from al-Kūfa. Imām al-Ḥusayn asked him of the situation of al-Kūfa and its current climate. In reply, the man said, "O grandson of the Prophet of Allāh! The people of Iraq have become united against you and have vowed to fight you." In response to this statement, Imām al-Ḥusayn recited the poem above.

Firm Resolve

One of the most important qualities of a victorious leader is having firm resolve. That is, the leader should not waver from his decision at the sight of any unfavorable incident or at the sight of any obstacle, nor should he portray any weakness. These qualities are evident in the character of Imām al-Ḥusayn when he spoke to the Kūfan traveler who informed him of the bitter and unexpected betrayal of the Kūfans. They had earlier announced themselves as the helpers and allies of Imām al-Ḥusayn and later became his enemies. This news caused no weakness or hesitation in the behaviour of Imām al-Ḥusayn. Rather, he insisted on his cause. In return, through composing some poems, which signify the worthlessness and pettiness of this worldly life and its wealth, he made himself and his entourage much more resolute in their decision. This is one of the lessons Imām al-Ḥusayn taught to humankind.

Notes to Chapter 29
At al-Shuqūq

1. This is a paraphrase of the notion expressed in the Holy Qur'ān, Sūrah al-Ra'd [13]: 31.
2. This is a paraphrase of the notion expressed in the Holy Qur'ān, *inter alia*, in the Sūrah Āl-i 'Imrān [3]: 40; and Ibrāhīm [14]: 27.

3. This is a paraphrase of the same concept expressed in the Holy Qur'ān, Sūrah al-Raḥmān [55]: 29.
4. Ahmad is another designation of Prophet Muḥammad, mentioned only once in the Holy Qur'ān, Sūrah al-Ṣaf [61]:6.
5. Ibn 'Asākir, *al-Ta'rīkh*, p. 164; Al-Khwārazmī, *Maqtal al-Ḥusayn*, vol. 1, p. 223; and Ibn Shahr Āshūb, *Manāqib*, vol. 4, p. 95.

30

At Zubāla

بسم الله الرّحمن الرّحيم

امّا بعد، فانّه قد اتانا خبر فظيع، قتل مسلم بن عقيل وهانى بن عروة وعبدالله بن يقطرو قد خذلتنا شيعتنا، فمن احبّ منكم الا نصراف فلينصرف، ليس عليه منّا ذمام.

"In the Name of Allāh, the All-compassionate, the All-Merciful. Now to our topic: Indeed a distressing piece of news has reached us: Muslim b. 'Aqīl, Hānī b. 'Urwa, and 'Abd Allāh b. Yaqṭur have been murdered, and our followers have forsaken us. Hence, any of you who may wish to return can go back; there is no longer any commitment to us on you." [1]

Context

After passing by al-Shaqūq, Imām al-Ḥusayn's caravan reached the station called Zubāla. It was there that Imām al-Ḥusayn was informed by a letter from al-Kūfa from one of his followers with the news of the martyrdom of Muslim b. 'Aqīl, Hānī b. 'Urwa, and 'Abd Allāh b. Yaqṭur. [2] Then Imām al-Ḥusayn conveyed the news to his entourage in the way indicated above.

Lucidity of Speech

One of the merits and distinguishing factors of true religious leaders is their plainness, sincerity, and expression of the truth as observable in the discourses of true religious leaders. Based on their firm conviction, the Imām is always sincere and frank in conveying to his followers whatever may concern their destiny, even if this honesty may harm him. This is because the aim of such leaders is to instill faith in the hearts of the people; all their efforts are to reach this aim. This cannot be achieved by pretention, fraud, and hiding facts, some acts which are unfortunately predominant in the world of politics.

This sincere attitude, loyalty, and truthfulness are evident in the conduct of all Imāms, and above all in the personality of Prophet Muḥammad who is the role model for humanity. This was evident in all aspects of the Prophet's life, and Imām al-Ḥusayn, the leader of liberality, was no different. In this way, he clearly made his companions aware of the danger he anticipated on various occasions on the way from Medina to Karbalā. Specific examples include, the speech he delivered when he left Mecca; while talking with the three 'Abd Allāhs (that is, 'Abd Allāh b. 'Abbās, 'Abd Allāh b. 'Umar, and 'Abd Allāh b. al-Zubayr); when he was talking with Muḥammad b. al-Ḥanafīyyah; and finally when he received a letter from one of his friends about the martyrdom of three of his loyal companions. For more emphasis, he showed the letter to his companions and read it out for them.

The Incentive and Effect of this Proposal

Al-Ṭabarī, the great historian, and the late Sheikh al-Mufīd, as one of the greatest Shi'i scholars, offer a similar analysis regarding the incentive and effect of this proposal. Al-Ṭabarī held that Imām al-Ḥusayn was aware that those who had joined him on the way had expected to arrive in al-Kūfa where there was support and obedience for Imām al-Ḥusayn. However, after the betrayl of the Kūfans, Imām al-Ḥusayn wanted the companions who accompanied him to have a clear view of the real situation. Some of his companions left him and returned as soon as they found out the reality of the journey, except for a small loyal group of companions who were faithful to the Imām to the last drop of their blood. Imām al-Ḥusayn conveyed to them the content of the letter.

According to al-Ṭabarī, the effect of conveying the content of the letter was that a number of those who had joined Imām al-Ḥusayn dispersed and left him so that only those who had joined him in Medina remained. The same analysis is also recorded in Ibn Sa'd's *al-Ṭabaqāt*.

Conclusion

In Zubāla, Imām al-Ḥusayn mentioned the same proposition that was repeated in various places and on a number of occasions: that there was no obligation on his companions and he would set them free without any commitment. Following this event, only his staunch companions remained. Again, at the next station, Baṭn al-'Aqaba, he communicated the same concern with his companions more candidly.

Notes to Chapter 30
At Zubāla

1. Al-Ṭabarī, *al-Ta'rīkh*, vol. 7, p. 294; and al-Mufīd, *Kitāb al-Irshād*, p.123.
2. Ibn Ḥajar in *al-Iṣābah* gives the following account about the way 'Abd Allāh b. Yaqṭur was murdered: When Imām al-Ḥusayn left Mecca, he dispatched 'Abd Allāh b. Yaqṭur with a letter for Muslim b. 'Aqīl; however, 'Abd Allāh b. Yaqṭur was arrested by Ḥuṣayn b. Numayr at al-Qādisīya and was taken to 'Ubayd Allāh b. Zīyād, the governor of al-Kūfa. 'Ubayd Allāh b. Zīyād ordered him to deliver a talk, abusing Imām 'Alī and Imām al-Ḥusayn. To seize this opportunity, 'Abd Allāh b. Yaqṭur apparently agreed to do so. However, he started praising Imām 'Alī and Imām al-Ḥusayn, and spoke ill of the Umayyads. He informed people that he was the envoy of Imām al-Ḥusayn, inviting people to join and help Imām al-Ḥusayn in defiance to Ubayd Allāh b. Zīyād. With this unexpected turn, 'Ubayd Allāh b. Zīyād ordered him to be thrown down to the ground from the roof of the Government Palace at al-Kūfa, while his hands were cuffed from behind. Fallen on the ground, his bones were broken. While he was still alive, a person by the name of 'Abd al-

Malik b. 'Umayr hurried and severed his head. Faced with the criticism of people, he justified his cruel act under the guise of freeing 'Abd Allāh b. Yaqṭur from pain! Islam does not permit a person to put an end to one's life and the severe pain being endured.

31

At Baṭn al-'Aqaba

a) ما ارانى الا مقتولا فانّى رايت فى المنام كلابا تنهشنى واشدّها علىّ كلب ابقع

b) يا عبدالله! ليس يخفى علىّ الرّاى وانّ الله لا يغلب على امره انّهم لن يدعونى حتّى يستخرجوا هذه العلقة من جوفى فاذا فعلوا ذلك سلّط الله عليهم من يذلّهم حتّى يكونوا اذلّ فرق الامم.

a) "I see myself only to be slain; for I dreamt that some dogs were attacking me, the most aggressive of which was a piebald dog."

b) ... "O servant of Allāh! The point is not unknown to me, and Allāh is undefeated in His affairs. [1] They have not called upon me until they would shed my blood. When they have done this, Allāh will certainly make a person dominate them who will denigrate them so that they will be the most humiliated of nations." [2]

Context

After Zubāla, Imām al-Ḥusayn's caravan reached Baṭn al-'Aqaba. On the authority of the sixth Imām, Imām Ja'far al-Ṣādiq, Ibn Qūlawayh mentioned that Imām al-Ḥusayn, on the basis of a dream [5], addressed his companions in the way mentioned above in the first fragment quoted (a).

According to the late Sheikh al-Mufīd in *Kitāb al-Irshād,* an old man by the name of 'Amr b. Lawdhān of the 'Akrama tribe met Imām al-Ḥusayn's caravan at Baṭn al-'Aqaba and he enquired about Imām al-Ḥusayn's destination. "To al-Kūfa." Imām al-Ḥusayn replied.

'Amr b. Lawdhān replied in the following way: "I ask you by Allāh to return from here, for I believe, in this journey you will be confronted only with spears and swords. However, it will be safe for you to move to those who have invited you provided that they have prevented any war or riot and they are ready for you. However, in the present condition of which you are also aware, I do not see it safe for you to go there."

In response to the old man's statement, Imām al-Ḥusayn informed him, as indicated above, that he did have a clear view of the situation; however, Allāh's will is unchangeable. Then Imām al-Ḥusayn informed him that the enemies had been determined to slay him, a shameful act after which Allāh will make someone dominate them who will make them the most despised nation.

Notes to Chapter 31
At Baṭn al-'Aqaba

1. Ibn Qūlawayh al-Qummī, *Kāmil al-Zīyārāt*, p. 75; and al-Tabarī, *Ta'rīkh*, vol. 7, p. 294.
2. Al-Mufīd, *Kitāb al-Irshād*, p. 223; Ibn 'Asākir, *Ta'rīkh*, p. 211; and Ibn Kathīral-Dimashqī, *al-Bidāya wa al-Nihāya*, vol. 8, p. 169.
3. The dreams of the prophets and the Infallibles are true, revelatory dreams, hence totally different from those of ordinary people.

32

Imām al-Ḥusayn's Speech After the Noon Prayer in Sharāf

ايّها النّاس! انّها معذرة الى اللّه واليكم و انّى لم اتكم حتّى اتتنى كتبكم وقدمت بها رسلكم ان اقدم علينا فانّه ليس لنا امام ولعلّ اللّه ان يجمعنا بك على الهدى فان كنتم على ذلك فقد جئتكم فاعطونى ما اطمانّ به من عهودكم ومواثيقكم و ان كنتم لمقدمى كارهين انصرف عنكم الى المكان الّذى جئت منه اليكم.

"O People! This is a dutiful statement before Allāh and a sound proof for you. I did not set out to you until your letters reached me together with your envoys inviting me to you, saying there would be no Imām for us and perhaps Allāh will direct us to the Right Path because of you. Hence, if you are still of the same opinion, I have come to you and you must pledge allegiance to me with the conviction that was evident in your pledges and covenants. However, if you have developed aversion to my arrival, I shall return to the place wherefrom I set out to you." [1]

Context

After Baṭn al-'Aqaba, Imām al-Ḥusayn's caravan reached another station, called Sharāf. Soon after, al-Ḥurr b. Yazīd al-Rīyāḥī reached the same place, with 1,000 swordsmen under his command to block Imām al-Ḥusayn's progression. It was at this place that Imām al-Ḥusayn delivered two lectures, explaining his standpoint to al-Ḥurr's army as well as the agenda of the Umayyads and the reason of his journey.

The Clemency of Imām al-Ḥusayn

Before dealing with Imām al-Ḥusayn's lectures, it is necessary to have a view of what historians have recorded on the way Imām al-Ḥusayn treated al-Ḥurr's army. The scene indicates the clemency of Imām al-Ḥusayn which is an example for all leaders of the world.

Having reached Sharāf, Imām al-Ḥusayn ordered the young men of his entourage to go to the River al-Furāt, the Euphrates, before sunrise. He ordered them to take more water than their usual requirment, and bring it to the tents. A few hours later, during the hottest part of the day just before noon, al-Ḥurr b. Yazīd reached the same place with 1,000 swordmen under his command. Imām al-Ḥusayn noticed the extreme fatigue and thirst of al-Ḥurr's swordsmen, coupled with the heavy burden of the war clothing and weapons and the dust of the road. Imām al-Ḥusayn ordered his companions to distribute water among al-Ḥurr's forces as well as their horses and spray water on them to cool and refresh them. Imām al-Ḥusayn's companions did so: they quenched the intense thirst of the swordsmen, gave water to their horses, and sprayed water on the horses' polls, crests, and feet.

'Alī b. Ṭa''ān al-Muḥāribī, a swordsman, commented: "Owing to intense thirst and fatigue, I was the last soldier to reach the Sharāf station and assumed a place at the rear of the army. As the companions of [Imām] al-Ḥusayn were busy distributing water to the rest of the soldiers, nobody paid attention to me. It was at this time that an impressively handsome man noticed me from beside the tents. This man, whom later on I identified to be [Imām] al-Ḥusayn b. 'Alī, hurried toward me and, carrying a leather flask of water, told me, *'Anikh al-rāwīya* (Make the camel kneel down!)', but I did not understand him, for *al-rāwīyah* is a Hejazi dialect word. Noticing this, he repeated it another way, saying *'Anikh al-jamal.'* I made my camel kneel down and started drinking water. Owing to intense thirst, I hurried and the water poured on my face; I could not drink water comfortably. Then Imām al-Ḥusayn said, '*Ikhnith al-saqqā*' (Squeeze the leather flask!).' Again, I could not understand! At this moment, [Imām] al-Ḥusayn, who was holding the leather flask, took its mouth and adjusted it in such a way that I could drink water and quench my thirst easily."

Beginning the Salat

After this graceful, small reception, and some rest, it was time to perform the noon prayer. At this time, Imām al-Ḥusayn ordered his special *mu'adhin*, al-Ḥajjāj b. Masrūq [2]: "May Allāh have mercy on you! Recite the *azan* and *iqāmah* so that we shall perform the prayer". Upon this order, al-Ḥajjāj b. Masrūq started reciting the *azan*. In the meantime, Imām al-Ḥusayn asked al-Ḥurr b. Yazīd whether he would perform his prayer together with them, or separately with his own army. "Nay, we will perform the prayer together with you in one line," returned al-Ḥurr. Then Imām al-Ḥusayn led the prayer together with his companions, while al-Ḥurr and his army followed him.

Imām al-Ḥusayn's Speech

Following the noon prayer, Imām al-Ḥusayn began his speech, while leaning on his sword and wearing slippers, he wore a simple Arabic shirt and abaya. He delivered his speech, as quoted in the beginning of this chapter. Al-Ḥurr's army did not say anything after Imām al-Ḥusayn's speech, neither positively or negatively.

In this way, the noon prayer was performed, until it was time for the afternoon prayer. The afternoon prayer was led by Imām al-Ḥusayn, his companions and al-Ḥurr's army prayed behind him. After the afternoon prayer, Imām al-Ḥusayn delivered another speech which is recorded in the following chapter.

Notes to Chapter 32 Imām al-Ḥusayn's Speech After the Noon Prayer in Sharāf

1. Al-Ṭabarī, *Ta'rīkh*, vol. 7, pp. 297-8; Ibn al-Athīr, *al-Kāmil*, vol. 3, p. 280; al-Mufīd, *Kitāb al-Irshād*, pp. 224- 225; Al-Khwārazmī, *Maqtal al-Ḥusayn*, pp. 231-232.
2. Al-Ḥajjāj b. Masrūq al-Mudhḥijī al-Ju'fī, a Shi'i resident of al-Kūfa, went to Mecca to meet Imām al-Ḥusayn; from then on he was the *mu'adhin* of Imām al-Ḥusayn. He was martyred on Ashurā.

33

Imām al-Ḥusayn's Second Speech in Sharāf

امّا بعد: ايّها الناس! فانّكم ان تتّقوا اللّه وتعرفوا الحقّ لاهله يكن ارضى للّه ونحن اهل بيت محمّدصلّى اللّه عليه و اله و سلّم اولى بولاية هذا الامر من هؤلاء المدّعين ما ليس لهم والسّائرين بالجور والعدوان وان ابيتم الا الكراهة لنا والجهل بحقّنا وكان رايكم الآن غير ما اتتنى به كتبكم انصرف عنكم.

"O People! Indeed if you observe piety and are cognizant of the right for (and with) its holders, it will be more desirable to Allāh, and that we are the *Ahl al-Bayt* of [the Prophet] Muḥammad – upon whom and his progeny may Allāh bestow graces – hence we are more deserved to superindent this affair [leadership] rather than those claimants [the Umayyads] and others who have been committing crimes and increasing animosity. And if you were reluctant to us and ignorant of our right, and if your view at present is different from that when your letters reached me, I shall leave you." [1]

Context

As mentioned in the previous chapter, it was at the station Sharāf that Imām al-Ḥusayn met al-Ḥurr b. Yazīd al-Rīyāḥī and his army, the first army dispatched by 'Ubayd Allāh b. Zīyād. After the noon prayer, both armies performed the afternoon prayer together and behind Imām al-Ḥusayn. Following this Imām al-Ḥusayn delivered the above speech.

After Imām al-Ḥusayn's speech, al-Ḥurr replied that he had not been aware of anything about the Kūfans' letters of invitation.

Upon this statement of al-Ḥurr, Imām al-Ḥusayn ordered 'Uqba b. Sam'ān [2] to bring the two bags packed with the Kūfans' letters. Again al-Ḥurr reaffirmed that he was ignorant of the Kūfans' letters. At this point, Imām al-Ḥusayn and al-Ḥurr had a conversation, which is recorded in the next chapter.

Three Important Points

Imām al-Ḥusayn's speech contains three important points. Firstly, he introduced the *Ahl al-Bayt* of Prophet Muḥammad and declared their chastity and sanctity for which Allāh has assigned to them the sublime status of Imāmate and religious leadership of the *ummah*.

Secondly, he introduced his enemies by declaring that they are corrupt, cruel people and have assumed control of the Muslims' affairs by force and oppression.

Lastly, Imām al-Ḥusayn emphasised the motivation behind his journey to al-Kūfa in both lectures, as opposed to his uprising and challenge. He stressed that his journey was based on invitations from the people of al-Kūfa themselves. He then gave them an opportunity to revoke their invitation by saying that if they were reluctant and regretful of their earlier invitations, Imām al-Ḥusayn was ready to leave them and return.

Was Imām al-Ḥusayn Willing to Return to Medina?

If they had let him go, would Imām al-Ḥusayn be willing to return to Medina and abandon the movement he had initiated? The answer to this question can be found in the two recent speeches of Imām al-Ḥusayn in Sharāf. His speeches were an ultimatum so as not to leave any excuse for the Kūfans. This is what Imām al-Ḥusayn expressed in the very beginning of his lecture, that it was the final say before Allāh and the audience being addressed.

Imām al-Ḥusayn intended to inform the Kūfans that his journey to their city was not to launch an attack on them. Rather, the corrupt situation caused by the agents of the Umayyad rulers was absolutely false and unreliable. It was a journey undertaken in response to an earlier mass invitation of the inhabitants of al-Kūfa.

Imām al-Ḥusayn's uprising was not a consequence of the Kūfans' invitations, neither was his mission dependent on the Kūfans' support. If that had been the case, then after the betrayl of the Kūfans Imām al-Ḥusayn would have also abandoned his struggle and sought seclusion. Rather, Imām al-Ḥusayn meant that if the Kūfans had changed their mind and were no longer willing to receive Imām al-Ḥusayn and would not cooperate with him, he would not enter into al-Kūfa and this confrontation and opposition would take place away from al-Kūfa. However, the principle of not pledging allegiance to Yazīd and opposing him remained intact and unaltered for the Imām, even if it would lead to martyrdom. Had the opposition realised what Imām al-Ḥusayn meant by his speech, that nothing would weaken his resolve, they would have abandoned their confrontation as they would have anticipated the heavy price they would have to pay for confronting him. Any confrontation with Imām al-Ḥusayn would certainly result in the Umayyads paying a heavy price.

Conclusion

The fact that the battle took place between Yazīd's army and Imām al-Ḥusayn is convincing proof that Imām al-Ḥusayn never gave up opposition. In addition, the speeches of Imām al-Ḥusayn from the moment he left Medina until his tragic martyrdom confirms his unwavering resolve and firm decision. Imām al-Ḥusayn's speeches are replete with examples of his dedication to the cause; some of these fragments are as follows: "For this man, being slain by sword in the way of Allāh is more virtuous"; "I am moving toward death, and death is not unprestigeous for a freeman"; "Admitting humiliation is far from us"; "I will never succumb to them like a despised man, nor will I run away from them like a slave"; "Such a personality like me will never pledge allegiance with such a person like him [Yazīd]"; and "By Allāh! I will never pledge humiliation to them myself." With such views, Imām al-Ḥusayn would never give up his struggle or aim.

In conclusion, the Kūfans' actions had no effect, positive or negative, on Imām al-Ḥusayn's uprising, as their initial invitations were not the *incentive* behind his struggles, challenges, or uprising.

Notes to Chapter 33
Imām al-Ḥusayn's Second Speech in Sharāf

1. Al-Ṭabarī, *Ta'rīkh*, vol. 7, pp. 297-8; Ibn al-Athīr, *al-Kāmil*, vol. 3, pp. 280; al-Mufīd, *Kitāb al-Irshād*, pp. 224-5; al- Khwārazmī, *Maqtal al-Ḥusayn*, pp. 231-2.

2. 'Uqabah b. Sam'ān was a servant of Rabāb and was once arrested and freed by 'Umar b. Sa'd. He was one of those who were injured in the Battle of Karbalā on Ashurā.

34

In Response to al-Ḥurr

افبالموت تخوّفنى؟ وهل يعدو بكم الخطب ان تقتلونى؟ وساقول ما قال اخو الاوس لابن عمّه وهو يريد نصرة رسول الله صلّى الله عليه و اله و سلّم:

سامضى و ما بالموت عار على الفتى   اذا ما نوى حقّاً وجاهد مسلماً

واسا الرّجال الصّالحين بنفسه   وفارق مثبورا وخالف محرما

اقدّم نفسى لا اريد بقاءها   لتلقى خميسا فى الهياج عرمرما

فان عشت لم اندم وان متّ لم الم   كفى لك ذلا ان تعيش وترغما

Do you frighten me with death? And, can you do anything other than kill me? I will repeat [in answer] what al-Aws' brother had said to his cousin while he intended to help the Prophet of Allāh – (May Allāh bestow His blessings upon him and his progeny):

"I shall rush towards death which is not a disgrace for a youth,
When he believes in Islam and fights as a Muslim.
When he wishes to support the good-doers by sacrificing his life,
By disagreeing with the criminals and those who are enemies of Allāh.
I am offering my life and do not wish to retain it,
So as to confront a magnificent army in a fierce battle.
If I live, I won't regret; and if I die, I will have no problem, while for you,
It is enough to live so disgracefully." [1]

Context

In Sharāf, after Imām al-Ḥusayn delivered his second speech and showed al-Ḥurr and his companions the Kūfans' letters of invitation, al-Ḥurr continued to express his ignorance regarding the letters. At that time, there was a discussion between Imām al-Ḥusayn and al-Ḥurr about the Imām's movement, for Imām al-Ḥusayn intended to continue his journey toward al-Kūfa. Despite Imām al-Ḥusayn's decision, al-Ḥurr intended to prevent him from doing so on the basis of a mission entrusted to him.

When al-Ḥurr noticed that Imām al-Ḥusayn was resolute and not willing to compromise, he said: "Now that you have decided to go on your way, you had better choose a way neither to reach al-Kūfa nor to return to Medina so that I would make use of this opportunity and write a peaceful letter to 'Ubayd Allāh b. Zīyād: I hope I am saved from a confrontation with you." Then al-Ḥurr added: "I remind you that if you resort to sword and start a battle, you will certainly be slain!"

When al-Ḥurr reached this point, Imām al-Ḥusayn delivered the talk mentioned in the beginning of this chapter.

It is mentioned that Imām al-Ḥusayn praised the above poems because of the issues they address, hence he quoted them in his speeches on various occasions. The fact that he quotes such poetry signifies his intention to assist the religion of Islam, to perform a *jihad* in the cause of Islam, to defend the Qur'ān, and to preserve its verdicts from deterioration. The *jihad* is one of the greatest Divine duties and it follows the praiseworthy practice of Prophet Muḥammad. He abandoned everything: position, life, and even the lives of his beloved family and companions. [2] Anybody who performs a *jihad* in this way and is martyred cannot be blamed. However, someone who is attached to their home and position in a way that prevents them from going for *jihad* will be reproached in this world and the next.

Notes to Chapter 34
In Response to al-Ḥurr

1. Al-Balādhurī, *Anṣāb al-Ashrāf*, vol. 3, p. 171.
2. Aḥmad al-Sāberī al-Hamādanī, *Adab al-Ḥusayn wa Ḥimāsatuhū* (Qom, 1395 AH/ 1973), p. 33.

35

At al-Bayḍa

ايّها النّاس! انّ رسول الله صلّى الله عليه و اله قال من راى سلطانا جائرا، مستحلا لحرامالله، ناكثا عهده، مخالفا لسنّة رسول الله، يعمل فى عباد الله بالاثم والعدوان، فلم يغيّر عليه بفعل ولا قول كان حقّا على الله ان يدخله مدخله الا وانّ هؤلاء قد لزموا طاعة الشّيطان وتركوا طاعة الرّحمن واظهروا الفساد وعطّلوا الحدود واستاثروا بالفىء و أحلّوا حرام الله وحرّموا حلاله وانا احقّ ممّن غيّر وقد اتتنى كتبكم وقدمت علىّ رسلكم ببيعتكم انّكم لا تسلّمونى ولا تخذلونى، فان اتممتم علىّ بيعتكم تصيبوا رشدكم فانا الحسين بن علىّ و ابن فاطمة بنت رسول الله نفسى مع انفسكم واهلى مع اهلكم ولكم فىّ اسوة و ان لم تفعلوا ونقضتم عهدكم وخلّفتم بيعتى من اعناقكم ما هى لكم بنكر لقد فعلتموها بابى واخى و ابن عمّى مسلم، فالمغرور من اغترّ بكم فحظّكم اخطاتم ونصيبكم ضيّعتم ومن نكث فانّما ينكث على نفسه وسيغنى الله عنكم والسّلام عليكم ورحمةالله وبركاته.

"O People! Indeed the Prophet of Allāh – May Allāh bless him and his progeny – remarked: 'Anybody who sees a tyrant ruler who treats the *ḥarām* (prohibited) prescribed by Allāh as *ḥalāl* (permitted); infringes His covenant in defiance to the *sunnah* (practice) of the Prophet of Allāh; and treats the servants of Allāh by means of committing sins and enmity; and they do not revolt against him in words or deeds, Allāh has every right to drive them to their abode [in Hell].'

"Beware that they – the Umayyads – have preferred obeying Satan and have abandoned obeying the All-Merciful Allāh. They have supported corruption, delayed practicing the Divine punishments, usurped the *fay'* (special money to be paid to the Prophet's household), and have declared permissible (*ḥalāl*) what has been declared unlawful and forbidden."

"I am more deserved to make this change, and your letters have reached me with your envoys coming to me to express your allegiance (*bay'a*) that you would not render me to the enemies, nor would you leave me alone."

"Now, if you are still constant in your allegiance, you have indeed advanced, for I am al-Ḥusayn son of 'Alī and Fāṭima, daughter of the Prophet of Allāh; my life is associated with yours, my family is associated with yours [your families are as important to me as mine], and I am a role model for you. And, if you do not do this and break your promise and have already neglected your allegiance, this will not be a surprise, for you did the same with my father, brother, and cousin, Muslim. Hence, anybody who has confidence in you is deceived. You have gone the wrong way in gaining your share and have wasted your profits, 'and anyone who breaks his pledge does so to his own detriment' [1]. And, Allāh will make me independent of you. And, may Allāh's peace and blessing be bestowed on you." [2]

Context

After Sharāf, both caravans were travelling side by side and whenever there was water and places to rest, they would stop. One such resting place was a station called al-Bayḍa. There, Imām al-Ḥusayn had an opportunity to talk to al-Ḥurr's forces and make them aware of some facts and explain the reasoning behind his uprising and movement. The speech Imām al-Ḥusayn delivered is quoted at the beginning of this chapter. [3]

Imām al-Ḥusayn's Incentive to Start the Movement

In this speech, Imām al-Ḥusayn exposed the atrocities and corruption of the powerful enemy of Islam, the Umayyads. He also compared their situation to his position with respect to religion and the leadership of the Muslims. He therebye explained the rationale for his movement and uprising with a reference to a *hadith* related from Prophet Muḥammad. He declared that he was entitled to oppose and challenge the Umayyad leadership as a religious duty and responsibility, as they had started manipulating the Islamic rules mentioned in the Holy Qur'ān and those practiced by Prophet Muḥammad. It was exactly what he had remarked in his last will and testament just before he left Medina for Mecca and of the same reason he had given Muḥammad b. al-Ḥanafīyyah.

For Imām al-Ḥusayn the incentive to rise up came from the emergence of tyranny and corruption in practicing Islam. Hence his objective in this revolutionary movement was to enjoin the good and prohibit evil, to wipe away modes of corruption and implement the neglected rules of Islam. This is what he expressed earlier when he said: "I intend to enjoin the good and prohibit evil and conduct the practice of my grandfather [Prophet Muḥammad]." And, at the time, he remarked that "anybody who sees a tyrant ruler... and does not oppose him in words or deeds... it is their right that Allāh would direct them to their place in the Hell." This was Imām al-Ḥusayn's incentive in his own words.

The Holy Qur'ān has an explanation for disintegration of former peoples and breaking down of the prophets' programs and laws. The Holy Qur'ān remarks that neglecting the practice of enjoining good and prohibition from evil was the cause of and the collapse of previous civilizations. The Qur'ān is explicit in this regard: "If only there had been men endued with virtue in the ages before you who could preserve men from doing evil in the world, other than the few we saved from among them!" [4]

Bearing Witness or Admitting a Fact

There is a fragment in a ziyārah-text of Imām al-Ḥusayn which reads as follows: "I bear witness that you have indeed established the *salat*, paid the *zakat*, commanded to enjoin what is right and lawful, and prohibited doing what is wrong and unlawful." [5] Here being a witness cannot be taken merely in its everyday sense, that is, like a witness before a court of law. Rather, it is a manifest expression of a spiritual fact and admitting a reality, [6] on the basis of a holy aim and a spiritual end. To put it another way, it means that "I realise this point and understand it that your (Imām al-Ḥusayn's) movement and uprising was for commending the people to do good and to prohibit them from evil, not because of the Kūfans' invitations." However, all the efforts done were just some steps taken toward reaching this aim and the ultimate purpose was that "you (Imām al-Ḥusayn) have done the right *jihad* in the cause of Allāh."

Did Imām al-Ḥusayn Pay Attention to the Condition of Commending the Good in his Uprising?

Muslim scholars state a number of conditions for the practice of commending good and prohibiting evil. They explain that in addition to having a positive effect, this practice must not be hazardous for the one who practices it. However, this condition seems neglected in the movement of Imām al-Ḥusayn, such that he rushed toward the greatest danger, his and his companions' being martyred and the captivity of his family.

This question proves to be of utmost significance, for the fiqh-oriented rules are nothing but the lessons taken from the lives of Prophet Muḥammad and the Infallible Imāms.

The answer is that the above condition is a general one, hence inapplicable to special and exceptional cases. Concerning this case, two points must be clarified, firstly, the position of the sinner, and secondly, the status of the one who enjoins good and prohibits evil.

If the sinner is a person who has a high social and political position and their deeds set an example for others, their conduct will lead to a heresy, and any learned and pious Muslim's silence will be counted as an unforgivable sin. Such a Muslim must challenge and rise against corruption, even if it would endanger their life and property. This would be to prevent heresy from being established in society and to weaken its practitioner. If circumstances prevent a physical opposition, pious Muslims must announce their opposition in words without any care for the effect of the opposition or receiving any loss or damage in return.

The behaviour of some special companions of Imām 'Alī against the tyrants and heretics serve as a model and evidence in this regard. These special companions include: Maytham al-Tammār, Ḥujr b. 'Uday, Abū Dhar al-Ghifārī, and tens of other devout Shi'is and adherents of the Shia denomination who resisted against the tyrants. Their struggles and resistance were to prevent the emergence of a deviated or mixed line and to preserve the original and authentic Islamic mainstream. They resisted and showed opposition even against the slightest deviation, over a single issue, and a simple practical Islamic statement. They sacrificed their lives and properties to this end.

The status of the one who prohibits evil is also important. Those who are founders of religion and entrusted to disseminate the tenets of religion and the Divine statements, such as the prophets and the Infallible Imāms, the religious leaders, and their successors, have a special duty with regard to the Divine statements, a duty which is different to that of ordinary people. The prophets, their real successors, and the true guardians of Islam are entrusted with unique and significant duties that stand much higher than others' duties. Had it been the case that prophets accepted the corrupt ways of the people, there would have been no conflict or battle between them and their foes, nor would there have been any trace of their teachings and religious verdicts. To cite an example, when the Prophet Ibrāhīm rose up to challenge idol-worshipping, he stood against a large number of people and tyranical forces, but he smashed all the idols one by one, without any care.

In a similar manner, Prophet Yaḥyā – who was not a prophet of a distinct religion but was in charge of safeguarding religions before him – stood against the tyrant of his time in opposition to an illegal marriage and persisted so firmly that his severed head was presented in a basin as a gift to the tyrant.

Imām al-Ḥusayn referred to this event on the way to Karbalā, explicitly stating that the head of Prophet Yaḥyā was given as a gift to a Jewish tyrant. This signifies that the guardians of revelation and religion have a responsibility far higher than ordinary people.

Blasphemous Silence

Blasphemous silence is the sin which Imām 'Alī pointed to in the Battle of Ṣiffin. There was an elderly man from the Umayyad army who came forward to stand between the two armies and called on Imām 'Alī for a short meeting. Imām 'Alī came out and went toward the old Syrian soldier. At that time, the old Syrian soldier maintained that he knew that Imām 'Alī had a good profile with praiseworthy contributions to Islam, and enquired if he could come up with a suggestion to prevent bloodshed.

Imām 'Alī expressed his willingness to listen to his suggestion. The old Syrian soldier's suggestion was that Imām 'Alī would return to Iraq with his forces and they would return to Syria, too.

In response to this suggestion, Imām 'Alī confirmed that the old Syrian soldier's intentions were good; however, Imām 'Alī's answer was as follows:

"I also pondered about this war a lot and spent several nights reflecting on it. I found myself at the crossroads of the battle between war and blasphemy, and preferred the war to blasphemy. This is because Allāh will never be satisfied with His servants when a sin is committed on Earth and they are silent and remain content with the prevailing situation, and stop encouraging people to do the good and lawful, and forbidding others from committing the undesirable. Hence, I have found battling these people [Mu'āwīya and his associates] easier than enduring the chains of the Hell." [8]

As shown above, Imām 'Alī regarded silence against sins in itself a greater sin and comparible to blasphemy and keeping away from Islam. Hence, he regarded the silence of religious people against sin as a reason for dissemination of the sins, as it stands against Allāh's dissatisfaction.

Notes to Chapter 35
At al-Bayḍa

1. This is adopted from the Holy Qur'ān, Sūrah al-Fatḥ [48]: 10.
2. Al-Ṭabarī, *al-Ta'rīkh*, vol. 6, p. 229; Ibn al-Athīr, *al-Kāmil fī al-Ta'rīkh*, vol. 3, p. 280; al-Khwārazmī, *Maqtal al-Ḥusayn*, vol. 1, p. 229; al-Balādhurī, *Anṣāb al-Ashrāf*, vol. 3, p. 171.
3. Al-Khaṭīb al-Khwārazmī, the author of *Maqtal al-Ḥusayn*, believes that Imām al-Ḥusayn expressed the above text in the form of a letter to the Kūfan noblemen soon after his arrival to the region of Karbalā. I [viz., Ayatollah Najmī] believe that it might be in both ways, oral and written, due to the significance of the material.
4. The Holy Qur'ān, Sūrah Hūd [11]: 116.
5. This fragment is quoted in several ziyārah-texts in favour of Imām al-Ḥusayn. It is taken from al-Wārith ziyārah-text.
6. This is similar to Allāh's bearing witness, as in the following Qur'ānic verse: "Allāh is witness there is no Allāh but He, and so are angels and men full of learning ..." (Sūrah Āl-i 'Imrān [3]: 18)
7. Naṣr b. Muzāḥim, *Waq'ah Ṣiffin*, p. 474.

36

In Response to Abū Hiram

يا ابا هرم! انّ بنى اميّة شتموا عرضى فصبرت واخذوا مالى فصبرت وطلبوا دمى فهربت، وايم الله ليقتلونى فيلبسهم الله ذلا شاملا وسيفا قاطعا ويسلّط عليهم من يذلّهم حتّى يكونوا اذل من قوم سبا اذ ملكتهم امراة فحكمت فى اموالهم و دمائهم.

"O Abā Hiram! Indeed the Umayyads belittled my reputation, but I endured; they confiscated my property, but I endured; and wanted to shed my blood, so I felt insecure and departed. By Allāh, they shall slay me, and Allāh shall make them completely deprived with a sharp sword over them. He shall make a person suppress them, the one who shall denigrate them so that they shall be lower than the people of Saba' – Sheba – when their queen was a lady who was controlling their properties and lives." [1]

Context

It was at the station called al-Ruhayma that a Kūfan by the name of Abū Hiram [2] met Imām al-Ḥusayn and asked him, "O Grandson of the Prophet of Allāh! What has urged you to leave the *ḥaram* (sanctum) of your grandfather?"

In response to this query, Imām al-Ḥusayn gave the above answer.

Conclusion

Contrary to Imām al-Ḥusayn's speeches and addresses, his conversations with various people were short and concise. His answer to Abū Hiram was one of such cases. Despite its brevity in portraying the real face of the Umayyads, it anticipated two further points: Imām al-Ḥusayn's martyrdom, and the fall of the Umayyads as well as their denigration.

Imām al-Ḥusayn's reply indicates that he chose martyrdom with full knowledge and anticipated exactly what would take place in the future.

Notes to Chapter 36
In Response to Abū Hiram

1. Al-Khwārazmī, *Maqtal al-Ḥusayn*, vol. 1, p. 226; Ibn Ṭāwūs, *al-Luhūf*, p. 62; and Ibn Namā al-Ḥillī, *Muthīr al-Aḥzān*, p. 46.
2. In some sources, e.g., the copy of al-Khwārizmī's *Maqtal al-Ḥusayn*, this person's name is recorded as "Abū Ḥurra" which seems to be a misspelt form.

37

In Response to al-Ṭirimmāḥ b. ʿUday and his Associates

a) اما والله! انّي لارجو ان يكون خيرا ما اراد الله بنا، قتلنا ام ظفرنا ...

b) فمنهم من قضى نحبه ومنهم من ينتظر وما بدّلوا تبديلاً. اللّهمّ! اجعل لنا ولهم الجنّة واجمع بيننا وبينهم في مستقرّ من رحمتك و رغائب مذخور ثوابك..

c) انّ بيننا وبين القوم عهدا وميثاقا ولسنا نقدر على الا نصراف حتّى تتصرّف بنا و بهم الامور في عاقبة.

(a) "By Allāh! I do hope that whatever Allāh has determined for us will be good for us, whether we will be slain or victorious ...."

(b) "Some of them have fulfilled it by death, and some are still waiting, they have not changed in the least." [1] O Allāh! Reward us and them with Paradise, and take us and them to the place of Your Grace and the most ardently-desired and deposited rewards of Yours."

(c) "There is indeed a covenant between us and the people [of al-Kūfa], and we cannot turn away [due to the covenant] so long as we would see where our end would be" [2]

Context

According to al-Ṭabarī, four people by the names of ʿAmr b. Khālid, Saʿd, Mujmaʿ, and Nāfiʿ b. Hilāl set out from al-Kūfa together with al-Ṭirimmāḥ b. ʿUday. They met Imām al-Ḥusayn at ʿUdhayb al-Hijānāt, and informed him that while they were route, al-Ṭirimmāḥ used to recite the following lines:

"O My camel! Never get annoyed by my force,
And take me [to the destination] before dawn as soon as possible.
Give a ride to your best rider, your best traveler,
To take him to a man in whose genes are nobility and grace.
He is a nobleman and a prince and is the most tolerant,
So that Allāh has dispatched him here for performing the best tasks.
O Allāh! Protect him forever!"

When al-Ṭirimmāḥ's poem about his zeal to reach the Imām reached this line, Imām al-Ḥusayn replied as in (a) above, expressing his wish for good in whatever Allāh had determined for them.

Then Imām al-Ḥusayn asked these travellers about the thoughts and temperament of the people of al-Kūfa. They remarked in the following way: "O Grandson of the Prophet of Allāh! The heads of Kūfan tribes received heavy bribes from 'Ubayd Allāh b. Zīyād. Regarding others, their hearts are with you, but their swords are against you." After this, they informed Imām al-Ḥusayn of the sad news that his envoy Qays b. Mūsahhir al-Ṣaydāwī was martyred. Upon receiving this news, Imām al-Ḥusayn recited the Qur'ānic verse cited above, that is, Sūrah 33: 23. Following this, Imām al-Ḥusayn prayed for them to be in the most splendid place in Paradise.

After the above speech, al-Ṭirimmāḥ replied: "O Grandson of the Prophet of Allāh! When I was leaving al-Kūfa, I noticed a huge crowd of people. Upon enquiry, I found out that they were gathering there to get ready to fight (Imām) al-Ḥusayn b. 'Alī. O Grandson of the Prophet! I implore to you by Allāh to return from this journey, for I cannot think that even one person of the Kūfans would come to your aid. Even the crowd I noticed would be enough to defeat you, while their number and weapons are constantly increasing."

Al-Ṭirimmāḥ then made following suggestion: "O Grandson of the Prophet of Allāh! I believe that you, and I in your company, would better move to the region al-Aḥbā' where my tribe al-Ṭayy reside and it has very high mountains. The region is so safe and secure, away from the reach of the enemies, that throughout history our tribe has withstood attacks of the Ghassān monarchs. No enemy has ever had success to conquer this region. Apart from the geographical security and location, if you stay there for ten days, all members of the Ṭayy tribe, horsemen and infantry, would rush to your help, and I promise to provide you with 20,000 brave swordsmen who would fight with you.

In response to al-Ṭirimmāh's suggestion, Imām al-Ḥusayn replied, "May Allāh reward you and your tribe!" Then, he continued that there had been a covenant between him and the people of al-Kūfa, as mentioned (c) above.

When al-Ṭirimmāḥ realised Imām al-Ḥusayn's firm resolve, he sought permission from him to provide his family in al-Kūfa with some food he had obtained for them. He intended to get back to Imām al-Ḥusayn as soon as possible. Imām al-Ḥusayn then permitted him to set out.

Following this exchange, al-Ṭirimmāḥ hurried to get to his family in al-Kūfa. However, just before reaching Karbalā on his way back, he was informed of the martyrdom of Imām al-Ḥusayn and his companions.

Reinforcing Human Values

The words of Imām al-Ḥusayn are pearls of wisdom; there are several noteworthy points within his present discourse. Here only one of them is explained.

One who stands against the enemy seeks victory and the enemy's defeat. Imām al-Ḥusayn was no exception. However, defeat and victory had a different meaning for the Imām. Hence, there have been some misinterpretations concerning Imām al-Ḥusayn's uprising, and sometimes occassionally unfair conclusions have been drawn by disregarding some dimensions of this movement.

In Imām al-Ḥusayn's opinion, victory means discharging one's divine duty, carrying out one's religious mission, and reinforcing the human values. This holds true whether the apparent victory, which is an aim in all wars and challenges, is attained or not. On the basis of this philosophy, when al-Ṭirimmāḥ, an earlier companion of Prophet Muḥammad and a staunch follower of both Imām 'Alī and Imām al-

Ḥusayn, spoke of the situation in al-Kūfa and alluded to the apparent defeat of Imām al-Ḥusayn as unavoidable and suggested a solution, Imām al-Ḥusayn in response prayed for him and asked Allāh to place him together with other martyrs and to provide him with rewards and merits. Additionally, Imām al-Ḥusayn directed al-Ṭirimmāḥ's attention to a significant point: the divine responsibility and mission, and reinforcing the human values. That is to say, Imām al-Ḥusayn had an agreement with the people of al-Kūfa through meetings and correspondence. Imām al-Ḥusayn had promised to set out to al-Kūfa and to assume their leadership and Imāmate, and they promised him their full-fledged support. Hence, Imām al-Ḥusayn regarded it as his responsibility to fulfill his promise even if they would face danger, and it would be up to the Kūfans' whether to keep their promise or to break it. Such is the difference between an Infallible Imām and religious leader on the one hand, and political leaders on the other, in the past, today, and at any time throughout the history.

Notes to Chapter 37
In Response to al-Tirimmāḥ b. 'Uday and his Associates

1. The Holy Qur'ān, Sūrah al-Aḥzāb [33]: 23.

2. Al-Ṭabarī, *al-Ta'rīkh*, vol. 6, p. 230; see also Ibn al-Athīr, *al-Kāmil fī al-Ta'rīkh*, vol. 3, p. 281; al-Muqarram, *Maqtal al-Ḥusayn*, p. 220. The text analysed here is on the basis of the quotation available in al-Muqarram's *Maqtal al-Ḥusayn*.

38

A Conversation with ‘Ubayd Allāh b. al-Ḥurr al-Ju‘fī

a) يابن الحرّ! انّ اهل مصركم كتبوا اليّ انّهم مجتمعون على نصرتى وسالونى القدوم عليهم وليس الامر على مازعموا وانّ عليك ذنوبا كثيرة فهل لك من توبة تمحو بها ذنوبك؟ ...

b) تنصر ابن بنت نبيّك وتقاتل معه.

c) امّا اذا رغبت بنفسك عنّا فلا حاجة لنا فى فرسك ولا فيك وما كنت متّخذ المضلّين عضدا وانّى انصحك كما نصحتنى ان استطعت ان لا تسمع صراخنا ولا تشهد وقعتنا فافعل. فوالله! لا يسمع واعيتنا احد ولا ينصرنا الا اكبّه الله فى نار جهنّم.

(a) “O Ibn al-Ḥurr! Indeed the inhabitants of your city wrote to me that they were united to help me and requested me to come to them, but the reality of the affair is the reverse of what they had expressed. And, as you have committed a lot of sins, would you like (having) a repentance (opportunity) to nullify them?”

(b) “... You help the son of your Prophet’s daughter and fight together with him.”

(c) “... However, if you wish to turn away from us, we no longer need your horse and you, for ‘I would not take as helpers those who lead (men) astray.’ [1] And, as you advised me, I (do) advise you, if you can, take refuge at a place far away from us so as not to hear our cry (of help) and not to witness our battle. By Allāh! Nobody hears our cry of help and abstains from helping us unless Allāh shall throw them in the Fire.” [2]

Context

It was at Banī Muqātil that Imām al-Ḥusayn was informed that 'Ubayd Allāh b. al-Ḥurr al-Ju'fī [3] was residing at the same place. At first, Imām al-Ḥusayn dispatched al-Ḥajjāj b. Masrūq toward him. Al-Ḥajjāj said to 'Ubayd Allāh b. al-Ḥurr that he had brought a valuable gift for him if he would accept. By this, he meant that Imām al-Ḥusayn had arrived at the same place and called upon him, hence it was time to join him to attain a great felicity. If 'Ubayd Allāh would fight together with Imām al-Ḥusayn, he would enjoy ample merits and virtues, and if he would be martyred, he would have attained the grace of martyrdom.

In response to this statement, 'Ubayd Allāh told al-Ḥurr that he had seen a large crowd of people who were getting ready to fight against Imām al-Ḥusayn and his followers. He continued that he was sure that Imām al-Ḥusayn would be defeated, and that he would no longer support Imām al-Ḥusayn, hence he would avoid any contact with Imām al-Ḥusayn.

When al-Ḥajjāj got back to Imām al-Ḥusayn and conveyed the answer to him, Imām al-Ḥusayn himself went to his tent. 'Ubayd Allāh welcomed Imām al-Ḥusayn.

According to 'Ubayd Allāh b. al-Ḥurr al-Ju'fī, when he looked at Imām al-Ḥusayn, he realised that he had not seen anybody more handsome and striking than him, but he had a pitiful feeling for Imām al-Ḥusayn. It was a very moving situation, especially because a few little children accompanied the Imām.

'Ubayd Allāh b. al-Ḥurr noticed that Imām al-Ḥusayn's beard was black, and enquired whether it was its natural colour. In reply, Imām al-Ḥusayn's said that he had become old too early. Hence, he realised that Imām al-Ḥusayn had dyed his beard black.

After some initial conversation, Imām al-Ḥusayn addressed him as mentioned above in section (a) saying, the people of al-Kūfa had invited him but later betrayed him, and that he ('Ubayd Allāh) might want a chance to repent and nullify past sins. Then 'Ubayd Allāh b. al-Ḥurr enquired about how to get cleansed of his sins, and Imām al-Ḥusayn directed him to helping the son of the Prophet's daughter to fight in his company against the enemy.

At this point, 'Ubayd Allāh b. al-Ḥurr's reply was as follows: By Allāh! I do know that whoever follows you, they will attain eternal felicity. However, I do not think my help would benefit you, for I have not noticed anybody in al-Kūfa determined to help you. By Allāh! I ask you to exempt me from helping you because I am very much afraid of death. However, I would offer you my horse al-Mulhaqah: I have not pursued any enemy with this horse unless it caught him, and it helped me escape all enemies.

In response to 'Ubayd Allāh b. al-Ḥurr's statements, Imām al-Ḥusayn expressed what was mentioned in section (b) above. Imām al-Ḥusayn maintained that since 'Ubayd Allāh was reluctant to sacrifice his life, he no longer felt any need to him or to his horse, for he never sought help from those who have gone astray.

Following the above exchange, Imām al-Ḥusayn advised 'Ubayd Allāh as mentioned in section (c) above. Imām al-Ḥusayn reminded him that Allāh would throw into the Fire whoever would hear his cry of help but would deny him their help.

Despite all the above exchanges, 'Ubayd Allāh learnt nothing from the directive of Imām al-Ḥusayn and never joined him. However, later on he regretted the lost opportunity. He used to recite the following lines of poetry in which he reproached himself:

"Alas! This is a heavy loss which has made me restless,
When al-Ḥusayn sought help from the likes of mine to fight the oppressors.
When al-Ḥusayn asked my help to eradicate hypocrisy.
Had I assisted him, I would have attained a sublime status on the Resurrection Day."

Endeavor to Rescue Others

Having studied the above account of the meeting between Imām al-Ḥusayn and 'Ubayd Allāh b. al-Ḥurr and the former's suggestion to him for help, one may question why Imām al-Ḥusayn sought help from a well-known Arab criminal who was notorious for his hostility towards Imām al-Ḥusayn and Imām 'Alī. How can this gesture be justified together with Imām al-Ḥusayn's permission for his most loyal companions to leave him? Why did he permit his companions to leave him? And, how can an invitation sent to such a person like 'Ubayd Allāh b. al-Ḥurr be justified?

The answer to the above questions can be found out through reflecting on the role of the Infallible Imāms and their conduct in peace and war. This is because the Imāms continue the line of the prophets who intended to rescue the whole of mankind, whether individually or in groups.

Imām al-Ḥusayn's act of going to a sinner's tent is like the example of Prophet Isa who went to the house of a customs official, and visited the house of a woman of ill repute. Prophet Isa's explanation about his going to the house of the lady, together with his apostles, was that sometimes a doctor must go to the patient. [6] Similarly, Imām al-Ḥusayn went to 'Ubayd Allāh b. al-Ḥurr to ask if he would like to find a way to have his sins forgiven.

Imām al-Ḥusayn realised that 'Ubayd Allāh b. al-Ḥurr would not benefit from his guidance. Instead he had asked the Imām to accept his horse, and viewed everything from a materialistic perspective. He interpreted everything in terms of apparent triumph and defeat. Consquently, Imām al-Ḥusayn reminded him that he would no longer be in need of his horse or sword, and recited the above-mentioned Qur'ānic verse, reaffirming that he would not seek help from those who have gone astray.

Notes to Chapter 38 A Conversation with 'Ubayd Allāh b. al-Ḥurr al-Ju'fī

1. The Holy Qur'ān, Sūrah al-Kahf [18]: 51.
2. Al-Balādhurī, *Anṣāb al-Ashrāf*, vol. 3, p. 174; al-Ṭabarī, *al-Ta'rīkh*, vol. 6, p. 306; Ibn al-Athīr, *al-Kamīl fī al-Ta'rīkh*, vol. 3, p. 282; al-Khwārazmī, *Maqtal al-Ḥusayn*, vol. 1, p. 226; al-Dīnawarī, *al-Akhbār al-Tuwāl*, p. 246; al-Ṣadūq, *al-Amālī*, Session 30.
3. 'Ubayd Allāh b. al-Ḥurr al-Ju'fī was a proponent of 'Uthmān. After 'Uthmān was killed, he joined Mu'āwīya and fought Imām 'Alī among the former's army in the Battle of Ṣiffīn.

There are several accounts of 'Ubayd Allāh's lootings in history books. For further information, see al-Ṭabarī, *al-Ta'rīkh*, vol. 6, p. 231; al-Khwārazmī, *Maqtal al-Ḥusayn*, vol. 1, p. 226; and Ibn Ḥazm, *Jamhara*, p. 385.

4. Likewise, Imām 'Alī described Prophet Muḥammad as a doctor who used to visit his patients.

39

In Response to 'Amr b. Qays and his Cousin

انطلقا فلا تسمعا لی واعیة و لا تریا لی سوادا، فانّه من سمع واعیتنا او رای سوادنا فلم یجبنا او یغثنا کان حقّا علی الله عزّ و جلّ ان یکبّه علی منخریه فی النّار.

"Will you [two] move away so that you will not hear any of my calls for help or notice my calamity? Anybody who hears our cry or notices our calamity and has not responded or helped us, it is indeed Allāh's right to throw them into the Fire on their nose." [1]

Context

It was again at the station of Banī Muqātil that 'Amr b. Qays al-Mushriqī and his cousin had the honour of meeting Imām al-Ḥusayn. Thereupon, Imām al-Ḥusayn enquired whether they had come to help him. Their reply was negative; they maintained: "Because we have got a lot of children, people's properties have been entrusted to us, and we are uncertain about your fate, hence it is not fair that people's properties be wasted!"

In response to their reply, Imām al-Ḥusayn issued the above speech, signifying that anybody who would receive his cry of help but does not help him will be thrown into the Fire with humility.

A Severe Punishment

It can be concluded from Imām al-Ḥusayn's well-intended statement to 'Ubayd Allāh b. al-Ḥurr, and his reply to Harthama b. Abī Muslim (to be discussed in the Ashurā events) that those who denied their help to Imām al-Ḥusayn while he was in need of their assistance, would certainly receive the most severe punishment together with humiliation, as the worst type of punishment. In this regard, Imām al-Ḥusayn's prediction was that such people would not only be driven towards the Fire, they will endure the punishment with utmost humilitation, as expressed in Imām al-Ḥusayn's speech. Such people will receive this type of punishment because Imām al-Ḥusayn's appeal for help is in fact the Qur'ān's and Islam's appeal for help. Is it not the case that this appeal is that of the Prophet and that of the religion of Islam?

This punishment is not something personal. Rather, it is concerned with the status of the leadership which finds expression initially in the personality of the Prophet, and then subsequently in the Infallible Imāms, and yet some time later in the top-ranking Shi'i 'Ulamā'.

Another Instance of a Great Deprivation

While 'Ubayd Allāh b. al-Ḥurr lost the golden opportunity of attaining felicity that was already within his reach, and the honour of helping Imām al-Ḥusayn, and felt very much sorry for making this great mistake, there was a yet greater instance of losing this opportunity: 'Amr b. Qays.

Although 'Ubayd Allāh b. al-Ḥurr was so engrossed in the worldly life that he was blinded and answered Imām al-Ḥusayn in such a tone that he was scared of death. 'Amr b. Qays was impressed by Imām al-Ḥusayn's speech and character, left his cousin Mālik b. al-Naḍr al-Arḥābī and joined Imām al-Ḥusayn's companions. However, he stipulated a condition for helping Imām al-Ḥusayn that his assistance should be beneficial for him and effective for Imām al-Ḥusayn's victory; otherwise, he would be free to leave Imām al-Ḥusayn. Imām al-Ḥusayn accepted his condition Consequently, in the harshest moments of the Ashurā Battle, just when Imām al-Ḥusayn was in need of assistance, 'Amr b. Qays left Imām al-Ḥusayn and lost the grace of joining the Ashurā martyrs.

According to al-Ṭabarī, [2] 'Amr b. Qays reported his escape in the following way: On Ashurā, when he realised that the Kūfan soldiers intended to cut off the legs of the horses of Imām al-Ḥusayn's companions, he hid his own horse in a tent and attacked the enemy on foot. He killed two enemy soldiers and cut off a third one's hand. Noticing all of this, Imām al-Ḥusayn encouraged him for his efforts. According to 'Amr b. Qays, when he noticed that Imām al-Ḥusayn's companions were martyred except Suwayd b. 'Amr and Bishr al-Ḥadramī, he went to Imām al-Ḥusayn and mentioned his condition. At that time, Imām al-Ḥusayn confirmed his condition and asked him how he could escape the battle.

In the words of 'Amr b. Qays, when he obtained Imām al-Ḥusayn's permission, he took his horse out of the tent, mounted it, and left the battlefield. Upon escaping the battlefield, fifteen enemy soldiers pursued him until they got close to him at the village of Shufaya on the River Euphrates. When he turned to them, three of them knew him and let him go. In this way, he rescued his own life.

Notes to Chapter 39
In Response to 'Amr b. Qays and His Cousin

1. Al-Ṣadūq, *'Iqāb al-A'māl*, ed. A. A. Ghaffārī, p. 409; and al-Kashshī, *al-Rijāl*, p. 74.
2. The name of this person is recorded as 'Amr b. Qays al-Mushriqī in al-Saduq's *'Iqāb al-A'māl*, Kashshī's *Rijāl*, and al-Khu'ī's *Mu'jam Rijāl al-Ḥadīth* where the account is reported. However, in al-Ṭabarī's *al-Ta'rīkh*, vol. 6, pp. 238- 255, his name is recorded as Ḍaḥḥāk b. 'Abd Allāh al-Mushriqī. The *rijāl* scholars' and al-Ṭabarī's accounts suggest that 'Amr and Ḍaḥḥāk were two different persons, albeit they traveled independently of one another and met Imām al-Ḥusayn at different places, while their excuses were the same and they received the same answer from him. However, the one who left Imām al-Ḥusayn on Ashurā and in the heat of the war was Ḍaḥḥāk al-Mushriqī.

Notwithstanding, I [Ayatollah Najmi] believe that 'Amr b. Qays al-Mushriqī was the same person as Ḍaḥḥāk al-Mushriqī, with this copying mistake as a usual scribal phenomenon among *hadith* transmitters and *rijāl* scholars, an instance of which will be tackled with under the title of "A Historical Mistake". This is especially true of Ḍaḥḥāk or Qays al-Mushriqī whose biography was not dealt with by *rijāl* scholars, owing to his refusal to help Imām al-Ḥusayn. In any case, this great loss will be that of Ḍaḥḥāk al-Mushriqī whose joining and leaving Imām al-Ḥusayn were reported by al-Ṭabarī on the account of Abū Mikhnaf.

40

Near Karbalā

انّا لله و انّا اليه راجعون والحمد لله ربّ العالمين ... انّى خفقت براسى فعنّ بى
فارس وهو يقول: القوم يسرون والمنايا تسرى اليهم فعلمت انّها انفسنا نعيت
الينا ... جزاك الله من ولد خير ما جزى ولدا عن والده.

"'Surely we are for Allāh, and to Him we shall return.' [1] 'And, may all praise be to Allāh.' [2] … I took a short nap, and dreamt a horseman who was heralding: 'The people travel at night and death travels to them', so I learned that it was the news of our death … May Allāh reward you the best of the rewards." [3]

Context

Late at night at Banī Muqātil, Imām al-Ḥusayn ordered the youth to fill their leather-flasks with water and they continued their journey toward the next station. While they were traveling, Imām al-Ḥusayn recited the verse of *al-istirjā'* [4] several times and praised Allāh.

Hearing this, 'Alī al-Akbar, [5] Imām al-Ḥusayn's brave and elder son, enquired of the reason for this recitation. Imām al-Ḥusayn answered what he dreamt in the short nap he took, signifying that death was following them.

At this point, 'Alī al-Akbar asked: "May Allāh deter any unfavourable incident; are we not on the Right Path?" Then Imām al-Ḥusayn replied: "By Allāh, we do not take any step save in the Right Path." Thereupon,

'Alī al-Akbar stated: "In that case, we do not care about death if we are destined to be slain in the Right Path."

At this moment, Imām al-Ḥusayn prayed for him to have the best of the rewards.

In conclusion, if an uprising, a revolution, killing, and being killed are conducted in the Right Path, one must not be scared of death. This is yet another lesson the school of Imām al-Ḥusayn taught not only his son but to all his followers.

Notes to Chapter 40
Near Karbalā

1. The Holy Qur'ān, Sūrah al-Baqara [2]: 156.
2. The Holy Qur'ān, Sūrah al-Fātiḥa [1]: 1.
3. Al-Balādhurī, *Anṣāb al-Ashrāf*, vol. 3 p. 185; al-Ṭabarī, *al-Ta'rīkh*, vol. 6, p. 251; Ibn al-Athīr, *al-Kāmil fī al-Ta'rīkh*, vol. 3, p. 291; al-Khwārazmī, *Maqtal al-Ḥusayn*, vol. 1, p. 226; and Ibn Sa'd, *al-Ṭabaqāt*. According to Ibn Ṭāwūs in *al-Luhūf*, this incident took place at al-Tha'labīyya.
4. The Verse of *al-Istirjā'* is the same as the one indicated in No. 1 above. It is indicative of death.
5. 'Alī al-Akbar was Imām al-Ḥusayn's eldest son. Born in 33 AH/ 654 AD, he was the first Hāshimid youth who joined the battlefield on Ashurā and was martyred. He is buried at the feet of Imām al-Ḥusayn in the same monument.

Part Three

In Karbalā

41

On Arriving in Karbalā

ما كنت لابداهم بالقتال. ارض كرب و بلا. قفوا و لا نرحوا و حطوا و لا ترحلوا. فها هنا و اللّه! محط رحالنا و هاهنا و الله! سفک دمائنا و ها هنا و الله! تسبى حريمنا و ها هنا و الله! محل قبورنا و ها هنا و اللّه! محشرنا. ومنشرنا و بهذا وعدنى جدّى رسول الله صلّى اللّه عليه و اله ولا خلاف لوعده.

"I would not start fighting them; this is the land of sorrow and calamity. Stop here and do not (make any further) move, put down the luggage, and do not depart here, for by Allāh this is our landing site; and by Allāh this is the place where our blood will be shed; and by Allāh this is the place where our families will be arrested as captives; and by Allāh here is the location of our tombs, and by Allāh here is where we will be resurrected, and this was what my grandfather, the Prọphet of Allāh – may the grace of Allāh be granted to him and his progeny – promised me. There has been nothing untrue in his promise." [1]

Context

The caravan of Imām al-Ḥusayn and al-Ḥurr's army were marching ahead parallel to one another until they reached the region of Naynawā. There, both parties saw a horseman who was the messenger of 'Ubayd Allāh b. Zīyād, with a letter for al-Ḥurr. The letter read: "As soon as you read my letter, take al-Ḥusayn to an uncomfortable place, to a desert devoid of water and without any fort." Al-Ḥurr then read out the letter for Imām al-Ḥusayn, and informed him of his new mission.

Upon Imām al-Ḥusayn's enquiry to settle in the deserts of Naynawā, al-Ghaḍirīyāt, or Shufayya, al-Ḥurr replied that he could not agree with his request, for he was no longer free to decide. This was because the same messenger was 'Ubayd Allāh b. Zīyād's agent to supervise al-Ḥurr's conduct and deeds.

At this time, Zuhayr b. al-Qayn [2] suggested to Imām al-Ḥusayn that fighting that small number of enemy soldiers would be easier than confronting the huge army who would shortly arrive. He added: "By Allāh! Soon a massive army will reach here in support of them, and then we will not be able to resist them."

In response to this suggestion, Imām al-Ḥusayn said to Zuhayr b. al-Qayn that he would not start fighting them.

Then Imām al-Ḥusayn suggested al-Ḥurr go further and find a better place to camp. Al-Ḥurr agreed, and the two groups continued their way until they reached the region of Karbalā. It was at this place where al-Ḥurr and his men prevented Imām al-Ḥusayn from going any further because that place was near the Euphrates, hence a place suitable for Imām al-Ḥusayn's stay.

As Imām al-Ḥusayn decided to camp there, he enquired about its name and designations. The place was called al-Ṭaff. He enquired about any other name or designation, and the name Karbalā was mentioned.

According to Ibn Jum'ah al-Ḥuwayzī in his *Tafsīr Nūr al-Thaqalayn* on the authority of Abū Mikhnaf, Imām al-Ḥusayn shed tears profusely on hearing the name Karbalā. [3] Then Imām al-Ḥusayn delivered the above speech mentioned in the beginning of this chapter.

Conclusion

There are three important and interesting points in Imām al-Ḥusayn's discourse:

Firstly, Imām al-Ḥusayn mentioned the tragedy of Karbalā on several occasions, explicitly and implicitly. This sermon is yet another example where he predicted its details and place of occurrence, that is, the region of Karbalā, on the authority of a Prophetic *hadith*.

Secondly, Imām al-Ḥusayn's approach was significant. Although embarking on a war might seem beneficial to the camp of Imām al-Ḥusayn, as Zuhayr b. al-Qayn anticipated, Imām al-Ḥusayn stated his agenda: not to wage war.

This is the same as what Imām 'Alī instructed his men in the Battle of the Camel. Although Imām 'Alī's enemies attacked the city of Baṣrah, southern Iraq, twice and killed a large number his followers and the Shi'is, he ordered his followers not to initiate the war. Instead, he ordered them to have a peaceful dialogue with their enemies. [4]

Thirdly, one of the aims of the Infallible Imāms was to *correct* people's conduct and behaviour and to prevent religious and moral diversion. This is what Imām al-Ḥusayn expressed as encouragement to do good and prevention from doing evil. However, war remains the last resort once all other ways are exhausted.

In conclusion, Imām al-Ḥusayn's reply to Zuhayr b. al-Qayn is further evidence that Imām al-Ḥusayn's aim was not simply gaining an apparent victory in a military confrontation; rather, Imām al-Ḥusayn was pursuing an objective much higher and more sublime, with broader horizons.

Notes to Chapter 41
On Arriving in Karbalā

1. Al-Ṭabarī, *Ta'rīkh*, vol. 6, p. 232; Ibn al-Athīr, *al-Kāmil fī al-Ta'rīkh*, vol. 3, 282; al-Khwārazmī, *Maqtal al-Ḥusayn*, vol. 1, p. 234.
2. A resident of al-Kūfa, Zubayr b. al-Qayn al-Bijilī was a prominent man in his clan. Formerly, he was a proponent of 'Uthmān b. 'Affān. On the way back from Mecca to al-Kūfa, Zuhayr was moving in such a way as not to meet up with Imām al-Ḥusayn. However, at a station, he set up his tent at a spot not too far from the camp of Imām al-Ḥusayn. There, Imām al-Ḥusayn sent an envoy to invite him to meet with Imām al-Ḥusayn. Zuhayr got annoyed at receiving this invitation; his wife Dalham bt. 'Amr urged and encouraged him to rush to

meet Imām al-Ḥusayn. Back from meeting Imām al-Ḥusayn, he decided to let his wife join her clan so that he could serve Imām al-Ḥusayn. He stayed with Imām al-Ḥusayn and fought the enemies and attained the eternal felicity, martyrdom, on Ashurā.

3. 'Abd 'Ali Ibn Jum'a al-Ḥuwayzī, *Tafsīr Nūr al-Thaqalayn*, vol. 4, p. 221.

4. Abī 'Abd Allāh al-Ḥakīm al-Nayshābūrī, *al-Mustadrak*, vol. 2, p. 371; al-Muttaqī al-Hindī, *Kanz al-'Ummāl*, vol. 6, p. 85, *hadith* No. 1311.

42

Imām al-Ḥusayn's Sermon after Arriving in Karbalā

امّا بعد، فقد نزل بنا من الا مر ما قد ترون و انّ الدّنيا قد تغيّرت و تنكّرت وادبر معروفها و لم يبق منها الا صبابة كصبابة الا نا و خسيس عيش كالمرعى الوبيل. الا ترون الى الحقّ لا يعمل به و الى الباطل لا يتناهى عنه! ليرغب المؤمن فى لقاء الله فانّى لا ارى الموت الا سعادة و الحياة مع الظّالمين الا برما، النّاس عبيد الدّنيا والدّين لعق على السنتهم يحوطونه مادرّت معايشهم فاذا محّصوا بالبلاء قلّ الدّيّانون.

"Now then, the situation has happened to us in the way you consider, and (the affairs of) the world have changed, reached an unfavourable state, ignored its good deeds of which nothing has been left except a residual drop like a drop that remains in the bottom of a container, and a vile life like a stony farmland. Do you not notice that the right is not practiced and the wrong is not renounced? Hence a believer must wish to meet Allāh, for I do not consider death except with happiness and living together with the oppressors except with misery. People are slaves of the world, and religion is but a lickerish on their tongues preserved so long as their lives go well with it; however, when they are subject to an examination, the believers decrease in number." [1]

Context

Imām al-Ḥusayn arrived in the region of Karbalā on 2nd Muharram 61 AH/680 AD. After a short while, he delivered the above sermon.

Conclusion

In the above sermon which was the first talk Imām al-Ḥusayn delivered in Karbalā, he mentioned two significant points. Firstly, he indicated his incentive for the movement. As pointed out in the aforementioned speeches of Imām al-Ḥusayn, he mentioned several reasons for his movement, they included his opposition against Yazīd's rulership, diversion and change in the rules of Islam, and finally promoting the good and prohibiting the evil, all of which have been summarised and paraphrased above.

In such a situation, it is rightly expected that a conscientious believer must be willing to be martyred for making a radical change. As the most conspicuous example of such a virtuous believer is the Infallible Imām, he does not consider death except with happiness and life but a constant torture and calamity.

Secondly, Imām al-Ḥusayn spoke of how believers decrease in number when they are subjected to examination. Testing is the best way to find out the truth, people's thoughts, and their conviction of faith. Many people may pretend to be believers, chant slogans, and have acquired positions of truth-seeking and religious figures. However, their real character cannot be determined except when they are faced with clashes, calamities, and hardships. While the son of Fāṭima al-Zahrā, entered the arena of sacrifice and devotion, and was running toward Allāh, many of those who used to boast of Islam had fled.

Imām al-Ḥusayn was ready to sacrifice his life and the lives of his family members and have the survivors of his family members held as captives, all in support of Islam and the Qur'ān, to invite people to do good, and in opposition to the long-established enemy of Islam, the Umayyad rulers. However, in such a critical situation, there was no trace of such pseudo-religious figures like 'Abd Allāh b. 'Abbās, 'Abd Allāh b. al-Zubayr, and 'Abd Allāh b. 'Umar who regarded themselves as prominent religious figures. Although they had some position before the public, now that the question of martyrdom was a realistic outcome, those personalities never surfaced, as if they had not been in existence.

It is in the light of these events that really outstanding figures can be differentiated from those who claim to be Muslims who may seem more ardent and more religious in calm situations. Such hardships unveil their true faces, hence when they are tested, the believers decrease in number.

Note to Chapter 42
Imām al-Ḥusayn's Sermon after Arriving in Karbalā

1. Ḥasan b. Shu'bah al-Ḥarrānī, *Tuḥaf al-'Uqūl*, p. 174; al-Ṭabarī, *Ta'rīkh*, vol. 6, The Events of the Year 61 AH; Ibn Namā al-Ḥillī, *Muthīr al-Aḥzān*, p. 22; Ibn 'Asākir, *Tārīkh*, p. 214; al-Khwārazmī, *Maqtal al-Ḥusayn*, vol. 1, p. 237; and Ibn Ṭāwūs, *al-Luhūf*, p. 64. According to al-Ṭabarī and Ibn Namā, Imām al-Ḥusayn made this speech at Dhū Ḥusam. In some of the above-mentioned sources, the sentence "People are slaves of the world" appears in the beginning of this sermon; however, what appears here is the same as the one cited in *Tuḥaf al-'Uqūl*.

43

A Letter to Muḥammad b. al-Ḥanafīyyah

بسم اللّٰه الرحمن الرحيم من الحسين بن على عليهما السلام الى محمد بن على عليهما السلام و من قبله من بنى هاشم امّا بعد، فكانّ الدّنيا لم تكن و الاخرة لم تزل والسّلام .

"In the Name of Allāh, the Most Beneficent, the Most Merciful. (This is a letter) From al-Ḥusayn b. 'Alī – May both be granted with salām – to Muḥammad b. 'Alī and via him to the Hāshimids. Now then, it is as if the world has not been in existence, and the Hereafter would not terminate. Peace be to you." [1]

Context

Ibn Qūlawayh al-Qummī in his book *Kāmil al-Zīyārāt* relates on the authority of Imām Muḥammad al-Bāqir that soon after reaching Karbalā, Imām al-Ḥusayn wrote the above letter to his step-brother Muḥammad b. al-Ḥanafīyyah and those of the Hāshimids who had not joined him.

Conclusion

Imām al-Ḥusayn's present discourse reflects his outlook, the same as those of other Infallible Imāms, about this world and the Hereafter, explaining that life is not worthwhile without discharging one's religious duties. This is because a transient phenomenon does not have any worth more than this. Hence, all life, together with its gains, joys, status, and wealth, will be equivalent to despairs and tortures if it is devoid of discharging one's religious duties.

On the other hand, the Hereafter, from Imām al-Ḥusayn's perspective has boundless grandeur which cannot be measured in any way. The Hereafter is eternal, hence its felicity and joy are eternal. More importantly, Allāh's satisfaction is the highest form of delight: "And the blessings of Allāh are above all."[2] Likewise, its torture and punishment are ceaseless. In consequence, this view makes it easy to leave this world and join the Hereafter, even if it means enduring hardships. Imām al-Ḥusayn illustrated this outlook in his speech and put it into practice.

In this discourse, Imām al-Ḥusayn expressed the reality of this world and the Hereafter in a short and simple sentence in a letter to his step-brother Muḥammad b. al-Ḥanafīyyah and his relatives. Hence he provided them with his advice and direction. Simultaneously, he showed the world and all religious leaders the way and outlook they should undertake to direct people.

Notes to Chapter 43
A Letter to Muḥammad b. al-Ḥanafīyyah

1. Ibn Qūlawayh al-Qummī, *Kāmil al-Zīyārāt*, p. 75.
2. The Holy Qur'ān, Sūrah al-Tawba [9]: 73.

44

In Response to Ibn Zīyād's Letter

a) لا افلح قوم اشتروا مرضات المخلوق بسخط الخالق ...

b) ما له عندى جواب لانّه حقّت عليه كلمة العذاب

(a) "Any person who prefers the satisfaction of the created [people] over that of the Creator [Allāh], they will never reach felicity.

(b) He does not deserve my reply, for it has been proven that he shall be chastised (by Allāh)." [1]

Context

In a letter, al-Ḥurr informed 'Ubayd Allāh b. Zīyād [2] of Imām al-Ḥusayn's arrival in Karbalā. Consequently, 'Ubayd Allāh b. Zīyād issued the following letter to Imām al-Ḥusayn:

"Now then, I have been informed of your arrival in the region of Karbalā, and the Leader of Believers [3], Yazīd b. Mu'āwīya, has ordered me not to take any rest, nor to get satisfied with food until I kill you, or you would succumb to my order and pledge allegiance with Yazīd's administration."

Upon reading 'Ubayd Allāh b. Zīyād's letter, Imām al-Ḥusayn threw it to the ground and said what is mentioned in (a) above.

Then the courier sought a reply to the letter. Thereupon, Imām al-Ḥusayn answered what is indicated in (b) above, signifying that 'Ubayd Allāh b. Zīyād did not deserve an answer, for he had chosen to receive the Divine punishment.

When the courier returned to ʻUbayd Allāh b. Zīyād and informed him of Imām al-Ḥusayn's reaction to his letter, he was furious.

Conclusion

Imām al-Ḥusayn's answer was the same as his message on Ashurā: "The illegitimate one, son of the illegitimate one, has pressed me between two choices of submission and degradation; however, we never deserve degradation ...".

Notes to Chapter 44
In Response to Ibn Zīyād's Letter

1. Al-Khwārazmī, *Maqtal al-Ḥusayn*, vol. 1, p. 239; and al-Majlisī, ed., *Biḥār al-Anwār*, vol. 10, p. 189.
2. ʻUbayd Allāh b. Zīyād was the Umayyad governor of Baṣrah, southern Iraq. When Yazīd was informed of the Kūfans' leaning towards Muslim b. ʻAqīl, he nominated him as the governor of al-Kūfa to suppress the public uprise. He was the same person who dispatched the army to Karbalā to fight Imām al-Ḥusayn.
3. The Leader of Believers (*amīr al-mu'minīn*) was an honourific title earlier applied to Imām ʻAlī. However, Umayyad rulers urged people to refer to them in that way.

45

With ‘Umar b. Sa‘d

a) يابن سعد! ويحك اتقاتلنى؟ اما تتقى الله الّذى اليه معادك فانا ابن من علمت. الا تكون معى وتدع هؤلا فانّه اقرب الى الله تعالى ...

b) ما لك؟! ذبّحك الله على فراشك عاجلا ولا غفر لك يوم حشرك فو الله انّى لارجو ان لا تاكل من برّ العراق الا يسيرا.

(a) “O Son of Sa‘d [1]! Woe unto you! Do you intend to fight me? Do you not fear Allāh to Whom is your return? I am the son of whom you know [2]. Do you not want to be with me? This is indeed closer to Allāh the Sublime.”

(b) “What are you insisting on? May Allāh kill you at your home very soon and not forgive you on the day you are resurrected. By Allāh, I hope you will not eat of the wheat of Iraq but a little.” [3]

Context

According to al-Khaṭīb al-Khwārazmī, Imām al-Ḥusayn sent a message through one of his companions, ‘Amr b. Qurẓa al-Anṣārī, to ‘Umar b. Sa‘d to meet at night time. [4] When ‘Umar b. Sa‘d agreed, a tent was set up between the two camps. Imām al-Ḥusayn took twenty of his companions there but allowed only his step-brother al-‘Abbās b. ‘Alī and his elder son ‘Alī al-Akbar to enter the tent.

‘Umar b. Sa‘d did the same and he entered the tent with his son Ḥafṣ and his own servant.

At this meeting, Imām al-Ḥusayn addressed ʻUmar b. Saʻd in the way quoted above in (a). ʻUmar b. Saʻd expressed his anxiety that his house in al-Kūfa would be destroyed if he showed disloyalty to the Umayyads. Imām al-Ḥusayn promised to build a house for him in return. Then ʻUmar b. Saʻd expressed his anxiety for the safety of his own garden and date palms. Again, Imām al-Ḥusayn promised him a better garden in Hejaz. Then ʻUmar b. Saʻd said that he had been concerned with the security of his family in al-Kūfa and that they might be killed upon his withdrawal and refusal.

After listening to ʻUmar b. Saʻd's excuses, Imām al-Ḥusayn stood up and addressed him in the way indicated in (b) above, wishing him a fruitless and short life. In return, ʻUmar b. Saʻd replied quite mockingly, that he was content with Iraq's barley!

Conclusion

The above exchanges of Imām al-Ḥusayn contain two significant points. Firstly Imām al-Ḥusayn spoke as a well-wisher, even while talking with his enemy. In this way, he tried to rescue him from falling into misery. Although ʻUmar b. Saʻd mentioned his house and garden as excuses, Imām al-Ḥusayn still answered positively and promised him to reciprocate (2). Having lost the hope to direct ʻUmar b. Saʻd to the Right Path, Imām al-Ḥusayn predicted ʻUmar b. Saʻd's future, that he would neither live a long life nor gain any official position, a topic to be dealt with elsewhere.

Notes to Chapter 45
With ʻUmar b. Saʻd

1. Ibn Saʻd, full name ʻUmar b. Saʻd b. Abī Waqqās, was born in the year 23 AH/ 645. He reached the plain of Karbalā on 3 Muharram with 4,000 soldiers to fight Imām al-Ḥusayn. On Ashurā, he shot the first arrow toward Imām al-Ḥusayn's encampment and thus initiated the battle.
2. "Whom you know" refers to Imām ʻAlī and Prophet Muḥammad, Imām al-Ḥusayn's father and grandfather.

3. Al-Khwārazmī, *Maqtal al-Ḥusayn*, vol.1, p. 245.
4. Apparently this meeting took place on the eve of 8th or 9th Muharram.

46

Imām al-Ḥusayn's Discourse in the Tāsū'ā Afternoon

a) انّى رايت رسول الله صلّى الله عليه و اله فى المنام فقال لى : انّك صائر الينا عن قريب ...

b) اركب بنفسى انت يا اخى! حتّى تلقاهم فتقول لهم ما لكم وما بدا لكم وتسالهم عمّا جاء بهم...

c) ارجع اليهم فان استطعت ان تؤخّرهم الى غدوة وتدفعهم عنّا العشيّة نصلّى لربّنا اللّيلة وندعوه ونستغفره فهو يعلم انّى احبّ الصّلوة وتلاوة كتابه وكثرة الدّعاء والاستغفار.

(a) "I dreamt of the Prophet of Allāh (Prophet Muḥammad – May Allāh bless him and his progeny) who told me: "You are returning to us very shortly."

(b) "O My dear brother! May my soul be sacrificed for you! Ride (on your horse) to meet them and ask them of their purpose and incentive, and enquire of any news they have received."

(c) "Return to them, and if you can, delay them until early [next] morning, and get tonight as respite so that we will be performing *salat* (ritual prayer) for our Lord. Tonight we will appeal to Him and ask His forgiveness, for He knows that I do adore *salat*, reciting His Book [the Holy Qur'ān], profusion of supplications, and seeking forgiveness." [1]

Context

According to al-Ṭabarī, it was Thursday afternoon, 9th Muharram, [2] when 'Umar b. Sa'd ordered his army to attack the camp of Imām al-Ḥusayn and they began to move towards the camp of the Imām. At that time, Imām al-Ḥusayn was leaning on his sword and had a light nap.

Upon noticing the movement of 'Umar b. Sa'd's army, Lady Zaynab, Imām al-Ḥusayn's sister, rushed to him and addressed him thus: "O Brother! The enemy has got near the encampment."

When Imām al-Ḥusayn raised his head, his first statement was that which is mentioned in (a) above, signifying that Imām al-Ḥusayn would meet Prophet Muḥammad soon.

Imām al-Ḥusayn then addressed his step-brother al-'Abbās b. 'Alī, as quoted in (b) above, to meet the army and enquire of their purpose.

To fulfill this request, al-'Abbās, with 20 of his men, including Zuhayr b. al-Qayn and Ḥabīb b. Maẓāhir, approached the enemy forces and enquired of the reason of their movement.

The army soldiers of 'Umar b. Sa'd informed al-'Abbās that they had just received a new command from their amir, 'Ubayd Allāh b. Zīyād. It was that either Imām al-Ḥusayn had to pledge allegiance with Yazīd, or they would start the war. Al-'Abbās conveyed their mission to Imām al-Ḥusayn.

Upon this, Imām al-Ḥusayn recommended al-'Abbās to return to the enemy soldiers with the message indicated in section (c) above. In it, Imām al-Ḥusayn expressed his adoration for prayer and supplication for which he sought one night respite.

Al-'Abbās returned to the enemy and conveyed the Imām's request for one night of respite. As 'Umar b. Sa'd was hesitant to accept the suggestion, he consulted his army officers in this regard.

'Amr b. al-Ḥajjāj, an army officer, expressed that had they been of Turk or Daylam tribes, 'Umar b. Sa'd was supposed to give them a positive answer, while they were descendants of Prophet Muḥammad.

Qays b. al-Ash'ath, another enemy commander, believed that Imām al-Ḥusayn deserved a positive reply. He reasoned that the respite sought was neither for withdrawal nor for reconsidering the case of paying allegiance; rather Imām al-Ḥusayn's camp would start the war sooner than the enemy the next day.

Upon these consultations, 'Umar b. Sa'd was confused whether to agree to one night's respite. In the end, 'Umar b. Sa'd's answer to al-'Abbās b. 'Alī was that he would agree to one night respite provided that the following day would be critical in that their consent with paying allegiance would be accepted; otherwise, upon their denial to pay allegiance, they would not leave Imām al-Ḥusayn's camp at peace: the battle would determine everything. In this way, Imām al-Ḥusayn's camp received one night respite.

The Significance of Salat

The respite sought by Imām al-Ḥusayn indicates his whole-hearted attention to *salat*, supplication, and reciting the Holy Qur'ān. It was his ardent love of these matters that made him seek a night respite even from his brutal enemy. Such a gesture was not unexpected, for Imām al-Ḥusayn had come to that site to establish the *salat*, the Holy Qur'ān, and other Divine tenets. No doubt, supplication to Allāh made the most joyful moments of his life. Hence, any nation who rises up in the Divine cause must take lessons from these acts. It is because of this gesture that the ziyārah-text says: "I bear witness that you have established the *salat*, have paid the *zakat*, directed the public toward doing the right, prevented them from doing the evil, have followed Allāh and His Prophet – Prophet Muḥammad – until death reached you." [3]

Notes to Chapter 46 Imām al-Ḥusayn's Discourse in the Tāsū'ā Afternoon

1. Al-Balādhurī, *Anṣāb al-Ashrāf*, vol. 3, p. 185; al-Ṭabarī, *Ta'rīkh*, the Events of the Year 61; Ibn al-Athīr, *al-Kāmil fī al-Ta'rīkh*, vol. 3, p. 285; al-Mufīd, *Kitāb al-Irshād*, p. 230.

2. Whereas the 10th of Muharram is called 'Ashūrā', commonly spelt as 'Ashurā' in English texts, the 9th of Muharram is called Tāsū'ā.

3. These lines are taken from al-Wārith ziyārah-text, related on the authority of Imām Ja'far al-Sādiq and quoted in most of Shi'i ziyārah-collections, including Ibn Qūlawayh's *Kāmil al-Zīyārāt* in Ch. 79, all devoted to the Ziyārah-texts in favour of Imām al-Ḥusayn.

47

Imām al-Ḥusayn's Sermon on the Eve of Ashurā

a) اثنى على الله احسن الثّنا واحمده على السّرّاء والضّراء اللّهمّ! انّى احمدك على ان اكرمتنا بالنّبوّة وعلّمتنا القران و فقّهتنا فى الدّين وجعلت لنا اسماعا وابصارا وافئدة ولم تجعلنا من المشركين. امّا بعد: فانّى لا اعلم اصحابا اولى و لا خيرا من اصحابى و لا اهلبيت ابرّ و لا اوصل من اهل بيتى فجزاكم الله عنّى جميعا خيرا. وقد اخبرنى جدّى رسول الله صلّى الله عليه و اله بانّى ساساق الى العراق فانزل ارضا يقال لها عمورا وكربلا وفيها استشهد و قد قرب الموعد.

الا و انّى اظنّ يومنا من هؤلاء الاعداء غدا و انّى قد اذنت لكم فانطلقوا جميعا فى حلّ، ليس عليكم منّى ذمام وهذا اللّيل قد غشيكم فاتّخذوه جملا ولياخذ كلّ رجل منكم بيد رجل من اهلبيتى فجزاكم الله جميعا خيرا و تفرّقوا فى سوادكم ومدائنكم فانّ القوم انّما يطلبوننى ولو اصابونى لذهلوا عن طلب غيرى... يا بنى عقيل! حسبكم من القتل بمسلم اذهبوا قد اذنت لكم.

b)... انّى غدا اقتل وكلّكم تقتلون معى و لا يبقى منكم احد حتّى القاسم وعبد الله الرّضيع.

(a) "All praise is for Allāh the best of praises and all thanks be to Him in comfort and in distress. O Allāh! All praise is for You, for You have granted us prophethood and taught us the Qur'ān, granted us a profound understanding of religion. You have enabled us to hear, see and reflect, and have not made us of the polytheists."

"I do not know of any companions more loyal and better than mine, and no family members more truthful and confident than mine. Hence, may Allāh grant all of you the best of rewards."

"And, my grandfather, the Prophet of Allāh, has indeed informed me that I would be called to Iraq and would arrive at a land called 'Amūrā as well as Karbalā; and, I would be martyred here and the time has already approached."

"Beware that I believe that the enemies will start the war tomorrow, and that I have absolved you of your obligation, so all of you may leave, with no obligation to me. Use the darkness of night to depart. Let any one of you take one of my family members, so that Allāh may reward you all and you may get dispersed in your towns and cities. This is because the enemies want only me and if they have caught me, they will forget about anybody else. Hence, make the most of this opportunity."

Thereupon, his step-brothers, sons, nephews, and the sons of 'Abd Allāh b. Ja'far addressed him thus: "May it not happen for us to outlive you! May Allāh not show us this incident." From among them, al-'Abbās b. 'Alī started talking and after him, the rest of the companions spoke in the way he did. Then Imām al-Ḥusayn turned to the sons of Muslim [b. 'Aqīl] and said: "Your family have suffered enough with the killing of Muslim, return home; I give you permission." [1]

(b) "... Tomorrow I will be slain, and all of you will be slain together with me; nobody will survive, even al-Qāsim and 'Abd Allāh al-Raḍī' [the Infant]." [2]

Context

After the evening *salat* of Tāsū'ā, on the eve of Ashurā, and just a short while after gaining the respite, Imām al-Ḥusayn, gathered his companions and the Hāshimid youths and delivered a speech, as mentioned in (a) above.

The Last Test

Imām al-Ḥusayn declared his destined martyrdom on various occasions and throughout the route from Medina to Karbalā. He also gave his companions permission to leave him and freed them from the obligation and commitment. For the last time, on the eve of Ashurā, he remarked that the time for martyrdom had arrived, hence he declared his companions free from any obligation and commitment to himself, so that they could use the darkness of the night and head for their cities and towns.

This suggestion was Imām al-Ḥusayn's last test for his companions. In return, his companions responded reiterating their loyalty to him to the last drop of their blood. In this way, they successfully passed this test. The first person who spoke after Imām al-Ḥusayn was his step-brother al-'Abbās. He urged that they [the companions] would never leave Imām al-Ḥusayn.

Other Hāshimids spoke in a similar way as al-'Abbās did. Then Imām al-Ḥusayn turned to the sons of Muslim b. 'Aqīl and reminded them that the martyrdom of Muslim b. 'Aqīl would exempt them from taking part in the ensuing day's battle, hence they were already permitted to go back. Nevertheless, they replied that they would not be able to justify deserting their Imām and leader. Rather, they insisted on their loyalty, would sacrifice their property, lives, and sons, and would fight in company with him to the last drop of their blood.

Another companion who spoke was Muslim b. 'Awsaja who said: "How should we stop helping you? If so, what would be our justification before Allāh? By Allāh! I will never part with you until I pierce the chests of your enemies with my spear; I will fight them so long as my sword is with me, and when I remain weaponless, I would confront them by throwing rocks and stones at them until I breathe my last."

Sa'd b. 'Abd Allāh, another companion of Imām al-Ḥusayn, said: "By Allāh! We will never abstain from helping you until Allāh knows that we protected the sanctity of Prophet Muḥammad that is preserved in you. By Allāh! If I knew that I would be killed and burned and my ashes would be given life again 70 times, I would never abandon you;

however, I know that death will be only once after which there is the Divine boundless grace."

Zuhayr b. al-Qayn said: "O Grandson of the Prophet of Allāh! By Allāh! I would rather be killed and then revived 1,000 times in support of you; moreover, I wish by my being killed I would sacrifice my life for you and of the Hāshimid youths."

At this time, Muḥammad b. Bashīr al-Haḍramī, a companion of Imām al-Ḥusayn received the news that his son had been arrested. Imām al-Ḥusayn said to him that he was free to go and rescue his son. In response, Muḥammad b. Bashīr said: "By Allāh! I will never leave you." And then he added: "I wish to be killed by the beasts of the desert if I leave you alone." To contribute to rescuing Muḥammad b. Bashīr's son, Imām al-Ḥusayn gave him a few costly clothes to give to those who may help his son get rescued. [3]

Upon noticing such an admirable reaction from the Hāshimids and his companions, which indicated their knowledge, sensibility, and loyalty to the sublime status of Imāmate, Imām al-Ḥusayn wished them all the best of rewards. Thereupon, he stated explicitly that he would be killed the next day, together with the companions, and even Qāsim b. al-Ḥasan and 'Abd Allāh the Infant.

Following the response and sermon of Imām al-Ḥusayn, the companions unanimously expressed that they were thankful to Allāh for He bestowed them with a high status for helping him and would gratify them with superiority through getting martryed in his army. They further addressed Imām al-Ḥusayn and said: "O Grandson of the Prophet! Should we not be delighted that we shall be with you in Paradise?"

According to al-Rāwandī's *al-Kharā'ij*, Imām al-Ḥusayn showed them with the scenes they will be granted in Paradise, and they discerned them. [4]

An Untrue Remark

Some *maqtal*-texts record a controversial point on the reactions of a group of Imām al-Ḥusayn's companions on the eve of Ashurā. Some elegizers accord the following statement to Sakīna, a daughter of Imām al-Ḥusayn, from whom it is quoted thus: "I was sitting in my tent, and my father was talking about his martyrdom; meanwhile, he told his companions that those who might not like to be martyred on the ensuing day, they would be allowed to return to their towns and cities. In consequence, his companions started leaving him in groups of 10 to 20 people, until only a bit more than 70 of them remained." The above statement is untrue regarding the events of the eve of Ashurā for the following reasons:

First-hand and authoritative historical texts have not recorded such a scene. This is a remark available in third- or fourth-hand texts, among them in Sepehr's *Nāsikh al-Tawārīkh*, without any footnote to any text, and in *Ma'ālī al-Sibṭayn*, quoting from *Nūr al-'Ayn*. [5] Secondly, the above point contradicts what was quoted from the late al-Mufīd and al-Ṭabarī. [6] The point is that the companions of Imām al-Ḥusayn who anticipated some material gain left him in Zubāla as soon as he declared that they were no longer committed to him, and that only the loyal companions remained.

Another proof comes from Sheikh al-Ṭabarasī's comment. He mentions Imām al-Ḥusayn's sermon in which he declared that his companions were no longer under any obligation. In the response to this speech, Sheikh al-Ṭabarasī quotes some of the replies expressed by the companions. At the end of this scene, he remarks that Imām al-Ḥusayn wished his companions well and returned to his tent. [7]

Had some of the companions of Imām al-Ḥusayn left the scene on the eve of Ashurā, al-Ṭabarsī would have certainly documented it. Perhaps the quote from Sakina bt. al-Ḥusayn, could be true, but it must make reference to the events which took place in Zubāla: there is no mention of the eve of Ashurā in her statements. Rather, she mentions that the incident took place "one night"; however, some authors and mostly some preachers believe that "eve" to be on the eve of Ashurā, instead of the eve spent at Zubāla.

Notes to Chapter 47
Imām al-Ḥusayn's Sermon on the Eve of Ashurā

1. This sermon is quoted in the following sources: al-Ṭabarī, *Ta'rīkh*, Events of the Year 61 AH; Ibn al-Athīr, *al-Kāmil fī al-Ta'rīkh*, vol. 3, p. 285; Ibn Ṭāwūs, *al-Luhūf*, p. 79; al-Khwārazmī, *Maqtal al-Ḥusayn*, vol. 1, p. 246; Abū al-Faraj al-Isfahānī, *Maqātil al-Ṭālibīyyīn*, p. 82; and Ibn Sa'd, *al-Ṭabaqāt*. However, the sentence "qad akhbaranī jaddī [my grandfather has informed me]" is not recorded in al-Ṭabarī's volume.
2. This sentence is quoted in 'Abbās al-Qummī's *Nafas al-Mahmūm* ed. Ayatollah Reza Ustādī (Qom, 1405 AH/ 1974), p. 230.
3. The above six responses are recorded in the following works: al-Ṭabarī, *Ta'rīkh*, the Events of the Year 61 AH; Ibn al-Athīr, *al-Kāmil fī al-Ta'rīkh*, vol. 3, p. 285; al-Mufīd, *Kitāb al-Irshād*, p. 321; al-Ṭabarasī, *I'lām al-Warā*, p. 235; Ibn Ṭāwūs, *al-Luhūf*, p. 81; and al-Khwārazmī, *Maqtal al-Ḥusayn*, vol. 1, p. 247.
4. This is quoted in al-Mūsawī al-Muqarram, *Maqtal al-Ḥusayn*, p. 258.
5. There are two books, both entitled as *Nūr al-'Ayn*, that are mentioned in Āghā Buzurg al-Tehranī's *al-Dharī'a*. Both of them are *maqtal*-texts and published in India. One of them was written by a recent author, and the other one's author is still unknown. However, such a text cannot be regarded as an authority in itself.
6. See Chapter 30, above.
7. Al-Ṭabarasī, *I'lām al-Warā*, p. 236.

48

Another Epic in the Words of Imām al-Ḥusayn

واللّٰه! لقد بلوتهم فما وجدت فيهم الا الاشوس الاقعس يستانسون بالمنّية دونى استيناس الطّفل الى محالب امّه.

"By Allāh! I have tested them and found them all courageous and staunch, they are as associated with me like the association of the infant with the breasts of its mother." [1]

Context

The late Iraqi scholar Sayyid 'Abd al-Razzāq al-Mūsawī al-Muqarram describes how on the eve of Ashurā Imām al-Ḥusayn moved away from the tents. Nāfi' b. Hilāl al-Jumalī [2], a companion of Imām al-Ḥusayn, rushed out, met him and asked for his reason for leaving the encampment. Then, he said "O Grandson of the Prophet of Allāh! Your coming out toward the army of this rebellious man, 'Umar b. Sa'd, at this moment of night has made me very anxious and agitated."

In response to Nāfi' b. Hilāl, Imām al-Ḥusayn said: "I have left to become aquainted with the terrain [around the encampment] lest there might be a hiding place for the enemy to attack you or reciprocate your attacks from that point."

At that time, while holding Nāfi' b. Hilāl's hand Imām al-Ḥusayn remarked: "By Allāh! Tonight is the same night. A promise with no breach."

Then Imām al-Ḥusayn pointed to the mountains visible in the

moonlight and asked whether Nāfi' might desire to escape, he asked: "Don't you desire to escape toward these two mountains in the dark and rescue your life?"

Upon this, Nāfi' bowed down, prostrated over the feet of Imām al-Ḥusayn, and replied: "I wish to die! I have bought this sword at 1,000 dirhams and this horse at the same price. By Allāh Who has conferred devotion to you on me, there will be no separation between me and you unless this sword gets blunt and this horse runs out of breath."

The late Sayyid 'Abd al-Razzāq al-Mūsawī al-Muqarram related from Nāfi' b. Hilāl that having searched the plains around the encampment, Imām al-Ḥusayn returned and went to the tent of his sister Lady Zaynab al-Kubrā and Nāfi' was standing guard outside the tent. Thereupon, Lady Zaynab asked Imām al-Ḥusayn if he had tested his companions and was sure of their steadfastness. She was worried whether they might leave him alone amidst the foes.

In response to her concern, Imām al-Ḥusayn replied in the way quoted in the beginning of this chapter.

Upon noticing this scene, Nāfi' was about to burst into tears, and went to Ḥabīb b. Maẓāhir al-Asadī [3] to report what he had just noticed.

In reaction to this report, Ḥabīb b. Maẓāhir stressed that had it not been the case that they had been awaiting Imām al-Ḥusayn's command, they would have certainly attacked the enemy on the same night. At that time, Nāfi' suggested to him that he, together with a group of the companions, should move towards the tent of the women and children to emphasize their loyalty once more so that they would be reassured and calm.

Upon this suggestion, Ḥabīb b. Maẓāhir called on Imām al-Ḥusayn's companions, and they rushed out of their tents. Ḥabīb asked the Hāshimid companions to return to the tents and to continue either taking rest or offering prayers. Then he reported Nāfi''s message for the rest of the companions. At that time, all of them maintained that had it not been because of Imām al-Ḥusayn's command, they would have certainly attacked the enemy at that moment. They assured Ḥabīb of their loyalty.

This reconfirmation of loyalty delighted Ḥabīb and he prayed for the companions. Then Ḥabīb suggested that they get closer to the tent of the women to assure them of this loyalty.

By that tent, Ḥabīb addressed the Hāshimid ladies: "O Granddaughters of the Prophet and the *ḥarām*-relatives of the Prophet of Allāh! These are your courageous youths and these are their shining swords. They have all sworn not to sheathe their swords and not to put aside their long and pointed spears until they have pierced them into the chests of your enemies."

At that time, a lady answered their call as follows: "O Brave men! Defend the granddaughters of the Prophet of Allāh and the ladies of the Commander of the Faithful!"

At hearing the above response, the men could not hold back their tears and returned to their tents.

May my parents be sacrificed for you! You have become cleansed of all impurities, the land into which you are entombed is cleansed, and you have attained a sublime felicity, martyrdom.

Notes to Chapter 48 Another Epic in the Words of Imām al-Ḥusayn

1. The materials in this section are all taken from Sayyid 'Abd al-Razzāq al-Mūsawī al-Muqarram's *Maqtal al-Ḥusayn*, p. 262.

2. Nāfi' b. Ḥilāl al-Jumalī was a fearless commander, a renowned Qur'ān reciter, and a *hadith* recorder. He was a companion of Imām 'Alī in his Iraq wars, too. In Karbalā, when he was one of those who went to the Euphrates to bring water to the camp of Imām al-Ḥusayn, he never drank a drop of water, for Imām al-Ḥusayn and his entourage were still thirsty. In the Battle of Karbalā, he was injured and then was taken to al-Kūfa as a captive. He was then martyred by Shimr.

3. Ḥabīb b. Maẓāhir al-Asadī was a companion of Prophet Muḥammad. In the time of Imām 'Alī's government, he was

a resident of al-Kūfa, served as one of his companions, and participated in the wars. Ḥabīb b. Maẓāhir was one of those who wrote a letter of invitation to Imām al-Ḥusayn. Upon Muslim b. 'Aqīl's coming to al-Kūfa, Ḥabīb was one of those who stressed his loyalty to Imām al-Ḥusayn. He was martyred at the age 75 on Ashurā. For further information, see the following book: S. A. al-Qaṣīr, *Ḥabīb b. Maẓāhir al-Asadī* (Karbalā, 1432 AH/ 2011)

49

Imām al-Ḥusayn's Poems and Advice to his Sisters and Wives on the Eve of Ashurā

a) يا دهر افّ لك من خليل   كم لك بالا شراق والا صيل
من صاحب اوطالب قتيل   والدّهر لايقنع بالبديل
وانّما الامر الى الجليل   وكلّ حىّ سالك سبيل

b)... يا اختاه! تعزّى بعزاء الله واعلمى انّ اهل الارض يموتون و اهل السّماء لا يبقون و انّ كلّ شىء هالك الا وجه الله الذّى خلق الارض بقدرته ويبعث الخلق فيعودون و هو فرد وحده. ابى خير منّى وامّى خير منّى واخى خير منّى و لى و لهم و لكلّ مسلم برسول الله اسوة ...

c) يا اختاه! يا امّ كلثوم! يا فاطمة! يا رباب! انظرن اذا قتلت فلا تشققن علىّ جيباً ولا تخمشن وجهاً ولا تقلن هجراً.

(a) *"O Time! Woe unto your friendship,*
When at sunrise and sunset you
Kill so many of your friends and,
Never feel content with a substitute.
Affairs all depend on [Allāh] the Glorious
And any living creature takes this cause."

(b) "O Sister! Be patient, and know that all the living creatures on the earth shall die, those in the heavens will not survive, that everything will perish save Allāh Who created the earth with His might and will resurrect the creatures so they will come into being again, and He is Alone in this regard. My father was better than me, my mother was better than me, my brother was better than me; they all left this world for the world Hereafter. All Muslims, they, must follow the Prophet of Allāh who passed away and departed here for the world Hereafter."

(c) "O My sister! O Umm Kulthūm! O Fāṭima! O Rabāb! Pay attention to me and, when I am killed, never tear off your collars, scratch your faces, or utter anything irrelevant." [1]

Context

It is reported on the authority of the Imām 'Alī b. al-Ḥusayn "al-Sajjād", that on the eve of Ashurā Imām al-Ḥusayn was in a tent with some of his companions, and Jawn [2] (a former servant of Abū Dhar al-Ghifārī) was sharpening Imām al-Ḥusayn's sword. At that time, Imām al-Ḥusayn was reciting the poem cited in (a) above. From these verses, Imām 'Alī b. al-Ḥusayn realised they were a prophecy of death and martyrdom, and his eyes filled with tears; but he held them back. However, his aunt Zaynab was then sitting by his bed. [3] After Imām al-Ḥusayn's companions left him alone, his sister Lady Zaynab rushed to him and expressed her concern and distress: "Woe unto me! I wish I had died so that I could not witness such a time. O Remainder of my parents! O Shelter of my descendants! I feel as if I have lost all my beloved relatives; this very incident has renewed the calamities of the loss of my father 'Alī, my mother Fāṭima al-Zahrā, and my brother [Imām] al-Ḥasan."

Imām al-Ḥusayn tried to console her and instructed her in the way mentioned in (b) above. After this, he addressed his sisters, daughter, and wife as mentioned in (c) above.

Notes to Chapter 49
Imām al-Ḥusayn's Poems and Advice to his Sisters and Wives on the Eve of Ashurā

1. Al-Balādhurī, *Anṣāb al-Ashrāf*, vol. 3, p. 185; al-Ṭabarī, *Ta'rīkh*, the Events of the Year 61, p. 240; Ibn al-Athīr, *al-Kamīl fī al-Ta'rīkh*, vol. 3, p. 286; al-Mufīd, *Kitāb al-Irshād*, p. 232; al-Khwārazmī, *Maqtal al-Ḥusayn*, vol. 1, p. 237; al-Ya'qūbī, *Ta'rīkh*, vol. 2, p. 244; al-'Ubaydlī, *Akhbār al-Zaynabāt*.
2. Jawn b. Ḥuway was a servant of Abū Dhar al-Ghifārī. After Abū Dhar, he served the *Ahl al-Bayt*, and accompanied Imām al-Ḥusayn from Medina to Mecca and finally to Karbalā.
3. It was obviously a Divine will for Imām 'Alī b. al-Ḥusayn to catch a fever on the eve and day of Ashurā. Due to this illness, he was religiously exempted from joining the battlefield. Hence, the Divine line of Imāmate was preserved for the Shi'is.

50

Imām al-Ḥusayn's Qur'ān Recitation on the Eve of Ashurā

و لا يحسبنّ الّذين كفروا انّما نملى لهم خير لانفسهم انّما نملى لهم ليزدادوا اثما و لهم عذاب مهين. ما كان الله ليذرالمؤمنين على ما انتم عليه حتّى يميز الخبيث من الطّيّب.

"And let not those who disbelieve think that Our granting them respite is better for their souls; We grant them respite only so that they may add to their sins; and they shall have a disgraceful chastisement. On no account will Allāh leave the believer in the condition which you are in until He seperates evil from the good."[1]

Context

On the eve of Ashurā, Imām al-Ḥusayn's tents were buzzing with activity. One was preparing his weapon for the battle; another was engrossed in supplications; someone else was reciting verses of the Holy Qur'ān. There was a continuous hum caused by their prayers and supplications.

On the authority of Ḍaḥḥāk b. 'Abd Allāh al-Mushriqī [2], it is reported that on the eve of Ashurā there were several teams of horsemen dispatched from the army of 'Umar b. Sa'd to report what was going on in the camp of Imām al-Ḥusayn. One of the enemy forces overheard Imām al-Ḥusayn's voice reciting the above Qur'ānic verse. Upon hearing this, the enemy soldier shouted: "By Allāh! We are the good people whom Allāh separated from you (the camp of Imām al-Ḥusayn)."

In response to this false claim, Burayr b. Khuḍayr stepped forward and answered him in this way: "O shameless man! Allāh has placed you in the line of the corrupt people. Return to us and repent of your grave sin, for we are the honest people by Allāh."

Mockingly, the enemy soldier returned: "I bear witness by Allāh that this is true." He then returned to the enemy camp. [3]

A Scene of Testing

By selecting the above Qur'ānic verses, Imām al-Ḥusayn intended to convey the condition of the two armies on the eve of Ashurā.

The first verse provides the reason for the apparent dominance of the oppressor, while the believer must remember that this domination is short-lived. It is a transitory victory so that, by the Divine will, the oppressor will sink deeper and deeper in the abyss of corruption and sin. It can be regarded as a tactful respite for them. Therefore, any group, government, or individual with cruel and ruthless conduct that is provided with such respite must be prepared for a day when the most dreadful and painful Divine punishment will certainly embrace them.

The second verse concerns the believers. Although they are put to the test one day and receive an apparent defeat, this test is to make a distinction between the noble people and the unreliable ones. Such a test is not limited to the events of Ashurā and the plain of Karbalā which were, no doubt, one of the most significant tests. Rather, throughout time, this world has been a testing ground for people. This explains the famous quote "Every day is Ashurā and every land is Karbalā."

Notes to Chapter 50
Imām al-Ḥusayn's Qur'ān Recitation on the Eve of Ashurā

1. The Holy Qur'ān, Sūrah Āl-i 'Imrān [3]: 178-179.
2. Ḍaḥḥāk b. 'Abd Allāh al-Mushriqī was a person who used to fight on Imām al-Ḥusayn's side; however, he escaped the scene once he realised that there were only two men left among Imām al-Ḥusayn's battling companions.
3. Al-Ṭabarī, *Ta'rīkh*, the Events of the Year 61 AH, pp. 324-5; and al-Mufīd, *Kitāb al-Irshād*, p. 233.

51

Imām al-Ḥusayn's Dream on the Eve of Ashurā

... انّى رايت فى منامى كانّ كلابا قد شدّت علىّ تنهشنى وفيها كلب ابقع رايته اشدّها واظنّ انّ الذّى يتولّى قتلى رجل ابرص من هؤلاء القوم. وانّى رايت رسول الله بعد ذلك ومعه جماعة من اصحابه وهو يقول انت شهيد هذه الامّة وقد استبشر بك اهل السّماوات واهل الصّفيح الاعلى وليكن افطارك عندى اللّيلة. عجّل ولا تؤخّر! فهذا ملك قد نزل من السّما لياخذ دمك فى قارورة خضرا فهذا ما رايت وقد انف الامر واقترب الرّحيل من هذه الدّنيا لا شكّ فيه.

"I dreamt that it was as if some dogs were attacking and biting me, and there was a dog mottled black and white which was the severest in his attack. I feel the person who will kill me must be a leper from among those people (his enemies). And after that I dreamt the Prophet of Allāh, with a group of his companions around him, told me: 'You are the martyr of this *ummah*, and the residents of the heavens and Paradise has announced good tidings of your arrival, and that you will break your fast in my presence this coming evening, [so] hurry up and do not delay. And, this is an angel who has come down from the heavens to collect your blood in a green bottle.' This is what I dreamt and the time has already come, and no doubt the time of departure from this world has gotten closer." [1]

Context

The late Sheikh 'Abbās al-Qummī reports, on the authority of the late Sheikh al-Ṣadūq, that in the last hours of the eve of Ashurā, Imām al-Ḥusayn had a short nap, after which he reported his dream in the way mentioned above.

A Dream-Based Depiction of Reality

Whatever was going to take place in reality had appeared to Imām al-Ḥusayn in his dream. He then reported it to his companions to give them a vivid picture.

The scenes he witnessed included: his martyrdom on the ensuing day; the characteristics of his killer and that he was leprous such that he was shown in the form of "a mottled black and white dog"; being a guest of the Prophet of Allāh; the welcome of the angels for the soul of the Sublime Martyr of Islam; and preservation of his blood which must be retained afresh for good and all. These facts were what he had discerned in his dream; certainly all of them took place on Ashurā.

Note to Chapter 51 Imām al-Ḥusayn's Dream on the Eve of Ashurā

1. Al-Khwārazmī, *Maqtal al-Ḥusayn*, vol. 1, p. 252; and 'Abbās al-Qummī, *Nafas al-Mahmūm*, p. 234.

52

Seek Help from Perseverance and Prayer

a)... انّ الله تعالى اذن فى قتلكم وقتلى فى هذا اليوم فعليكم بالصّبر والقتال.

b) ... صبرا يا بنى الكرام! فما الموت الا قنطرة تعبر بكم عن البؤس والضّرّاء الى الجنان الواسعة والنّعم الدّائمة فايّكم يكره ان ينتقل من سجن الى قصر؟ وما هو لاعدائكم الا كمن ينتقل من قصر الى سجن وعذاب. انّ ابى حدّثنى عن رسول الله انّ الدّنيا سجن المؤمن وجنّة الكافر والموت جسر هؤلاء الى جنانهم وجسر هؤلاء الى جحيمهم، ما كذبت ولا كذبت.

(a) "Indeed Allāh the Sublime has granted me and you the permission to fight on this day, so you must be patient and fight." [1,2]

(b) "Be patient, O Sons of the noblemen! Death is nothing save a bridge which leads you from calamity and distress to the lofty paradise gardens and eternal grace, so who of you resents to be taken from a prison to a castle? This castle is not for your enemies except that it would be like being taken from a castle into a prison and chastisement. Indeed my father [3] related a *hadith* for me from the Prophet of Allāh: 'This world is a prison for the believer and a paradise garden for the disbelievers, and that death is a bridge for the believers, toward their paradise gardens; and a bridge for the other group toward their Hellfires.' I have not been told a lie, nor have I told a lie." [4]

Context

According to Ibn Qūlawayh and al-Mas'ūdī [5], having performed the dawn *salat*, Imām al-Ḥusayn glorified Allāh and turned to those who were performing the *salat* behind him. He addressed them in the way indicated in (a) above.

The late Sheikh al-Ṣadūq reported from Imām 'Alī "al-Sajjād" the following account [6]:

"On the day of Ashurā when the war became very fierce and it was a difficult time for Imām al-Ḥusayn, some of his companions felt weak and pale when they saw the mutilated bodies of their comrades and friends and that such an end would await them. On the contrary, Imām al-Ḥusayn and some of his special companions became more tranquil and at peace as the tension of the battle increased and the time for marytdom approached. Some of the first group became surprised at this and noticed the spiritual and delightful countenance of Imām al-Ḥusayn and expressed that he was by no means scared of death."

Upon hearing the above remark from his companions, Imām al-Ḥusayn addressed them in the way quoted in (b) above.

After this observation, Imām al-Ḥusayn organised the lines of his army which reportedly consisted of 72 people. [7] The right flank was entrusted to Zuhayr b. al-Qayn, the left one to Ḥabīb b. Maẓāhir, and the standard to his step-brother al-'Abbās b. 'Alī. Imām al-Ḥusayn himself and his relatives stood in the middle of the army.

Emphasis on Steadfastness

Immediately after the dawn prayer, Imām al-Ḥusayn reminded his companions of two principles, both connected with prayer (*salat*). Firstly, that they would be killed which was the Divine will, and secondly, the importance of being steadfast against the enemies. This is because there are several verses in the Holy Qur'ān that indicate statements about the *salat* which is a sign of Islam and having faith. Performing the prayer is mandatory in all situations even in situations where apparent defeat and being killed is certain. However, those who perform the *salat* but ignore joining the *jihad*, are mentioned in the

Holy Qur'ān as those who are reproached for saying "We believe in some [rules] but reject others." [8] The spirit of steadfastness and resistance in *jihad* must also be obtained from the *salat* and communication with Allāh; one must gain strength from worshipping and spirituality, as explicitly mentioned in the Holy Qur'ān in this way: "Seek (Allāh's help with patient perseverance and prayer." [9]

Notes to Chapter 52
Seek Help from Perseverance and Prayer

1. Ja'far b. Muḥammad b. Qūlawayh al-Qummī, *Kāmil al-Zīyārāt*, Ch. 23, *hadith* Nos. 7, 8, and 10.
2. This is very close in phrasing to the supplication the Prophet Muḥammad offered on the day of the Battle of Badr in 2 AH/ 624. See, 'Alī b. Tāwūs al-Hillī, comp., Muhaj al-Da'awāt wa Manhaj al-'Ināyāt, ed. Jawād al-Qayyumī al-Isfahānī (Tehran, 1422 AH/ 1380 Sh/ 2001), p. 157. (NB. [1] The vowels preceding the star mark (*) must bear a macron over. [2] A dot is needed under T in Tawus, and H in Hilli.)
3. The First Infallible Imām 'Alī
4. Sayyid Mustafā Mūsawī Āl-i I'timād and Muḥammad-Hoseyn Mūsawī-Meshkāt, eds., *Balāgha al-Ḥusayn*, p. 190.
5. Al-Mas'ūdī, *Ithbāt al-Wasīya*, p. 139.
6. Al-Ṣadūq, *Ma'ānī al-Akhbār*, p. 289.
7. Historians record the number of Imām al-Ḥusayn's combatants in different ways. This number sometimes reaches 150 people, both cavalry and infantry.
8. The Holy Qur'ān, Sūrah al-Nisā' [4]: 150.
9. The Holy Qur'ān, Sūrah al-Baqara [2]: 45.

53

Imām al-Ḥusayn's Supplication on Ashurā Morning

اللّهمّ! انت ثقتى فى كلّ كرب و رجائى فى كلّ شدّة وانت لى فى كلّ امر نزل بى ثقة وعدّة. كم من همّ يضعف فيه الفؤاد للّه وتقلّ فيه الحيلة ويخذل فيه الصّديق ويشمت فيه العدوّ انزلته بك وشكوته اليك رغبة منّى اليك عمّن سواك فكشفته وفرّجته فانت ولىّ كلّ نعمة ومنتهى كلّ رغبة.

"O Allāh! You are my trustee in every calamity and my hope in every distress. And, You are with me as a trustee and a support in every affair that concerns me. How numerous are the concerns in which hearts weaken, solutions decrease, the intimate friends separate, and the enemies joyfully celebrate. I have appealed to You and complained about the situation to You out of my devotion to You and in negligence of anything except You, hence You have rescued and revived it. So, You are the source of every grace and the purpose of every (act of) devotion." [1]

Context

In the previous chapter, Imām al-Ḥusayn organised his small army after the dawn prayer and briefed the commanders of each flank about their duties and tasks. At the same time, 'Umar b. Sa'd was also busy organizing his army. When Imām al-Ḥusayn noticed the large army of the enemy, he raised his hands towards the heavens and offered the above supplication.

Note to Chapter 53
Imām al-Ḥusayn's Supplication on Ashurā Morning

1. Al-Ṭabarī, *Ta'rīkh*, vol. 7, p. 327; Ibn 'Asākir, *Ta'rīkh Dimashq*, p. 211; Ibn al-Athīr, *al-Kāmil*, vol. 3, p. 287; and al-Mufīd, *Kitāb al-Irshād*, p. 233.

54

Imām al-Ḥusayn's First Speech on Ashurā

Part One: The Ultimatum

ايّها النّاس! اسمعوا قولى ولا تعجلوا حتّى اعظكم بما هو حقّ لكم علىّ و حتّى اعتذر اليكم من مقدمى عليكم فان قبلتم عذرى وصدّقتم قولى و اعطيتمونى النّصف من انفسكم، كنتم بذلك اسعد ولم يكن لكم علىّ سبيل وان لم تقبلوا منّى العذر ولم تعطوا النّصف من انفسكم فاجمعوا امركم وشركاكم ثمّ لا يكن امركم عليكم غمّة ثمّ اقضوا الىّ و لا تنظرون. انّ وليّي الله الّذى نزّل الكتاب وهو يتولّى الصّالحين.

O People! Listen to my speech and do not make haste until I have given you a piece of advice concerning your duty towards me, and I seek your pardon for my coming here. If you accept my explanation, verify my truthfulness and deal with me with justice, you will attain prosperity, and then there would remain no way for you to fight me. And, if you reject my explanation, deny my reason and do not make a fair judgment, 'Then plan your move, and call your associates, and make certain of your plan; then do whatever you intend against me, allowing me no respite.' [1] 'My savior is Allāh who has revealed the Book; and He protects those who are righteous.' " [2-3]

Context

Imām al-Ḥusayn intended to prevent the battle from taking place. When he realised that the enemy was completely ready to start the battle and had long prevented his encampment from reaching water, Imām al-Ḥusayn felt reluctant to initiate the war. He had expressed this principle from the moment they reached the plains of Karbalā. Moreover, Imām al-Ḥusayn's intent was to advise them, so that they would be able to make a distinction between the Right Path from the wrong one, so that there would not be anyone among them who would take part in shedding the blood of Imām al-Ḥusayn out of ignorance.

Sibṭ b. al-Jawzī's account is noteworthy in this regard. In *Tadhkira al-Khawāṣ*, he described: "When Imām al-Ḥusayn noticed that the people of al-Kūfa were insisting on killing him, he took a copy of the Holy Qur'ān, opened it, and placed it on his head and stood in front of the enemy's lines of troops, then he addressed the enemy soldiers in the following way: 'O People! This is the Book of Allāh and my grandfather shall be the arbiter between you and me. O People! Why do you regard it lawful to shed my blood? Am I not the son of your Prophet's daughter? Have you not heard the remark of my grandfather about me and my brother in that 'These two are the Princes of the Inhabitants of Paradise'? In case you do not believe my words, ask Jābir, Zayd b. Arqam, and Abū Sa'īd al-Khidrī. Isn't Ja'far al-Ṭayyār my uncle?"

Nobody from the crowd responded but Shimr. He shouted: "Now, you will go to the Hell." Thereupon, Imām al-Ḥusayn returned: "Allāh is the Greatest! My grandfather has informed me in a dream that a dog was sucking the blood of his *Ahl al-Bayt*. I believe that you must be that same dog." [4]

This is the benevolence of the Infallible Imām, a philanthropist and Divine leader, even toward such a brutal enemy. This was the practice of Imām al-Ḥusayn who never turned away from the Divine Path even in the harshest situation. In this way, nobody would say "Our Lord! If only You had sent us a messenger, we would have followed Your revelations before we suffered humiliation and disgrace!" [5]

Although there was not much time nor opportunity on the Day of Ashurā, Imām al-Ḥusayn delivered a series of sermons and guidelines. The first sermon has been quoted above. As it is a long sermon, it is quoted here in four fragments.

In the first and introductory fragment, Imām al-Ḥusayn reminded the enemies of a series of facts. He reminded the people of al-Kūfa and the army of ʻUmar b. Saʻd that he never intended to pledge or to compromise with the enemies. Rather, he intended to express a range of basic and important facts concerning the role of Imāmate and leadership, which were his duty. Hence, he advised them to listen to him and not make haste.

Part Two: After a Pause in Imām al-Ḥusayn's Sermon

According to books of Islamic history, when Imām al-Ḥusayn reached the end of the above sermon, a large number of the ladies who were listening to him began to cry and started sobbing. In response to this, Imām al-Ḥusayn paused for a short while and asked his step-brother al-ʻAbbās and his son ʻAlī al-Akbar to ask them to be quiet. He said "Quieten them, for by my life, there will be much more to weep in the future".

When they were silent, Imām al-Ḥusayn started delivering another sermon. After praising Allāh, he delivered the following sermon.

عباد اللّه! اتّقوا اللّه وكونوا من الدّنيا على حذر! فانّ الدّنيا لو بقيت على احد او بقى عليها احد لكانت الا نبيا احقّ بالبقا واولى بالرّضاء وارضى بالقضا غير انّ اللّه خلق الدّنيا للفناء فجديدها بال ونعيمها مضمحلّ وسرورها مكفهرّ والمنزل تلعة والدّار قلعة فتزوّدوا فانّ خير الزّاد التّقوى واتّقوا اللّه لعلّكم تفلحون.

"O Servants of Allāh! Fear Allāh, and be wary of the worldly life, for if the world had been eternal or anybody had been destined to live forever, the prophets would have been most worthy of survival and most content with the [Divine] destiny. However, Allāh created the world for extinction, hence its new makes are antiquated, its graces are fleeting, its delight is sullen, its situation is located on a mountain-slope, and its house is transient. Hence, try to avail [yourselves] of some provisions, for 'The best of provisions is piety' [6], and 'Fear Allāh, so that you may reach felicity.' [7].

ايّها النّاس! انّ الله تعالى خلق الدّنيا فجعلها دار فناء وزوال متصرّفة باهلها حالا بعد حال فالمغرور من غرّته والشّقىّ من فتنته فلا تغرّنّكم هذه الدّنيا فانّها تقطع رجاء من ركن اليها وتخيب طمع من طمع فيها واراكم قد اجتمعتم على امر قد اسخطتم الله فيه عليكم واعرض بوجه الكريم عنكم واحلّ بكم نقمته فنعم الرّب ربّنا وبئس العبيد انتم اقررتم بالطّاعة وامنتم بالرّسول محمّد صلّى الله عليه و اله ثمّ انّكم زحفتم الى ذرّيّته وعترته، تريدون قتلهم. لقد استحوذ عليكم الشّيطان فانساكم ذكر الله العظيم فتبا لكم و لما تريدون انّا لله وانّا اليه راجعون. هؤلاء قوم كفروا بعد ايمانهم. فبعدا للقوم الظّالمين.

"O People! Allāh the Exalted created the world and has made it an abode of devastation and abatement that changes its inhabitants from one state to another. Hence the deceived person is one who has been fooled by the world, and the evildoer is one whom it has deceived. Therefore, be wary not to be deceived by this world, for it shatters the hope of anybody who has tended to it, and makes hopeless anybody who has had a hope in it.

"I see that you have decided on an act for which you have attained the wrath of Allāh against yourselves, and He has turned His graceful view away from you and has granted you His chastisement. Therefore, the best lord is our Lord and you are the worst servants [people]! You have promised to obey and accepted faith in Prophet Muḥammad – May Allāh grant him and his progeny His blessings – then you have advanced toward his progeny and house to slay them. Indeed Satan has gained control over you, so you have forgotten the remembrance of Allāh the Great. Hence, woe upon you and what you seek! 'Surely we belong to Allāh and to Him we shall return.' [8] They are the people who 'turned blasphemous after their faith' [9], "hence away with the evildoers.' [10]." [11]

Context

In the second part of his sermon, Imām al-Ḥusayn spoke of the transience of the world, as he regarded worldly life and riches as transitory. Had the worldly life been eternal, the prophets would have been more entitled and deserving to benefit from it.

In addition, Imām al-Ḥusayn stated the underlying cause for the people of al-Kūfa's going astray. He explained that they had abandoned and betrayed Islam, faith, and the descendants of Prophet Muḥammad and embarked on fighting and killing the grandson of the Prophet simply in the vain hope of gaining a portion of this temporary worldly life.

Imām al-Ḥusayn's aim was to awaken the enemy to the truth so that he would prevent the battle and blood-shed. In this way, he intended to guide to the Right Path those who were likely to be directed and to encourage them to give priority to the Hereafter instead of life in this world.

Part Three

In the third fragment of his sermon, Imām al-Ḥusayn continued giving advice and direction to the enemy:

ايّها النّاس! انسبونى من انا ثمّ ارجعوا الى انفسكم وعاتبوها وانظروا هل يحلّ لكم قتلى و انتهاك حرمتى؟ الست ابن بنت نبيّكم وابن وصيّه وابن عمّه و اوّل المؤمنين باللّه والمصدّق لرسوله بما جاء من عند ربّه؟ اوليس حمزة سيّدالشّهدا عمّ ابى ؟ او ليس جعفر الطّيّار عمّى ؟ او لم يبلغكم قول رسول اللّه لى ولاخى هذان سيّدا شباب اهل الجّنة ؟ فان صدّقتمونى بما اقول و هو الحقّ و اللّه! ما تعمّدت الكذب منذ علمت انّ اللّه يمقت عليه اهله ويضربه من اختلقه و ان كذّبتمونى فانّ فيكم من ان سالتموه عن ذلك اخبركم. سلوا جابر بن عبد اللّه الانصارى وابا سعيدالخدرى وسهل بن سعد السّاعدى و زيد بن ارقم وانس بن مالك يخبروكم انّهم سمعوا هذه المقالة من رسول اللّه لى ولا خى. اما فى هذا حاجز لكم عن سفك دمى؟

"O People! Reflect upon who I am, then look to yourselves and question your thought process. Do you think it is lawful for you to kill me and to violate my sanctity? Am I not the son of your Prophet's daughter, the son of the trustee of the Prophet and his cousin, the first believer in Allāh, and the first to embrace what His Prophet has brought from His Lord? Isn't Ḥamza, the Prince of Martyrs, my father's cousin? [12] Isn't Ja'far who flies with wings in heaven my uncle? [13] Hasn't the statement of the Prophet of Allāh regarding me and my brother reached you [14], 'These two are Princes of the youths of Paradise.'? If you accept what I have stated is the truth, and it is indeed the truth, for by Allāh, I have never told any lie since I realised that Allāh hates whoever tells a lie and shall defeat the liar. If you do not believe me, there are indeed among you some people whom if you asked, they could inform you of this. Ask Jābir b. 'Abd Allāh al-Anṣārī, Abā Sa'īd al-Khidri, Sahl b. Sa'd al-Sā'idī, Zayd b. Arqam, and Anas b. Mālik, and they will report to you, for they have heard this statement about me and my brother from the Prophet of Allāh. Is this not sufficient to prevent you from shedding my blood?"

Context

Some people from al-Kūfa who were subject to the Umayyads' propaganda were told that fighting Imām al-Ḥusayn was indeed defending the legal and approved Muslim caliph – Yazīd b. Mu'āwīya and as Imām al-Ḥusayn had risen against the welfare and interests of the Muslim public, it is obligatory for any Muslim to fight him. Therefore, in the third fragment of his sermon, Imām al-Ḥusayn reminded them of his identity, the distinction of his family members and their relation to the Holy Prophet.

He mentioned this in order to answer some of the rumors fabricated against him. These reminders struck a cord with every Muslim. Everybody knew well that Imām al-Ḥusayn was a grandson of Prophet Muḥammad, and the son of Fāṭima al-Zahrā and Imām 'Alī, a cousin of the Prophet and the first who embraced his faith in the religion of Prophet Muḥammad. When others were battling Islam, Imām 'Alī supported and defended Islam. Imām al-Ḥusayn mentioned the sacrifices of his two honourable uncles, Ḥamza and

Ja'far, that strengthened Islam and the Qur'ān; they were martyred in support of Islam.

About himself, Imām al-Ḥusayn emphasized one of his merits that no Muslim could deny. It was a Prophetic *hadith* which says "Al-Ḥasan and al-Ḥusayn are the Princes of the Youths of Paradise."

Imām al-Ḥusayn intended to direct the enemies' attention toward true Islam. He did this by means of reminding them of these virtues so that if they regarded the movement of Imām al-Ḥusayn to be against Islam, they would realise that the religion of Islam emerged in *their* house and was passed on to them and others due to the sacrifices of the *Ahl al-Bayt*. When Imām 'Alī embraced Islam, the ancestors of the enemies' ruler and caliph were followers of blasphemy. Those whom the enemies regarded as supporters of Islam and under whose leadership they were fighting had been some of the most staunch enemies of Islam. The uncles of Imām al-Ḥusayn were martyred in battle against them. Furthermore, how could it be possible that a person who was introduced by Prophet Muḥammad as "the Prince of the Youths of Paradise" could have abandoned Islam and the former enemies of Islam have proven to be the supporters of Islam?

Part Four: After Interrupting Imām al-Ḥusayn's Sermon

An enemy commander interrupted Imām al-Ḥusayn's sermon. At this time, Shimr b. Dhī al-Jawshan, noticed that Imām al-Ḥusayn's sermon could influence and awaken the enemy forces and cause them to abandon the battlefield. For this reason, he interrupted Imām al-Ḥusayn's speech and shouted: "He is wrong and does not know what he is talking about."

In response to this affront, Ḥabīb b. Maẓāhir al-Asadī answered him that he [Shimr] had been in abysmal ignorance, for Allāh had sealed his heart.

Following this short heated exchange, Imām al-Ḥusayn continued his sermon as follows:

a) فان كنتم فى شكّ من هذا القول، افتشكّون انّى ابن بنت نبيّكم؟ فو اللّه ما بين المشرق والمغرب ابن بنت نبي غيرى فيكم ولا فى غيركم. ويحكم! اتطلبونى بقتيل قتلته اومال استهلكته او بقصاص جراحة.

b) يا شبث بن ربعى! ويا حجّار بن ابجر! ويا قيس بن الا شعث! و يا يزيد بن الحارث! الم تكتبوا الىّ ان قد اينعت الثمار واخضرّ الجناب وانّما تقدم على جند لك مجنّدة؟

c) و اللّه! لا اعطيهم بيدى اعطاء الذّليل ولا افرّ منهم فرار العبيد. يا عباد اللّه! انّى عذت بربّى و ربّكم ان ترجمون اعوذ بربّى و ربّكم من كلّ متكبّر لا يؤمن بيوم الحساب.

(a) "Hence if you are still in doubt regarding this statement [of mine], do you doubt that I am the son of your Prophet's daughter [15]. By Allāh! Between east and west [in the world] there is no son of the daughter of a Prophet except me. Woe on you! Do you want me in revenge for a slain individual I have killed, for a property I have damaged, or for a wound I have inflicted?"

(b) … "O Shabath b. Rib'ī! O Ḥajjār b. Abjar! O Qays b. al-Ash'ath! And, O Yazīd b. al-Ḥārith! Did you not write to me, 'The fruits have ripened, the region has got verdant, and you will arrive at an army ready for you.' ?" [16]

(c) … "No! By Allāh! I shall never give them an inferior hand [to make a compromise] and shall not evade them in the way slaves do. O Servants of Allāh! 'I have taken refuge in my Lord and your Lord against your stoning me to death' [17]. 'I seek refuge in the sanctum of my Lord and your Lord from every insolent imposter who does not believe in the Day of Reckoning [18] .' " [19]

Context

Upon delivering part (a) of Imām al-Ḥusayn's lecture, the enemy army became completely silent. Then he addressed some of those who had written letters of invitation and were present in the enemy army.

His address was in the way indicated in (b) above. They had no answer, instead, they denied having written such letters.

At this moment, addressing Imām al-Ḥusayn in a loud voice, Qays b. al-Ash'ath enquired: "O Ḥusayn! Why don't you pledge allegiance to your cousin [Yazīd b. Mu'āwīya] to relieve yourself? In that case you will be treated as you wish and will have no problem."

In response to the above query and suggestion, Imām al-Ḥusayn delivered the above fragment of his speech mentioned in (c) above.

Conclusion

In the last and fourth fragment of his sermon, Imām al-Ḥusayn was explicit that even if all his merits were overlooked and if what Prophet Muḥammad stated about him was considered doubtful, could it be denied that he was the grandson of their Prophet? Was there any grandson of the Prophet on the earth except him? However, having stated all those facts, Imām al-Ḥusayn bravely stated that he would never come to a compromise with the enemy.

Notes to Chapter 54
Imām al-Ḥusayn's First Speech on Ashurā

1. The Holy Qur'ān, Sūrah Yūnus [10]: 71.
2. The Holy Qur'ān, Sūrah al-A'rāf [7]: 196.
3. This discourse is quoted with some minor variations in al-Ṭabarī, *Ta'rīkh*, The Events of the Year 61 AH; Ibn al-Athīr, *al-Kāmil fī al-Ta'rīkh*, vol.3, p. 287; al-Mufīd, *Kitāb al-Irshād*, p. 234; al-Khwārazmī, *Maqtal al-Ḥusayn*, vol.1, p. 253, and Ibn Sa'd's al-*Ṭabaqāt*.
4. Ṣibṭ b. al-Jawzī, *Tadhkirah al-Khawāṣ*, p. 262.
5. The Holy Qur'ān, Sūrah ṬāHā [20]: 134.
6. The Holy Qur'ān, Sūrah al-Baqara [2]: 197.
7. The Holy Qur'ān, Sūrah Āl-i 'Imrān [3]: 130, 200.

8. The Holy Qur'ān, Sūrah al-Baqara [2]: 156.
9. The Holy Qur'ān, Sūrah Āl-i 'Imrān [3]: 86, 90
10. The Holy Qur'ān, Sūrah al-Mu'minūn [23]: 41
11. Al-Khwārazmī, *Maqtal al Ḥusayn*, vol. 1, p. 253. The first fragment of this discourse of Imām al-Ḥusayn is also quoted by Ibn 'Asākir in *Ta'rīkh Dimashq*, p. 215.
12. The title Sayyid al-Shuhadā' [The Prince of Martyrs] was first applied to Ḥamza b. Abū Ṭālib who was martyred with a spear in the Battle of Uḥud near Medina in 3 AH/ 625.
13. Ja'far, a brother of Imām 'Alī, lost his arms and was martyred in the Battle of Mu'ta in 8 AH/ 630. He is called al-Ṭayyār, the Flying, because it is related from Prophet Muḥammad that Allāh shall give Ja'far two wings in the Hereafter for his severed arms.
14. That is, the second Infallible Imām al-Ḥasan al-Mujtabā, who was poisoned and martyred at the behest of Mu'āwīya b. Abī Sufyān.
15. That is, the son of Fāṭima al-Zahrā – Prophet Muḥammad's daughter.
16. Al-Balādhurī, *Anṣāb al-Ashrāf*, vol. 3, p. 188; and al-Khwārazmī, *Maqtal al-Ḥusayn,* vol.1, pp. 252-3.
17. The Holy Qur'ān, Sūrah al-Dukhān [44]: 20.
18. The Holy Qur'ān, Sūrah al-Mu'min [40]: 27.
19. Op. cit., note 16 (above).

55

Imām al-Ḥusayn's Second Speech on Ashurā

a)... ويلكم! ما عليكم ان تنصتوا الىّ فتسمعوا قولى و انّما ادعوكم الى سبيل الرّشاد. فمن اطاعنى كان من المرشدين ومن عصانى كان من المهلكين وكلّكم عاص لامرى غير مستمع لقولى. قد انخزلت عطيّاتكم من الحرام وملئت بطونكم من الحرام فطبع الله على قلوبكم. ويلكم! الا تنصتون؟ الا تسمعون؟

b) تبّا لكم ايّتها الجماعة وترحا! افحين استصرختمونا ولهين متحيّرين فاصرخناكم مؤدّين مستعدّين، سللتم علينا سيفا فى رقابنا وحششتم علينا نار الفتن الّتى جناها عدوّكم وعدوّنا فاصبحتم البا على اوليائكم ويدا عليهم لاعدائكم بغير عدل افشوه فيكم ولا امل - اصبح لكم فيهم الا الحرام - من الدّنيا انالوكم وخسيس عيش طمعتم فيه من حدث كان منّا و لا راى تفيل لنا مهلا لكم الويلات، اذ كرهتمونا وتركتمونا فتجهّزتم والسّيف لم يشهر والجاش طامن والرّاى لم يستصحف ولكن اسرعتم علينا كطيرة الدّبا وتداعيتم الينا كتداعى الفراش فقبحا لكم! فانّما انتم من طواغيت الامّة و شذاذ الاحزاب و نبذة الكتاب و نفثة الشّيطان و عصبة الاثام و محرّفى الكتاب ومطفىء السّنن وقتلة اولاد الانبيا ومبيرى عترة الا وصيا وملحقى العهار بالنّسب ومؤذى المؤمنين و صراخ ائمّة المستهزئين الّذين جعلوا القران عضين.

c) و انتم ابن حرب و اشياعه تعتمدون و ايّانا تخذلون؟ اجل و الله! الخذل فيكم معروف وشجت عليه عروقكم وتوارثته اصولكم وفروعكم ونبتت عليه قلوبكم وغشيت به صدوركم فكنتم اخبث شجرة شجى للنّاظر و اكلة للغاصب الا لعنة الله على النّاكثين الّذين ينقضون الايمان بعد توكيدها وقد جعلتم الله عليكم كفيلا فانتم والله هم الا انّ الدّعىّ بن الدّعىّ قد ركزنى بين اثنتين بين السلّة والذّلّة، وهيهات منّا الذّلّة! يابى الله لنا ذلك ورسوله والمؤمنون وحجور طابت وطهرت وانوف حميّة ونفوس ابيّة من ان تؤثر طاعة اللّئام على مصارع الكرام. الا انّى قد اعذرت وانذرت، الا انّى زاحف بهذه الاسرة على قلّه العدد وخذلان النّاصر.

فا ن نهزم فهزّامون قدما — و ان نهزم فغير مهزّمينا
وما ان طبّنا جبن ولكن — منايانا و دولة اخرينا
فقل للشّا متين بنا افيقوا — سيلقى الشامتون كما لقينا
اذا ما الموت رفع عن اناس — بكلكله اناخ باخرينا

اما والله! لا تلبثون بعدها الا كريث ما يركب الفرس حتّى تدور بكم دور الرّحى و تفلق بكم فلق المحور عهد عهده الىّ ابى عن جدّى رسول الله فاجمعوا امركم وشركاكم ثمّ لايكن امركم عليكم غمّة ثمّ اقضوا الىّ ولا تنظرون. انّى توكّلت على الله ربّى وربّكم ما من دابّة الا هو اخذ بناصيتها انّ ربّى على صراط مستقيم.

d) اللّهمّ! احبس عنهم قطرالسّما وابعث عليهم سنين كسنى يوسف وسلّط عليهم غلام ثقيف يسقيهم كاسا مصبّرة فلا يدع فيهم احدا قتلة بقتلة وضربة بضربة ينتقم لى ولاوليائى ولا هل بيتى واشياعى منهم، فانّهم كذّبونا وخذلونا و انت ربّنا عليك توكّلنا واليك المصير.

(a) "Woe unto you! Why do you not listen to me and hear what I say while I am inviting you to the way of righteousness? Whoever follows me will be amongst the guided ones; and whoever disobeys me will be amongst the perished. You are all disobedient towards me and do not pay attention to what I say. Your gifts are unlawful and your abdomens are filled with unlawful foods, hence Allāh has sealed your hearts. Woe on you! Do you not take heed? Do you not listen?"

(b)..."Woe on you, may you be grieved! When you called for our help you were infatuated and bewildered, so we came to your help with complete readiness. Then you raised against us a sword which was in our control and ignited against us the fire of turmoil which both our and your enemies had provided. Now you have become a support and a hand of your enemies against your friends without any justice among you and without any hope from them. From them you have received nothing but the unlawful (*ḥarām*) from the worldly life they have given to you and the ruined life you had hoped to go without for us to have erred or to have a malignant intention.

"Slow down! Woe unto you! When you disliked us, you left us alone, then you prepared [for the war]; the swords have not got unsheathed, and the hearts are still calm. The decision on the war is not settled, but you have rushed toward us like a swarm of locusts and have attacked us like insects. Woe unto you, for you are indeed the tyrants of this *ummah*; its dispersed parties; the people abandoned by the Book [the Qur'an]; what Satan let loose; the small bands of sinners; the falsifiers of the Book [the Qur'ān]; the extinguishers of (the light of) sound traditions; the descendants of the killers of the prophets; the annihilators of the progeny of the Divinely-appointed vicegerents; the ascribers of the illegitimate to lineages; the exasperators of the faithful; and the yelling shout of the heads of the mockers 'who have made the Qur'ān into shreds.' " [1, 2]

After this, Imām al-Ḥusayn continued his sermon in the following way:

(c) "And, you rely on Ibn Ḥarb [3] and his followers, and leave us? Yes, by Allāh! Betrayal is well known amongst you, it runs through your veins, your roots and branches have received it, your hearts have grown up with it, your hearts have developed roots in it, and it has covered your chests. Hence, you have been the most harmful tree for the gardener and the most poisonous fruit to the one who partakes of it. Behold! May the curse of Allāh be on the violators of promises who break promises after they had pledged them solemnly, 'and you have indeed taken Allāh as your surety.' [4] Hence, by Allāh, you are those people. Behold! The illegitimate one, son of the illegitimate one, [5] has pressed [me] between two choices, sword [6] and abasement. And, how far is abasement from us! Allāh withholds this from us, His Prophet, the believers, chaste mothers, self-esteemed minds, and unsubmissive souls to prefer obedience of the abased over the arena of the nobles. Beware that I have informed and warned you! Beware that I am advancing [toward my goal] with this family [of mine] with the small number of my companions and [the former] helpers' leaving [us]."

Following this, Imām al-Ḥusayn recited a poem:

"If we expel [the enemies], we have since been expellants
If we get defeated, defeatism has been our trait.
And, cowardice is not our natural disposition, but
Our death has arrived, and the power has gone to others.
Tell our rebukers: beware!
That they will face other rebukers as we have.
That if the camel of death leaves one's gate
It will kneel down at someone else's gate."

"By Allāh! You will not live save a short while as when a horse is mounted upon to take you around like the millstone and make you agitated like the center of the millstone, as this has been a promise that my father had quoted from Prophet Muḥammad. 'So conspire together, along with your partners, leaving nothing vague in your plan, then carry it out against me, without giving me any respite.' [7] 'Indeed I have put my trust in Allāh, my Lord and your Lord. There is no living being but He holds it by its forelock. Indeed my Lord is on a straight path.' " [8]

(d)... "O Allāh! Deny them rain, give them years such as the harsh years of Yusūf, and make a Thaqafīd youth victorious over them, who will make them quench their thirst with a cup of bitterness where none of them would be left unpunished such that killing would be the revenge of killing and hurt for hurt, in revenge of me, my family, companions, and followers, for they have told us a lie and abandoned us. 'You [Allāh] are our Lord, we place our trust in You, and to You is our returning.'" [9] [10]

Context

These words of Imām al-Ḥusayn deserve much reflection and exegeses. The lessons contained in this one sermon could fill an entire book.

In a very important section of this sermon, Imām al-Ḥusayn rebuked the people of al-Kūfa and reminded them of their betrayal. He spoke of how they had escaped the tyranny of the Umayyads and rushed toward him and then in an instant, reversed their allegiance, supported the Umayyads and betrayed him. In consequence, they used the sword they had received from the house of the Prophet against them. They kindled a fire against Imām al-Ḥusayn and the *Ahl al-Bayt.* Imām al-Ḥusayn rebuked them, saying that they acted as extinguishers of the light of guidance. He compared them to an ominous fruit that got stuck in the throat of the gardener who had cultivated it, causing him to die, while the same fruit had tasted sweet, ripe, and fresh for the unjust usurpers [the Umayyads] who made the most of treacherous plans.

In the beginning of the sermon, Imām al-Ḥusayn pointed to the root of their treason and betrayal. The reason was that they were accustomed to unlawful resources, hence they had taken unlawful food. In consequence, they decided to support the old enemy of Islam, the Umayyads. As for himself, Imām al-Ḥusayn declared his way and announced that he would not succumb to Yazīd b. Mu'āwīya; he bravely said: "How far is abasement from us!" Finally, he warned them about the denigrating future of the people of al-Kūfa. He appealed to Allāh to make a young man from the Thaqafī tribe victorious over them. There are some points here that need clarification.

The first point concerns the effect of unlawful food in divergence from the right path. No doubt, any sin, not followed by repentance, will prove effective in one's deviation from the Right Path and intellectual difficiency. This being so, unlawful food has the most undesirable effects. Therefore, it is important for everyone to be mindful of their intake, not only when one has reached maturity but also when one is a baby and even when one is yet in the form of an embryo. Although children are not considered responsible, the type of food will certainly influence their intellectual as well as spiritual development and character in adulthood. This is why Imām al-Ḥusayn said that the reason for their betrayal and reluctance to listen to his truthful words was due to their intake of unlawful food. Over the past years, they had received huge sums of money as gifts from Mu'āwīya to defeat Imām al-Ḥusayn's father [Imām 'Alī] and his elder brother [Imām al-Ḥasan] and to conspire against them politically. They used to receive those sums of illegal money in the guise of gifts which they spent on their provisions. Therefore, the effect of those unlawful provisions had been that their hearts darkened, their eyes became blind, and their ears deaf to receive the advice of Imām al-Ḥusayn.

The second important remark in Imām al-Ḥusayn's sermon draws the attention of the Kūfans to the point that they had arisen against Islam with the force that Islam itself had provided them. This point is by no means limited to the events in Karbalā and the Ashurā tragedy. Rather, this remains a reality in all challenges throughout history. Yet more shocking is when some people who owe their life to Islam and the Qur'ān remain hesitant in the face of anti-religious deeds which disrespect Islam. They also contribute to the opponent's movement by their silence. The danger of such people like Abū Mūsā al-Ash'arī [11], those who participated in the Battle of Ṣiffīn against Imām 'Alī, the hordes who were memorisers of the Qur'ān and kindled the flame of the Battle of Nahrawān were by no means less than the danger of Mu'āwīya and al-Ḥajjāj b. Yūsuf al-Thaqafī for Islam.

The last point concerns the firm resolution of Imām al-Ḥusayn. He was so firm in his decision and belief not to succumb to abasement. He constantly maintained his resolution even when he was forced to choose either submission to 'Umar b. Sa'd's proposal or an honourable death. He was still firm even when his body was trampled. His slogan always remained: "How far is abasement from us!"

The present author believes that the above slogan is extremely expressive and instructive. It is more inspirational than the red flag hoisted over the golden dome of Imām al-Ḥusayn's sacred sanctuary. It was beneficial defense against the enemy too, for Imām al-Ḥusayn was faced with a tyranical and ruthless enemy who attacked and raided his camp so mercilessly that the tragedy is far beyond description. However, the enemy found itself at a disadvantage when battling the firm resolve of Imām al-Ḥusayn. It was in this way that they preferred being killed over being defamed and dishonoured. This is expressed in the poem he recited.

As eloquently elegized in a poem by the late Sheikh Kāẓim al-Uzrī, the enemy's spears drastically mutilated and hurt their bodies; however, they had no effect whatsoever on the firm decision of the camp of Imām al-Ḥusayn.

Notes to Chapter 55
Imām al-Ḥusayn's Second Sermon on Ashurā

1. The Holy Qur'ān, Sūrah al-Ḥijr [15]: 91.
2. Part of this sermon is quoted in Ḥasan b. Shu'bah al-Ḥarrānī's *Tuḥaf al-'Uqūl* as Imām al-Ḥusayn's letter to the people of al-Kūfa.
3. "Ibn Ḥarb" refers to Yazīd b. Mu'āwīya b. Abū Sufyān. Abū Sufyān's given name was Ḥarb.
4. The Holy Qur'ān, Sūrah al-Naḥl [16]: 91.
5. "The illegitimate one son of the illegitimate one" refers to 'Ubayd Allāh b. Zīyād. Zīyād was known as "Zīyād b. Abīh" (Zīyād son of his [unknown/unidentifiable] father); this designation signifies that he was also born of out of wedlock.
6. The Arabic word used is *al-silla* 'the swords' which is a metaphor for war and killing.
7. The Holy Qur'ān, Sūrah Yūnus [10]: 71.

8. The Holy Qur'ān, Sūrah Hūd [11]: 56.
9. A Qur'ānic fragment, Sūrah al-Mumtaḥina [60]: 4.
10. With minor textual variations, this sermon is quoted in the following sources: Ḥasan b. Shu'ba al-Ḥarrānī, *Tuḥaf al-'Uqūl*, p. 171; al-Khwārazmī, *Maqtal al-Ḥusayn*, vol. 2, pp. 7-8; Ibn Ṭāwūs, *al-Luhūf;* 'Abd Allāh b. Nūr al-Dīn al-Baḥrānī, *Maqtal al-'Awālim*; and Ṣibṭ b. al-Jawzī, *Tadhkirah al-Khawāṣ*. The text quoted here is taken from al-Khwārazmī's book.
11. Abū Mūsā al-Ash'arī was an imbecile who was deceived by 'Amr b. al-'Āṣ. And the caliphate was quickly usurped by Mu'āwīya, leading to Imām 'Alī's apparent boycott, all owing to Abū Mūsā al-Ash'arī's stupidity.

56

The Curses Imām al-Ḥusayn Invoked

a) اللّهمّ! انّا اهل بيت نبيّك وذرّيّته وقرابته فاقصم من ظلمنا وغصبنا حقّنا انّك سميع قريب.

b) اللّهمّ! ارنى فيه هذا اليوم ذلا عاجلاً!

c) اللّهمّ! حزه الى النّار!

d) اللّهمّ! اقتله عطشا ولا تغفر له ابداً!

(a) "O Allāh! We are the house of Your Prophet [Muḥammad], his descendants, and relatives. Take revenge from whoever has done injustice to us and usurped our right. Indeed You are the All-Hearing and are near."

(b) "O Allāh! Show me today in him a swift despisedness."

(c) "O Allāh! Drive him toward the Fire!"

(d) "O Allāh! Kill him in a state of thirst and never forgive him!"

Context

Historians have recorded that on Ashurā three people individually confronted Imām al-Ḥusayn, all after his sermons. They insisted on denying the truth and making Imām al-Ḥusayn angry such that he invoked the Divine curse on them. In effect of such invocation, Imām al-Ḥusayn's curse on them was realised. For two of them, the curse was fulfilled almost instantly; for the third one, the effect of the curse appeared a little while after the Ashurā tragedy.

According to al-Khwārazmī, when Imām al-Ḥusayn found the enemies inattentive to his sermon and determined to attack, he looked to the sky and offered the prayer mentioned in (a) above.

Muḥammad b. al-Ash'ath, an enemy soldier, who was in the front row and heard Imām al-Ḥusayn's curse, moved closer to Imām al-Ḥusayn and mockingly enquired of the family relation between Imām al-Ḥusayn and Prophet Muḥammad.

Upon noticing such stubbornness, Imām al-Ḥusayn cursed him as mentioned in (b) above. Shortly after, when he went to a corner to relieve himself, a scorpion stung him and he died right away. [1]

On the accounts narrated by al-Balādhurī, Ibn al-Athīr, and some other historians, while the enemy's army was advancing toward Imām al-Ḥusayn's encampment, a man by the name of 'Abd Allāh b. Ḥawza al-Tamīmī came forward and enquired "Is there al-Ḥusayn amongst you?"; he repeated this three times. Thereupon, while pointing to Imām al-Ḥusayn, a companion of Imām al-Ḥusayn, replied "This is [Imām] al-Ḥusayn. What do you want of him?"

'Abd Allāh b. Ḥawza shouted at Imām al-Ḥusayn and said "Hellfire on you!"

Then Imām al-Ḥusayn said, "You told a lie, for I am moving to a Lord, Gracious, Beneficent, deserving obedience, and Intercessor. But, who are *you*?"

He replied "I am Ibn al-Ḥawza."

Then, Imām al-Ḥusayn raised up his hands toward the heavens and, in a way rhyming with the enemy's byname (Ibn al-Ḥawza), he cursed him as mentioned in (c) above.

Upon hearing Imām al-Ḥusayn's curse, 'Abd Allāh b. al-Ḥawza became angry and whipped his horse to run away from the scene. His horse made a sudden jerk movement, causing him to fall backwards from behind the horse in a bump, while his foot was still stuck in the horse's stirrup. His horse ran wild, and out of his control and it dragged him to a ditch full of fire. 'Abd Allāh's injured body fell down in the fire; he received his initial punishment in this world, with the fire in the Hereafter.

When Imām al-Ḥusayn realised that his prayer was answered immediately, he prostrated in appreciation of finding his request fulfilled. [2]

On the authority of Ibn al-Athīr, it is reported that al-Masrūq b. Wā'il al-Ḥaḍramī, who was in the front row of the Kūfan army, decided not to fight the camp of Imām al-Ḥusayn. He saw what happened to 'Abd Allāh b. al-Ḥawza; al-Masrūq and realised that Imām al-Ḥusayn and his family had a high status before Allāh; otherwise, he [al-Masrūq] would certainly be driven to the Fire.

Al-Balādhurī's narrated that: "On Ashurā, 'Abd Allāh b. Ḥusayn al-'Aḍudī addressed Imām al-Ḥusayn in a loud voice: 'O Ḥusayn! You see this water of the Euphrates that looks like azure and as lovely as the sky! By Allāh! We will never let a drop of it reach your throat until you die of thirst.' In response to this impudence, he received Imām al-Ḥusayn's curse as mentioned in (d) above.

According to al-Balādhurī, just as Imām al-Ḥusayn had cursed him, 'Abd Allāh died of thirst. He lived just a while after the Ashurā tragedy. However, he used to drink large quantities of water without feeling his thirst quenched. [3]

Notes to Chapter 56
The Curses Imām al-Ḥusayn Invoked

1. Al-Khwārazmī, *Maqtal al-Ḥusayn*, vol. 1, p. 241.
2. Al-Balādhurī, *Anṣāb al-Ashrāf*, vol. 3, p. 91; Ibn al-Athīr, *al-Kāmil fī al-Ta'rīkh*, vol. 4, p. 27; al-Khwārazmī, *Maqtal al-Ḥusayn*, vol.1, p. 294; Ibn 'Asākir, *Ta'rīkh Dimashq*, p. 256.
3. Al-Balādhurī, *Anṣāb al-Ashrāf*, vol. 3, p. 181.

57

An Address to ‘Umar b. Sa‘d

اى عمر! اتزعم انّك تقتلنى ويولّيك الدّعىّ بلاد الرّى وجرجان؟ و الله! لا تتهنّا بذلك! عهد معهود فاصنع ما انت صانع! فانّك لا تفرح بعدى بدنيا والاخرة! وكانّى براسك على قصبة يتراماه الصبيان بالكوفة ويتّخذونه غرضا بينهم.

“O ‘Umar! Do you hope that you will slay me and the illegitimate one [1] will entrust you with the regions of Ray [2] and Jurjān [3]? Never ever, by Allāh! Never will you rejoice it. This is a certain covenant, so do whatever you wish because you will never take delight in this world or in the Hereafter. I foresee that your head will be placed on a reed and children will stone it in al-Kūfa and take it as a target amongst themselves.” [4]

Context

After the second sermon, Imām al-Ḥusayn summoned ‘Umar b. Sa‘d. Although extremely reluctant to meet with Imām al-Ḥusayn, he came forward and Imām al-Ḥusayn gave his final statement, informing him of the dangerous consequences of his decision to initiate the battle. Imām al-Ḥusayn’s address is quoted in the beginning of this chapter.

When he heard Imām al-Ḥusayn’s sharp remark, ‘Umar b. Sa‘d became furious and turned his face. However, he returned to his group without uttering a word.

Imām al-Ḥusayn's Curse and the Fate of 'Umar b. Sa'd

Imām al-Ḥusayn tried hard to advise 'Umar b. Sa'd and to direct him to the Right Path. Imām al-Ḥusayn met him twice and even promised to compensate his financial losses. Imām al-Ḥusayn intended to direct him so he would not commit an action resulting in his misery in this world and in the Hereafter. However, love of governmental position and power made him so infatuated that he reacted negatively to the advice of Imām al-Ḥusayn. At the end of the first meeting, Imām al-Ḥusayn cursed him to be killed at home. Again, at the end of the second meeting, Imām al-Ḥusayn warned him and foretold that he would not attain any governorship, nor will he gain happiness in this world or the Hereafter.

Here a short account of the fate of 'Umar b. Sa'd is given. This will shed light on how the curses of Imām al-Ḥusayn came to fruition in the short while of 'Umar b. Sa'd's life after Karbalā. Just as Imām al-Ḥusayn had cursed him, he was beheaded on his bed at his home.

The misery of 'Umar b. Sa'd started right after the Ashurā tragedy when he returned to al-Kūfa with the surviving members of his army.

In al-Kūfa, he went to Dār al-'Imārah, the Government House, to present a report of his mission to 'Ubayd Allāh b. Zīyād. After his report, 'Ubayd Allāh b. Zīyād demanded to see the written command he had given him to confront and fight Imām al-Ḥusayn.

Upon this resolute demand, 'Umar b. Sa'd replied that the command was lost during the battle. In this way, he abstained from returning the written command to 'Ubayd Allāh b. Zīyād.

Ubayd Allāh b. Zīyād insisted on seeing it, 'Umar b. Sa'd then said: "O Amir! Why do you insist so firmly, while I obeyed your command and killed [Imām] al-Ḥusayn and his companions. However, that command of yours must remain with me to show it to the old women of the Quraysh tribe in Medina and other cities to use it as evidence."

According to Sibṭ b. al-Jawzī, 'Ubayd Allāh b. Zīyād became furious and the quarrel between 'Umar b. Sa'd and him turned fierce. While returning home from the Government House, 'Umar b. Sa'd said: "There has not been a traveler returning home so miserable like me, for I have lost both this world and the Hereafter."

After this episode, 'Umar b. Sa'd became homebound. His misery increased. He ignited the anger of 'Ubayd Allāh b. Zīyād and was abhorred and detested by the public in al-Kūfa. Any time he went to a mosque, people dispersed from around him. Anytime he went outdoors, everybody cursed him; they pointed to him, calling and reffering to him as "The Killer of Imām al-Ḥusayn."

At last, in 65 AH/ 684, only five years after the martyrdom of Imām al-Ḥusayn, he was killed at the command al-Mukhtār al-Thaqafī. A shortened version of the account is as follows.

Al-Mukhtār expressed his decision to kill 'Umar b. Sa'd by saying that he would kill a person with particular characteristics (those of 'Umar b. Sa'd) so that the angels and people will be delighted. A man by the name of al-Haytham who was there understood that 'Umar b. Sa'd was going to be the target. He dispatched his son 'Uryān to 'Umar b. Sa'd to warn him. The next day, 'Umar b. Sa'd sent his son Ḥafṣ, who was with him in Karbalā, to al-Mukhtār to begin a negotiation. When Ḥafṣ arrived, al-Mukhtār asked for Kaysān al-Tammār who was the headmaster of al-Mukhtār's police forces, and secretly informed him that it was time for beheading 'Umar b. Sa'd.

According to Ibn Qutayba, Kaysān arrived at 'Umar b. Sa'd's house on the mission he had received from al-Mukhtār. Kaysān found 'Umar b. Sa'd lying on his bed. Upon noticing the furious look of Kaysān, 'Umar b. Sa'd realised his death was near. He attempted to rise up but his foot got stuck within the blanket and made him fall down. Without a moment of delay, Kaysān beheaded him. In this way, 'Umar b. Sa'd's detestable life ended.

When Kaysān brought 'Umar b. Sa'd's severed head to al-Mukhtār, he asked Ḥafṣ if he could identify whose head it was. Ḥafṣ answered in the positive and said, "Life will no longer be worthwhile!"

Al-Mukhtār confirmed Ḥafṣ's expression, and ordered Ḥafṣ to be beheaded, too. After that, he had Ḥafṣ's severed head put next to his father's. Then al-Mukhtār remarked as follows: " 'Umar b. Sa'd in compensation for Imām al-Ḥusayn, and Ḥafṣ for 'Alī al-Akbar." Then he continued: "No, by Allāh! They never stand on a par with each other. If I kill three-quarters of all the Quraysh tribe, they will not be equal with just a finger joint of Imām al-Ḥusayn." [5]

Such was the effect of Imām al-Ḥusayn's curse and anticipation concerning 'Umar b. Sa'd, the cruelest tyrant of history, who never attained any happiness and delight and was killed on his bed at home.

Notes to Chapter 57
An Address to 'Umar b. Sa'd

1. 'Ubayd Allāh b. Zīyād b. Abīh, the then governor of al-Kūfa.
2. Ray was a city in north central Iran. The present city of Ray in southern Tehran is in the same location.
3. Jurgān was a city located to the east of the present city of Gorgan in northern Iran. Even today the older region of Gorgan is referred to as Jurjān.
4. Al-Khwārazmī, *Maqtal al-Ḥusayn*, vol. 2, p. 8; 'Abd Allāh Nūr al-Dīn al-Baḥrānī, *Maqtal al-'Awālim,* p. 253.
5. Ibn Qutayba, *al-Imāma wa al-Sīyāsa*, vol. 2, p. 24; al-Ṭabarī, *Ta'rīkh*, Events of the Year 61 AH; and Ibn al-Athīr, *Ta'rīkh*, Events of the Year 61 AH.

58

An Address to Harthama

فتول هربا حتى لا ترى مقتلنا! فوالذى نفس حسين بيده لا يرى اليوم مقتلنا احد ثم لا يعيننا الا دخل النار.

"So return swiftly so as not to see (the place of) our martyrdom! By Him [Allāh] Who possesses Ḥusayn's life, no one will witness our battle and then does not assist us unless they shall enter the Fire." [1]

Context

On the authority of Naṣr b. Muzāḥim, Ibn Abī al-Ḥadīd [2] reported from Harthama that he was one of the companions of Imām 'Alī in the Battle of Ṣiffīn. On the way back to al-Kūfa, the route passed through the region of Karbalā. There they stopped for a while and performed the dawn prayer together with Imām 'Alī. After the prayer, Imām 'Alī grasped a handful of the soil of Karbalā, smelled it, and said: "Wonderful! What a fragrant soil you are, O soil of Karbalā! Some people will be resurrected from this region who will enter Paradise without any question."

When he returned home, Harthama reported this experience to his wife Jardā' bt. Sumayr, who was a loyal follower of Imām 'Alī. Then he asked her if Imām 'Alī's statement could be reliable. She confirmed that Imām 'Alī said nothing but the truth.

Many years passed, and Harthama was a soldier in the army of 'Ubayd Allāh b. Zīyād. Soon after reaching the region of Karbalā, he identified it to be the same place. He then remembered Imām 'Alī's statement. He was disappointed to have joined 'Ubayd Allāh b. Zīyād's army. Hence he rode his horse to the place where Imām al-Ḥusayn was standing and reported what he heard from Imām 'Alī.

Imām al-Ḥusayn enquired whether Harthama was with him or with his enemy. Harthama replied: "O Grandson of the Prophet of Allāh! I am neither your supporter, nor your enemy's. I have left my wife and daughter in al-Kūfa; I am concerned about their safety owing to 'Ubayd Allāh b. Zīyād." Imām al-Ḥusayn issued the above address to Harthama. Harthama left there for al-Kūfa so he would not witness the battle and Imām al-Ḥusayn's martyrdom.

Notes to Chapter 58
An Address to Harthama

1. Ibn Abī al-Ḥadīd, *Sharḥ Nahj al-Balāgha*, vol. 3, p. 170.
2. 'Izz al-Dīn 'Abd al-Ḥamīd b. Hibah Allāh al-Mada'inī, known as Ibn Abī al-Ḥadīd (586-656 AH/ 1190-1257) was a renowned Mu'tazilite Arab poet. He is famous for his commentary on the *Nahj al-Balāgha.*

59

In Response to 'Amr b. al-Ḥajjāj

ويحك يا عمرو! اعلىّ تحرّض النّاس؟ انحن مرقنا من الدّين وانت تقيم عليه؟
ستعلمون اذا فارقت ارواحنا اجسادنا من اولى بصلى النّار.

"Woe unto you, O 'Amr! Do you instigate people against me? Have we abandoned the religion (of Islam), but you still believe in it? When our souls have left our bodies, you will realise who is more deserving of the Fire." [1]

Context

One of the enemy commanders named 'Amr b. al-Ḥajjāj encouraged his forces to fight Imām al-Ḥusayn. He used to speak against Imām al-Ḥusayn and say: "Fight the person who has abandoned the religion (of Islam) and has got separated (defiantly) from the (Muslim) community." Upon hearing this instigation, Imām al-Ḥusayn responded as quoted in the beginning of this chapter.

Note to Chapter 59
In Response to 'Amr b. al-Ḥajjāj

1. Al-Ṭabarī, *Ta'rīkh*, the Events of the Year 61 AH; al-Khwārazmī, *Maqtal al-Ḥusayn*, vol. 2, p. 15; and Ibn al-Athīr, *al-Kāmil*, vol. 3, p. 290.

60

Addressing His Companions at the Outset of the Battle

قوموا ايّها الكرام الى الموت الّذى لابدّ منه! فانّ هذه السّهام رسل القوم اليكم. فواللّه! ما بينكم وبين الجنّة والنّار الا الموت يعبر بهولا ء الى جنانهم و بهولا الى نيرانهم.

"O honourable ones! Rise up to the inevitable death, for the arrows are the envoys of the enemy to you. By Allāh! There is nothing between you and Paradise and the Fire except death; it [death] takes them to their Paradise gardens and them to their Hellfire." [1]

Context

When 'Umar b. Sa'd returned to his army after his public meeting with Imām al-Ḥusayn, he addressed his men in the following way: "Bear witness by the Amir ['Ubayd Allāh b. Zīyād] that I have been the first to initiate the attack on [Imām] al-Ḥusayn's tents."

The Kūfan army then started shooting arrows in the direction of the tents. A torrent of arrows showered the tents. It is said that in this attack there were only a few who were not shot.

At that time, Imām al-Ḥusayn addressed his companions as cited above. According to *al-Luhūf*, at that time, some companions of Imām al-Ḥusayn launched a group attack and a fierce battle took place. When the dust settled, about fifty of Imām al-Ḥusayn's companions were martyred.

The title "O honourable ones!" is the most expressive, valuable, and comprehensive expression used. It describes a lofty status and its beauty lies in the fact that it was assigned by Imām al-Ḥusayn. Not only is the honour of the companions observable in the last days of their lives and statements, it is a designation made by Prophet Muḥammad and the Archangel Gabriel. According to Imām al-Ḥusayn, once while the Prophet was walking together with some of his companions, he noticed a few children playing. Then the Prophet paused by one of the children and kissed him. A companion asked the reason for this, and the Prophet replied that once he had noticed that the child in question was playing together with Imām al-Ḥusayn and he gathered some dust from Imām al-Ḥusayn's sole and rubbed it against his face and eyes. Hence, he liked that child because he showed respect to Imām al-Ḥusayn. Prophet Muḥammad said: "Now the Archangel Gabriel has informed me that that child will be a companion of my grandson al-Ḥusayn on Ashurā." [2]

Notes to Chapter 60 Addressing His Companions at the Outset of the Battle

1. Ibn Ṭāwūs, *al-Luhūf*, p. 89; and al-Khwārazmī, *Maqtal al-Ḥusayn*, vol. 2, p. 9.
2. Khalīl Kamarehyī *Haftad-o-do Tan va Yek Tan*, vol. 5, p. 250, quoting al-Majlisī's *Biḥar al-Anwār*.

61

The Causes of Allāh's Wrath

a) اشتدّ غضب الله على اليهود اذ جعلوا له ولدا واشتدّ غضبه على النّصارى اذ جعلوه ثالث ثلاثة واشتدّ غضبه على المجوس اذ عبدوا الشّمس والقمر دونه واشتدّ غضبه على قوم اتّفقت كلمتهم على قتل ابن بنت نبيّهم.

b) اما والله! لا اجيبهم الى شيء ممّا يريدون حتّى القى الله وانا مخضّب بدمى. .

c) اما من مغيث يغيثنا؟ اما من ذاب يذبّ عن حرم رسول الله؟

(a) "Allāh's wrath on the Jews was provoked when they fabricated a son for Him; His wrath on the Christians was invoked when they fabricated a newborn baby for Him and made the Trinity; His wrath was invoked on the Zoroastrians when they worshipped the sun and the moon instead of Him, and His wrath was invoked on a people who agreed on killing the son of their Prophet's daughter." [1]

(b) "By Allāh! I will never answer them positively regarding what they desire until I meet Allāh with my face dyed with my blood."

(c) "Isn't there anyone [2] to help us? Isn't there anyone [3] to sacrifice his life in favour of the *ḥarām* [families] of the Prophet of Allāh?"

Context

After the initial phase of the battle in which some companions of Imām al-Ḥusayn were martyred, Imām al-Ḥusayn held his beard [4] and made the above statement as mentioned in (a). He then completed his speech with (b) above.

When Imām al-Ḥusayn recited the lines quoted in (c), the women in his camp were overcome with grief and started to sob and shed tears profusely.

According to one report, after hearing this, Sa'd and Abū al-Ḥutūf, two brothers who were in the Kūfan army changed their stance. They joined Imām al-Ḥusayn, defended him and were martyred. An account of their martyrdom will follow in the next chapters.

Notes to Chapter 61
The Causes of Allāh's Wrath

1. 'Abd al-Razzāq al-Mūsawī al-Muqarram, *Maqtal al-Ḥusayn*, pp. 239-240.
2. In the original text, it is "helper"; however, as it is put as "anyone", instead of "any helper" to sound better in English.
3. In the original text, it is "sacrifice". To sound better in English, this instance of "sacrifice" is put as "anyone".
4. This was a gesture of honesty.

62

Imām al-Ḥusayn's Statements at the Time of His Companions' Martyrdom

Introduction

Imām al-Ḥusayn encouraged his loyal companions to perform *jihad*, especially in the last moments of their lives. He attended to them in person either when they sought permission to go to the battlefield or when they were injured and about to be martyred. At such moments, he expressed kind statements and was soft-hearted towards them. Each of those statements gave them joy and encouraged them profoundly. It is hard to understand how much these statements meant to the companions, all we understand is that kind words from Imām al-Ḥusayn are like honour medals on their chests and will shine throughout history. These statements also shed light on the ways and manners of the companions. For example, when Imām al-Ḥusayn attended the mutilated body of Wāḍiḥ, his Turkish-speaking servant, he embraced him and put his face on his servant's to show his appreciation. His servant became extremely delighted with this gesture of appreciation of Imām al-Ḥusayn; Wāḍiḥ then replied: "Who else can be like me while the grandson of the Prophet of Allāh has put his cheek on mine?" He passed away shortly after and joined the rest of the martyrs. [1] When Imām al-Ḥusayn attended the injured body of Muslim [b. 'Awsaja], he embraced the him; Muslim smiled in appreciation and passed away. [2]

In this chapter, Imām al-Ḥusayn's responses are quoted. They are quoted in the same order as indicated in historical accounts and *maqtal*-texts. On the authority of al-Baḥrānī's *Maqtal al-'Awālim* (p. 85), and al-Khwārazmī's *Maqtal al-Ḥusayn* (vol. 2, p. 25), the companions of Imām al-Ḥusayn used to bid farewell to him on their way to the battlefield with this sentence:

"May peace (salām) be unto you, O Grandson of the Prophet of Allāh". In response to their farewell, Imām al-Ḥusayn said: "And, peace (salām) be unto you, and we are after you", and then he recited the Qur'ānic verse:

فمنهم من قضى نحبه ومنهم من ينتظر و ما بدّلوا تبديلا .

"Some of them fulfilled their vows and some still wait, and have not changed the least." [3]

Addressing Muslim b. 'Awsaja

When Muslim b. 'Awsaja [4] fell to the ground, bleeding and barely alive, Imām al-Ḥusayn went to him with Ḥabīb b. Maẓāhir, and sat by his mutilated body. Thereupon, Imām al-Ḥusayn said: "May Allāh have mercy upon you, O Muslim." He then recited the above Qur'ānic verse. At this time, Ḥabīb b. Maẓāhir addressed Muslim b. 'Awsaja and said: "Your being killed is very painful for me, but I give you the good tidings that you will enter Paradise within a few moments." Muslim replied: "May Allāh reward you the best."

Ḥabīb then expressed that he would have been ready to carry out Muslim's last will, had he not intended to give his life on the battlefield.

In a faint voice, Muslim recommended Ḥabīb to help Imām al-Ḥusayn to the last drop of his blood. In return, Ḥabīb assured him that he would fulfill his request. Meanwhile, Muslim b. 'Awsaja breathed his last and joined the martyrs of Islam.

Addressing 'Abd Allāh b. 'Umayr's Mother

a) جزيتم من اهل بيتى خيرا! ارجعى الى النّساء! رحمك الله! فقد وضع عنك الجهاد.

b) لا يقطع الله رجاک!

(a) "May you receive a good reward from my family. Return to the women! May Allāh have mercy on you! Jihād is not your task."

(b) "May Allāh not disappoint you!" [5]

Context

One of the companions of Imām al-Ḥusayn was named of 'Abd Allāh b. 'Umayr whose *kunya* (filial byname) was Abu Wahab. He was a member of the Banū Kalb tribe. He left al-Kūfa with his wife and mother to join and help Imām al-Ḥusayn.

'Abd Allāh b. 'Umayr was martyred with some other companions in an attack on the left flank of Imām al-Ḥusayn's army; it was carried out by a group enemies under Shimr's command. 'Abd Allāh b. 'Umayr fought valiantly in a counter-attack. After killing many of the enemy's infantry and cavalry forces, he lost his right arm and one of his feet. In consequence, he was taken as a prisoner of war, and was soon tortured and killed.

'Abd Allāh b. 'Umayr's wife rushed out from the tents to the battlefield. While wiping off the blood and dust from her martyred husband's face, she said: "Enjoy Paradise! I beseech Allāh Who has granted you Paradise to make me your companion there!"

At this time, Shimr ordered his servant Rustam to attack her. He split her head with a sharp blow, and she fell beside her husband's mutilated body. She was the only woman martyred on Ashurā.

Following this scene, Rustam decapitated 'Abd Allāh's head and threw it toward the encampment. 'Abd Allāh's mother, who was in the tent, wiped the blood and dust from her son's face and began to attack the enemy with a tent pole.

At this moment, Imām al-Ḥusayn ordered her to return to the tents. He then made the statement mentioned in (a) above.

At the strict order of Imām al-Ḥusayn, 'Abd Allāh's mother returned to the tents. Meanwhile, she was uttering this prayer: "O Allāh! Never disappoint me!" In return, Imām al-Ḥusayn said his prayer for her, as mentioned in (b) above.

A Historical Error

There are a number of accounts in *maqtal* (martyrdom accounts) and *rijāl* (authority) texts, which record that a person of the Banū Kalb tribe was in Karbalā with his wife and mother, whose martyrdom account is as mentioned above. His name is recorded as Abd Allāh b. 'Umayr al-Kalbī or Wahab b. 'Abd Allāh al-Kalbī. However, as there was a person by the name of Wahab who had recently converted from Christianity to Islam, some authors mistakenly attribute the story of 'Abd Allāh b. 'Umayr to this Christian Wahab, mentioning him as Wahab al-Kalbī.

As a result of this historical error, some Ashurā-oriented books mention amongst the companions of Imām al-Ḥusayn the following three people: 'Abd Allāh b. 'Umayr, Wahab b. 'Abd Allāh al-Kalbī, and Wahab the Christian. Yet, in some other *maqtal* texts, there is only one person by the name of Wahab and there is no mention of 'Abd Allāh b. 'Umayr who was certainly martyred in Karbalā. Likewise, sometimes only 'Abd Allāh b. 'Umayr is mentioned, excluding the second Wahab. [6] The error originates from historians who quote on the authority of their predecessors.

'Abd Allāh b. 'Umayr, or Wahab b. 'Abd Allāh?

The present author [Ayatollah Najmi] believes that it was not the case, as mentioned in Ibn Ṭāwūs's *al-Luhūf* or al-Khwārazmī's *Maqtal al-Ḥusayn*, that there was a martyr by the name of Wahab b. 'Abd Allāh. Rather, this person must be 'Abd Allāh b. 'Umayr al-Kalbī who is mentioned amongst the Ashurā martyrs in first-hand and authoritative history books and *maqtal*-texts. Furthermore, he is mentioned in some *rijāl* (authoritiy) books, such as al-Ṭusī's *Rijāl* and al-Māmiqānī's *Tanqīḥ al-Maqāl*, as a former companion of Imām 'Alī and a companion of Imām al-Ḥusayn b. 'Alī.

However, it is unlikely that both 'Abd Allāh b. 'Umayr al-Kalbī and Wahab b. 'Abd Allāh al-Kalbī took part in the battle on Ashurā due to the following reasons. Firstly, it is unlikely that two people among a small army had exactly the same characteristics; being from the same tribe, accompanied by their wives and mothers, and were martyred in exactly the same way, having the same conversation with Imām al-Ḥusayn for them. Secondly, there is no mention of Wahab in *Ziyārah al-Nāḥīya al-Muqaddasa*, while 'Abd Allāh b. 'Umayr is mentioned as a martyr. The *al-Nāḥīya al-Muqaddasa* ziyārah-text contains the names of the most renowned Ashurā martyrs together with those of their killers. [7] This being so, it is very unlikely that such a tragic story would not be mentioned there.

The Origin of this Error

This error originates from a confusion over the *kunya* (filial byname) of 'Abd Allāh b. 'Umayr. He was called Abū Wahab, and his wife was Umm Wahab. Historians and *maqtal*-writers paid less attention to the *kunya* of 'Abd Allāh, and focused on the *kunya* of his wife, Umm Wahab as the accounts mention a lady named Umm Wahab who joined the battlefield. This led them to conclude that this Umm Wahab must be the mother of a person by the name of Wahab who in turn must have been there and was martyred in Karbalā. Little by little, the *kunya* of 'Abd Allāh b. 'Umayr was misrecorded as Wahab al-Kalbī, instead of the correct from of Abū Wahab al-Kalbī. This misrecording has since been copied out in subsequent books and accounts over time.

The facts are as follows: Umm Wahab was not a martyr's mother, rather she was the wife of a martyr, called 'Abd Allāh b. 'Umayr, whose *kunya* was Abū Wahab. His mother was present in Karbalā for whom Imām al-Ḥusayn prayed, but her *kunya* was not Umm Wahab; her *kunya* was Umm 'Abd Allāh, for her son's name was 'Abd Allāh.

Errors concerning proper names are abundant in history and *rijāl* books, due to the number of personal names and titles. It is customary among Arabs that people may be called by a name, a *laqab*, or a *kunya*, and sometimes with all these three titles. A person may even have several *laqab*s and *kunya*s.

The aforementioned discourse was about 'Abd Allāh b. 'Umayr, Abū Wahab, Wahab b. 'Abd Allāh. However, Wahab the Christian deserves a separate mention elsewhere.

Imām al-Ḥusayn's Address to Abū Thumāma al-Ṣā'idī

a ذكرت الصّلوة جعلك الله من المصلّين الذّاكرين! نعم! هذا اوّل وقتها. سلوهم ان يكفّوا عنّا حتّى نصلّى.

b) تقدّم فانّا لاحقون بك عن ساعة.

(a) "You have mentioned '*salat*'; May Allāh make you one of those who establish prayer and remember Allāh. Yes! Now is the outset of the prayer time! Ask them [the enemies] to pause (so that) we perform the *salat*."

(b) "Proceed, for we will reach you shortly."

Context

'Amr b. Ka'b, better known as Abū Thumāma al-Ṣā'idī, who was a companion and a *mu'adhin* of Imām al-Ḥusayn, realised that it was the midday, and approached Imām al-Ḥusayn saying: "May my life be sacrificed for you! Although these people [the enemies] continue their attacks incessantly, by Allāh, they will never catch you so long as I am alive. However, I would rather perform another *salat* behind you before I meet Allāh!"

In response to the above statement, Imām al-Ḥusayn replied as mentioned in (a). Soon after requesting a short ceasefire, Ḥuṣayn b. Numayr, an enemy commander, yelled that their *salat* would not be accepted by Allāh. [8]

Ḥabīb b. Maẓāhir answered Ḥuṣayn b. Numayr and the confrontation led to a clash in which Ḥabīb was martyred. Despite these confrontations, Imām al-Ḥusayn performed the noon *salat* with his companions, while a heavy torrent of arrows showered over them. Meanwhile, some companions of Imām al-Ḥusayn were wounded and others martyred while performing *salat* behind Imām al-Ḥusayn. They maintained their places as those who establish the *salat* and remember Allāh.

After the noon prayer Abū Thumāma stepped forward, ahead of other companions, and expressed that he preferred to join the martyrs. He hated protecting himself at the cost of Imām al-Ḥusayn's loneliness amongst his family members.

In response to this earnest appeal, Imām al-Ḥusayn permitted him to join the battlefield and answered as indicated in (b) above.

A few moments later, Abū Thumāma attacked the enemy and was martyred by his cousin Qays b. 'Abd Allāh al-Ṣā'idī.[9]

A Lesson for the Combatants of the Right Path

Salat overshadows everything. This was the practice of Imām al-Ḥusayn and his companions on Ashurā. At the outset of the time of prayer, Imām al-Ḥusayn disregarded everything else and requested a respite from his enemy to perform the *salat*.

This is a lesson for all combatants of the Right Path, a lesson which Imām 'Alī gave to his followers at the most critical moment in the Battle of Ṣiffīn. [10] When Ibn 'Abbās noticed Imām 'Alī was agitated about something, he enquired about the reason. Imām 'Alī told him that he was waiting for the sun to reach meridian so that it will be the beginning of the time for *salat*. Ibn 'Abbās said it seemed impossible to pause for performing the *salat* to which Imām 'Alī replied that he was fighting the enemy for the sake of *salat*. Imām 'Alī never overlooked performing the mid-night *salat*, even during the Battle of Ṣiffīn and on the Eve of Whining. [11-12]

Who was Abū Thumāma?

Abū Thumāma was a brave Arab and a prominent figure of the Shi'i of al-Kūfa. He served as a companion of Imām 'Alī and accompanied him in all of his battles. After Imām 'Alī, he joined Imām al-Ḥasan al-Mujtabā; and after Imām al-Ḥusayn's return to Medina, he remained in al-Kūfa. After Mu'āwīya's death, Abū Thumāma was one of those who wrote a letter of invitation to Imām al-Ḥusayn and invited him to al-Kūfa. When Muslim b. 'Aqīl arrived in al-Kūfa, Abū Thumāma joined him and, at the command of Muslim b. 'Aqīl, he started purchasing weapons, an area in which he was an expert.

After Muslim b. 'Aqīl was martyred, Abū Thumāma escaped al-Kūfa. He hid himself in a safe place for a while, until he, and Nāfi' b. Hilāl, secretly left and joined Imām al-Ḥusayn on the way to Karbalā.

Abū Thumāma's Devotion

According to al-Ṭabarī, after 'Umar b. Sa'd reached Karbalā, he dispatched Kathīr b. 'Abd Allāh al-Sha'bī, who was a cruel person, on a mission to meet Imām al-Ḥusayn and question his reason for coming to Karbalā. Kathīr in return expressed his willingness to meet and murder Imām al-Ḥusayn. However, 'Umar b. Sa'd remarked that he only wanted to know of the reason for Imām al-Ḥusayn's arrival in Karbalā.

Kathīr started heading towards Imām al-Ḥusayn's encampment. When Abū Thumāma noticed him, he informed Imām al-Ḥusayn that Kathīr was the most cruel and impudent person on the earth. He then stepped ahead and blocked Kathīr's way and told him that he had to disarm if he wanted to meet the Imām.

Kathīr stressed that he had a message for Imām al-Ḥusayn. He aimed to accomplish his mission; otherwise, he would return.

Abū Thumāma replied: "Then, I must hold the hilt of your sword while you are meeting Imām al-Ḥusayn."

Kathīr did not accept the above suggestion. So Abū Thumāma suggested to Kathīr that he deliver the message to him to pass on and in return, he would bring him Imām al-Ḥusayn's answer. This was because he would never let such a cruel and ruthless person enter Imām al-Ḥusayn's tent.

According to al-Ṭabarī's account, their dialogue led to cursing one another. As a result, Kathīr returned to 'Umar b. Sa'd without any gain. After that, 'Umar b. Sa'd entrusted the same mission to Qurra b. Qays al-Tamīmī.

Ziyārah al-Nāḥīya al-Muqaddasa commends Abū Thumāma al-Ṣā'idī in the following way: "May salām be bestowed upon Abī Thumāma 'Abd Allāh al-Ṣā'idī."[13]

Addressing Sa'īd b. 'Abd Allāh al-Ḥanafī

.. نعم! انت امامی فی الجنّة.

"Yes, you are ahead of me in Paradise."

Context

The enemy did not honour Imām al-Ḥusayn's request for a brief ceasefire to perform the noon prayer. However, Imām al-Ḥusayn endeavored to perform the *salat* outside the encampment, regardless of the enemies' attack. In the meantime, some companions of Imām al-Ḥusayn stood in front of Imām al-Ḥusayn to protect him from the arrows. Some of them received a lot of arrows and fell to the ground.

Heavily bleeding, weak and lying on the ground, Sa'īd b. 'Abd Allāh whispered: "O Allāh! Send your curse upon these people, like the chastisement you sent for the people of 'Ād and Thamūd, pay my salām to Your Prophet [Muḥammad], and inform him of the calamity I am enduring due to this sacrifice. Enduring this calamity and affliction has been to attain Your reward through assisting (the religion of) Your Prophet." Then he cast a look at the face of Imām al-Ḥusayn and enquired:

"Have I fulfilled my commitment, O Grandson of the Prophet of Allāh?" In response to this query, Imām al-Ḥusayn made the statement indicated above in the beginning of this section.

Addressing 'Amr b. Qurẓa al-Ka'bī

نعم! انت امامی فی الجنّة فاقرا رسول الله منّی السّلام واعلمه انّی فی الاثر.

"Yes! You are ahead of me in Paradise. Pay my salām to the Prophet of Allāh, and inform him that I will follow soon." [14]

Context

Like Sa'īd b. 'Abd Allāh, 'Amr b. Qurẓa guarded Imām al-Ḥusayn at the time of prayer and was heavily wounded by arrows in his chest and head. 'Amr b. Qurẓa fell to the ground and heard Imām al-Ḥusayn's conversation with Sa'īd b. 'Abd Allāh. Hence he asked the same question that Sa'īd b. 'Abd Allāh had posed. In return, he received the above response from Imām al-Ḥusayn.

In a *ẓiyārah* issued by Imām al-Mahdi, he says: "May *salām* be bestowed unto 'Amr b. Qurẓa al-Anṣārī."

Ugly and Beautiful

What strength of character 'Amr b. Qurẓa must have had to become a human shield against the torrent of arrows. He received a countless number of arrows on the chest such that within a few moments he fell to the scorching sand of Karbalā. However, he was still uncertain if he had fulfilled his commitment conscientiously with a sense of utmost loyalty toward Imām al-Ḥusayn. This concern compelled him to seek Imām al-Ḥusayn's confirmation

This world manifests the ugly and the beautiful side by side; it shows both light and felicity juxtaposed to darkness and wretchedness. 'Alī b. Qurẓa was 'Amr b. Qurẓa's brother but his fate was very different to his brother's. Understanding the root of this difference lies in a comparison between Qurẓa b. Ka'b and 'Alī b. Qurẓa, that is, the father and the son, respectively. The story is an example of the Qur'ānic concept of "bringing forth the dead from the living." [15]

Qurẓa b. Ka'b was a companion of the Prophet, a transmitter of *hadith*, and a companion of Imām 'Alī. He participated in the Battle of Uḥud and the subsequent battles. In the Battle of Ṣiffīn, he was a standard-bearer of Imām 'Alī's army. Furthermore, Imām 'Alī entrusted him with the governorship of the Fars region in southern Persia. He passed away in 51 AH/670. It is also said that he was the first person after whose death, a formal lamentation gathering was held in al-Kūfa.

Qurẓa b. Ka'b had several sons. However, these two sons became very famous, namely, 'Amr and 'Alī; the former is well-known for his sacrifice in favour of Imām al-Ḥusayn on Ashurā, and the latter for his disgusting fate.

'Amr b. Qurẓa arrived in Karbalā on the same day Imām al-Ḥusayn did. Imām al-Ḥusayn entrusted him the mission of conducting the meetings with 'Umar b. Sa'd, and he accomplished this mission without fault through to the last of these dialogues. On Ashurā, he was one of the first companions of Imām al-Ḥusayn who sought permission, joined the battlefield, recited a *rajaz* – war poem – and returned to the encampment to restore his energy. He bravely guarded Imām al-Ḥusayn when he performed the noon prayer. As mentioned earlier, he was heavily wounded by arrows on the forehead and chest and was martyred.

However, 'Alī b. Qurẓa had a totally different fate. He arrived in Karbalā with 'Umar b. Sa'd, as a member of the Kūfan army, to fight Imām al-Ḥusayn. On Ashurā, when he was informed of his brother's martyrdom, he left the ranks of soldiers and screamed at Imām al-Ḥusayn: "O Ḥusayn! O liar and son of a liar! You deceived my brother and killed him."

In response to this, Imām al-Ḥusayn said: "I have not persuaded your brother, nor did I deceive him; however, Allāh has directed him and misguided you!"

Extremely furious, 'Alī b. Qurẓa shouted: "May Allāh kill me if I do not kill you!" He then made an attack toward Imām al-Ḥusayn. However, Nāfi' b. Hilāl prevented him from reaching and harming Imām al-Ḥusayn and attacked him with a spear. At this moment, 'Alī b. Qurẓa's comrades stepped in and took him back to their army. He received medical treatment and lived for a while thereafter. [16]

Imām al-Ḥusayn's Sermon after the Noon Prayer

يا كرام! هذه الجنّة قد فتحت ابوابها واتّصلت انهارها واينعت ثمارها وهذا رسول الله صلّى الله عليه و اله والشّهدا الّذين قتلوا فى سبيل الله يتوقّعون قدومكم و يتباشرون بكم فحاموا عن دين الله ودين نبيّه وذبّوا عن حرم الرّسول.

"O Noblemen! This is the Paradise whose gates have been opened up, its rivers are full of water, and its fruits are ripe. This is the Prophet of Allāh (may Allāh bless him and his progeny) and the martyrs, killed in the cause of Allāh, who look forward to your arrival and give each other the good tidings of your coming. Hence, support the religion of Allāh and the religion of His Prophet, and sacrifice yourselves for the *ḥarām* of the Prophet." [17]

Context

According to the late Iraqi scholar al-Muqarram, after performing the noon *salat* and answering the calls of Sa'īd b. 'Abd Allāh and 'Amr b. Qurẓa who had been martyred, Imām al-Ḥusayn turned to the rest of his companions, who were looking forward to sacrificing their lives and attaining martyrdom. He then issued the above short address.

At the Martyrdom of Ḥabīb b. Maẓāhir

عندالله احتسب نفسى وحماة اصحابى.

"I regard my supportive defendants' and my own martyrdom in favour of Allāh." [18] [19]

Context

When Imām al-Ḥusayn requested a temporary ceasefire, Ḥuṣayn b. Numayr shouted out: "What kind of *salat*? Your *salat* is not accepted!"

Hearing this, Ḥabīb b. Maẓāhir stepped ahead and returned: "O donkey! Do you think it (the *salaṭ*) will not be accepted from the progeny of the Prophet, but yours will be accepted?!"

At the above retaliation, Ḥuṣayn b. Numayr attacked Ḥabīb b. Maẓāhir, with the forces of each side supporting their own comrades.

In consequence, a harsh confrontation took place. Although Ḥabīb b. Maẓāhir was an old man, he killed several enemies. Eventually, he was martyred and his head severed.

The martyrdom of this beloved old companion [20] proved unbearable for Imām al-Ḥusayn, he sat down beside Ḥabīb's mutilated and decapitated body and made the statement mentioned above.

Imām al-Ḥusayn's Prayer for Abū al-Sha'thā'

اللّهمّ سدّد رميته واجعل ثوابه الجنّة!

"O Allāh! May you direct his arrow to the target and make Paradise his reward!"

Context

Yazīd b. Zīyād, known as Abū al-Sha'thā' al-Kindī, was a renowned and skillful archer in al-Kūfa and was part of the army of 'Umar b. Sa'd. However, when he heard Imām al-Ḥusayn's sermon and realised that nobody had answered him positively, he left 'Umar b. Sa'd's army, and joined the side of Imām al-Ḥusayn. He attained this felicity before al-Ḥurr b. Yazīd al-Rīyaḥī's joining Imām al-Ḥusayn.

Soon after joining Imām al-Ḥusayn, Abū al-Sha'thā' went to the battlefield on horseback. However, after his horse was hamstrung, he returned to the encampment, bent down on his knee in front of the tents, and shot toward the enemy some one hundred arrows he had with him.

Due to his bravery and repentance, Imām al-Ḥusayn prayed for him as mentioned above. Having shot all the arrows he had, he stood up and reported to Imām al-Ḥusayn that only five of his arrows went astray! Thereupon, he attacked the enemy forces, fought them, and was martyred. [21]

Addressing al-Ḥurr b. Yazīd al-Rīyāḥī

a) نعم! يتوب الله عليك ويغفرلك، قتلة مثل قتلة النّبيّين وال النّبيّين ... انت الحرّ كما سمّتك امّك وانت الحرّ فى الدّنيا والاخرة .

b) لنعم الحرّ حرّ بنى رياح — صبور عند مشتبك الرّماح

ونعم الحرّ اذ نادى حسينا — وجاد بنفسه عند الصياح

فيا ربّى اضفه فى جنان — وزوّجه مع الحور الملاح

(a) "Yes, Allāh shall certainly accept your repentance and forgive you. These are the slain, like the martyrs of the prophets and the families of the prophets." "You are free (al-Ḥurr) as your mother named you, and you are free both in this world and in the Hereafter.

(b)

"The best freeman is al-Ḥurr of Banī Rīyāḥ [22]
Who was patient when spears clashed. [23]
And the best al-Ḥurr was he when al-Ḥusayn called. [24]
And, he sacrificed his soul at the cry,
Hence, O Allāh, [May You] receive him as a guest in Paradise,
And marry him charming houris."

Context

According to Ibn al-Athīr, al-Ḥurr b. Yazīd al-Rīyāḥī [25] broke away from 'Umar b. Sa'd's army and went towards Imām al-Ḥusayn in a state of repentance. Al-Ḥurr then expressed that he could not imagine that they would fight Imām al-Ḥusayn, otherwise he would not have joined them. At that moment he was resolute to join Imām al-Ḥusayn and to sacrifice his life so that his repentance would be accepted.

In response to this gesture, Imām al-Ḥusayn assured him that Allāh would certainly forgive him. It was as indicated in (a) above. [26]

According to al-Ṭabarī and Ibn Kathīr, [27] al-Ḥurr attacked the enemy after Ḥabīb b. Maẓāhir was martyred. He and Zuhayr b. al-Qayn attacked the enemy together before performing the noon prayer.

When one was surrounded, the other would attack the enemies to rescue him. Finally, when al-Ḥurr's horse was injured, he continued fighting on foot. After killing over fourty of the enemy forces, a group of soldiers attacked and martyred him. Thereupon, some companions of Imām al-Ḥusayn attacked the enemies, pushed them back, took al-Ḥurr's body to the encampment, and placed it in the tent allocated for the martyrs' bodies.[28]

It was at this place that Imām al-Ḥusayn glanced at al-Ḥurr's body and he was still alive. Then Imām al-Ḥusayn expressed the statements quoted above in (a), signifying that his companions were sacrificing their lives for high humane and religious values, not for mercenary ends. After this, Imām al-Ḥusayn sat down by al-Ḥurr's body and recited the poem quoted in (b) above. [29]

The Real Meaning of Felicity

Al-Ḥurr and his comrades showed what it means to be truly free and attain felicity. They were once amongst the forces of the wrong side and members of the army of the enemies of Islam. They had arrived in Karbalā to fight and kill the grandson of the Prophet, and to extinguish the torch of guidance. However, they turned to their sense of conscience and intellect and gained the opportunity to receive the Divine grace and blessings. In consequence, they utilised the sword in support of Islam and the Qur'ān and they attained martyrdom.

It is not certain how many of the enemy forces repented and joined Imām al-Ḥusayn on the eve and day of Ashurā. Their names, manners of expressing repentance, and martyrdom have not been recorded in history books. However, there were two other notable individuals who repented. Like al-Ḥurr, they were fortunate to achieve the grace of repentance and joined Imām al-Ḥusayn in the last minutes his life. They attained eternal felicity and grace through martyrdom.

Sa'd b. al-Hārith and his Brother

Sa'd and his brother Abū al-Ḥutuf were sons of al-Hārith and lived in al-Kūfa. They used to believe in the extremism of the al-Kharijites (the Seceders) and believed that Imām 'Alī deserved to be executed. These two brothers accompanied 'Umar b. Sa'd and arrived in Karbalā to fight Imām al-Ḥusayn. However, on the day of Ashurā, when all the companions of Imām al-Ḥusayn had been martyred, Imām al-Ḥusayn made his cry of help, saying: "Isn't there anyone to help me?" On hearing this cry for help, the women and children began to cry and weep. At once, these two brothers said to each other that while their belief was that "There is no verdict other than that of Allāh, and anyone who has disobeyed Allāh does not deserve being followed" [30], wasn't Imām al-Ḥusayn the grandson of their Prophet? Rather, wasn't it the case that they looked forward to benefiting from his grandfather on the Day of Judgment? How was it that they were fighting him, while he was standing in the battlefield alone?

All of a sudden, they changed their direction and stance, and rushed toward Imām al-Ḥusayn. They unsheathed their swords and fought the enemies at a place closest to the place of Imām al-Ḥusayn.

After fighting the enemies for a short while, the two brothers were martyred. They succeeded to achieve the eternal felicity, as al-Ḥurr did. [31]

Addressing Zuhayr

a) نعم! يتوب الله عليك ويغفرلك، قتلة مثل قتلة النّبيّين وال النّبيّين ... انت الحرّ كما سمّتك امّك وانت الحرّ فى الدّنيا والاخرة .

b) لنعم الحرّ حرّ بنى رياح | صبور عند مشتبك الرّماح
ونعم الحرّ اذ نادى حسينا | وجاد بنفسه عند الصياح
فيا ربّى اضفه فى جنان | وزوّجه مع الحور الملاح

(a) "I shall join them after you."

(b) "May Allāh not keep you away from His grace! May He curse your slayers such a curse that metamorphosed some people into monkeys and pigs." [32]

Context

Zuhayr b. al-Qayn [33] returned to the encampment after fighting the enemies and joined Imām al-Ḥusayn. While he put a hand on Imām al-Ḥusayn's shoulder, he sought permission to go to the battleground by reciting this poem:

"May my life be sacrificed for you,
For it has attained the Right Path,
Today is the day that I shall meet up with
Your grandfather, the Prophet, al-Ḥasan, 'Alī,
And Ja'far al-Ṭayyār, and the brave Ḥamza the Martyr."

In reply, Imām al-Ḥusayn assured him that he would follow them shortly, as indicated in (a) above. When Zuhayr was martyred, Imām al-Ḥusayn went to his body addressed him in the way indicated in (b) above.

Indeed, those who lose their intellect and act like monkeys at the order of such people as 'Ubayd Allāh b. Zīyād and 'Umar b. Sa'd, they follow a pig-like existence in which life is only worth satisfying one's lusts; such people are subject to the Divine curse, and prove to be devoid of any trait of humanity.

Addressing Ḥanẓala al-Shibāmī

a) رحمك اللّه! انّهم قد استوجبوا العذاب حين ردّوا عليك ما دعوتهم اليه من الحقّ ونهضوا اليك ليستبيحوك واصحابك فكيف بهم الان وقد قتلوا اخوانك الصّالحين. ...

b) رح الى خير من الدّنيا وما فيها و الى ملك لا يبلى!

c).. امين امين!

(a) "May Allāh bless you! They have proven worthy of chastisement while they answered you by moving toward you to kill you and your companions when you invited them to the Right Path. Now that they have slain your good brethren, they will certainly be entrapped by the Divine chastisement."

(b) "Go towards felicity and away from the worldly life and whatever exists therein and to 'a kingdom that never gets deteriorated.' " [34]

(c) "Amen! Amen!" [35]

Context

One of the companions of Imām al-Ḥusayn was Ḥanẓala al-Shibāmī. [36] When he stood in front of the enemies, he started giving them advice and completed his address with a few Qur'ānic verses: "O People! What I fear for you is the day of gathering, crying, and calling. The day you will turn your backs and flee, with none to defend you against Allāh. Whoever Allāh allows to go astray has none to show him the way." [37]

After this, he returned to the encampment. Imām al-Ḥusayn praised him for his speech as in (a) above.

Then Ḥanẓala remarked: "You are right; May I sacrifice my life for you." He sought permission to go to the battlefield, and asked: "Shall we not go towards our Lord and meet up with our brethren?"

Imām al-Ḥusayn gave him permission in the way indicated in (b) above. On leaving the encampment, Ḥanẓala expressed his farewell: "May peace be to you, O Abā 'Abd Allah! May Allāh's peace be granted to you and your family! May Allāh make us known to each other in His Paradise!"

As indicated in (c) above, Imām al-Ḥusayn confirmed his prayer by uttering "Amen" twice. Ḥanẓala went to the battleground and fought bravely until he was martyred. [38]

Addressing Sayf b. al-Ḥārith and Mālik b. 'Abd

a) اى ابنى اخوى ما يبكيكما؟ فوالله انّى لارجو ان تكونا بعد ساعة قرير العين ...

b) جزاكما الله يا ابنى اخوى عن وجدكما من ذلك ومواساتكما ايّاى احسن جزا المتّقين ...

c) وعليكما السّلام ورحمةالله وبركاته.

(a) "O Sons of my brethren! What makes you shed tears? By Allāh! I wish you would be delighted after a while."

(b) "O You (two) cousins! May Allāh reward you for your find and consolation, the best reward for the pious."

(c) "May peace be with you (two) Allāh's grace and blessings [39] and May Allāh's peace, grace and blessing be with you!"

Context

As narrated by al-Ṭabarī, two cousins of the Hamdan tribe, Sayf b. al-Ḥārith b. Rabī‘ and Mālik b. ‘Abd Allāh b. Sarī‘ (born of the same mother) managed to reach Karbalā while the route to Karbalā was not blocked by the Umayyad agents; they joined Imām al-Ḥusayn's forces.

On Ashurā, they saw that Imām al-Ḥusayn's forces were so small in number, so they went to Imām al-Ḥusayn in a state of grief, sobbing profusely. Imām al-Ḥusayn enquired of what made them shed tears, as indicated in (a) above.

They replied: "May we be sacrificed for you! No, by Allāh! We do not weep for ourselves, but we weep for you! We see that you are already surrounded but we cannot defend you by anything other than sacrificing our lives."

On seeing such a sense of performing their duty, responsibility, and sacrifice, Imām al-Ḥusayn wished them the best of rewards, as quoted above in (b).

On the authority of Abū Mikhnaf, al-Ṭabarī remarked that when these two young men were talking with Imām al-Ḥusayn, Ḥanẓala b. As‘ad, whose account was given above, was giving some advice to the enemy forces and was martyred. Following this event, these two youths ran so fast toward the battlefield and they overtook one other.

On the way to the battlefield, they turned back a couple of times toward Imām al-Ḥusayn and bid farewell to him. In return, Imām al-Ḥusayn answered them as indicated in (c) above. In the battle, they supported one another such that when one was suddenly surrounded, the other one attacked the enemy and rescued him. They fought bravely until they were martyred. [40]

A Sense of Responsibility

It was the sense of responsibility to discharge one's duty that Imām al-Ḥusayn praised. In the above conversation, the most significant lesson is the importance of realising one's duty and responsibility, a characteristic which Imām al-Ḥusayn praised, and for which he requested enormous rewards from the Almighty. This reward is the best reward for the pious.

In the above account of the two youths, it is indicated that they shed tears over the small number of Imām al-Ḥusayn's companions and the large number of the enemy forces, and that they had nothing other than their lives to sacrifice. They competed with one another to reach the battlefield; they are described in the Holy Qur'ān as "For that may aspire (all) those who (wish to) aspire (for bliss)" [41]. Therefore, their emphasis on their covenant with Imām al-Ḥusayn and the way they turned back toward the tents to bid farewell to Imām al-Ḥusayn signifies their sense of responsibility.

Addressing Jawn b. Ḥuway

a) يا جون! انت فى اذن منّى! فانّما تبعتنا طلبا للعافية فلا تبتل بطريقننا ..

b) اللّهمّ! بيّض وجهه وطيّب ريحه واحشره مع الا برار وعرّف بينه وبين محمّد وال محمّد!

(a) "O Jawn! You are free (to leave me) because you have followed us in the quest for comfort, hence do not get yourself into trouble in our cause."

(b) "O Allāh! Whiten his face, perfume him, resurrect him with the nobles, and acquaint him with (Prophet Muḥammad and the progeny of (the Prophet) Muḥammad." [42]

Context

Jawn b. Ḥuway had formerly been the servant of Abū Dhar al-Ghifārī. [43] After Abū Dhar passed away, he was determined to serve Imām al-Ḥasan al-Mujtabā after whom he joined and served Imām al-Ḥusayn. He accompanied Imām al-Ḥusayn from Medina to Mecca and finally to Karbalā. On Ashurā, when the battle reached its peak, he went to Imām al-Ḥusayn and sought permission to go to the battleground. In response to Jawn's request, Imām al-Ḥusayn answered him in the way indicated in (a) above.

At this time, Jawn threw himself on the feet of Imām al-Ḥusayn and appealed: "O Grandson of the Prophet of Allāh! Is it fair that I used to be dependent on your favour in your time of comfort and convenience and leave you alone when you are in trouble in front of the enemy? Although my body has an unpleasant smell, my lineage is unknown, and my skin-colour is dark, please have mercy on me so that my body emits fragrance, my skin-colour brightens, and my lineage gets renowned in Paradise due to your favour. No, by Allāh! I will never part with you until my blood mixes with your fragrant blood."

At the sight of such loyalty, sincerity, and insistence, Imām al-Ḥusayn gave him permission to go to the battlefield. When Jawn was martyred, Imām al-Ḥusayn went to his body and offered the prayer quoted in (b) above.

Regarding 'Umar b. Junāda

هذا غلام قتل ابوه فى الحملة الاولى ولعلّ امّه تكره ذلك

"This is a young man whose father was killed in the first attack, and perhaps his mother resents this [his joining the battlefield]."

Context

After Junāda al-Anṣārī was martyred, his 11-year son 'Umar, who had come to Karbalā with his parents, stepped forward and requested Imām al-Ḥusayn's permission to join the battlefield. In response to this request, Imām al-Ḥusayn made the above statement.

This loyal young man, replied: "My mother ordered me to sacrifice my life in your favour."

Upon this definite answer, Imām al-Ḥusayn permitted him to the battlefield. On the battle ground, 'Umar recited the following *rajaz*:

My Amir is [Imām al-]Ḥusayn, and what a nice Amir he is!
The delight of the heart of the herald and the warner." [44]

'Alī and Fāṭima are his parents,
Do you know any parallel for him?"

'Umar was martyred in the battle. His head was severed and thrown back to the tents. 'Umar's mother took her young son's severed head, wiped off the dust, and threw it back to an enemy soldier standing nearby. Due to the impact of the blow to the enemy soldier's head, the soldier was killed as well. 'Umar's mother returned to the encampment and took a stick and attacked the enemy. While attacking the enemy, she cried the following *rajaz* (war poem):

"I am a woman amongst the women
A thin, feeble, old woman.
I deliver to you a severe blow,
Out of devotion for the descendants of Fāṭima the Noble."

Having injured two enemy soldiers, she returned to the tents at the order of Imām al-Ḥusayn. [45]

At the Martyrdom of 'Alī al-Akbar

a) اللّهمّ! اشهد على هؤلاء القوم! فقد برز اليهم اشبه النّاس برسولك محمّد صلّى اللّه عليه و اله خلقا وخلقا ومنطقا وكنّا اذا اشتقنا الى رؤية نبيّك نظرنا اليه.

اللّهمّ! فامنعهم بركات الارض وفرّقهم تفريقا ومزّقهم تمزيقا واجعلهم طرائق قددا ولا ترض الولاة عنهم ابدا! فانّهم دعونا لينصرونا ثمّ عدوا علينا ليقاتلونا. انّ اللّه اصطفى ادم ونوحا وال ابراهيم وال عمران على العالمين ذرية بعضها من بعض واللّه سميع عليم ...

b) مالك؟ قطع اللّه رحمك كما قطعت رحمى ولم تحفظ قرابتى من رسول اللّه وسلّط عليك من يذبحك على فراشك.

c) ... قتل اللّه قوما قتلوك! يا بنىّ! ما اجراهم على اللّه وعلى انتهاك حرمة رسول اللّه!؟ على الدّنيا بعدك العفا!

(a) "O Allāh! Bear witness concerning this group of people (the enemy) toward whom [a youth] has gone out bearing the closest resemblance to Your Prophet Muḥammad – May Allāh bless him and his progeny – in creation, manner, and speech such that when we yearned to look at Your Prophet, we cast a look at him.

"O Allāh! Deny for the enemies the graces of the earth, make them dispersed, disrupted, and groups 'of dissimilar ways' [46] and never make the rulers content with them for good, for they have invited us to help us but then expressed enmity against us to fight us. 'Indeed Allāh chose Adam and Noah, and the progeny of Abraham and the progeny of 'Imrān above all the nations; some of them are descendants of the others, and Allāh is All-Hearing, All-Knowing.' " [47]

(b) "What happened to you? May Allāh terminate your line of descent, for you have terminated my line of descendants [through 'Alī al-Akbar], you have not considered my [blood] relationship with the Prophet of Allāh; and may Allāh make someone dominant over you to kill you at your home."

(c) "May Allāh annihilate the people who have slain you. O my dear son! What has made them so forgetful about Allāh as to offend the sanctity of the Prophet of Allāh. After you, may the world be obliterated!" [48]

Context

'Alī al-Akbar was the first of Imām al-Ḥusayn's relatives to go to the battlefield. After all other companions were martyred, it was his relatives' turn to go to the battlefield. In doing so, 'Alī al-Akbar was the first to sacrifice his life for the protection Islam and the Holy Qur'ān.

When Imām al-Ḥusayn professed the martyrdom of his companions and his own end, 'Alī al-Akbar commented as follows: "In that case, we do not care about death if we are destined to be killed in the Right Path."

Imām al-Ḥusayn praised 'Alī al-Akbar. On the basis of his description, 'Alī al-Akbar had several moral and physical virtues. In terms of features, manner, and speech he was so similar to Prophet Muḥammad that if at any time a member of Imām al-Ḥusayn's relatives yearned to look at the countenance of Prophet Muḥammad, they could look at 'Alī al-Akbar. This is an evidence for the fact that he perfectly mirrored Prophet Muḥammad, both physically and morally.

According to al-Khwārazmī in *Maqtal al-Ḥusayn*, 'Alī b. al-Ḥusayn, that is, 'Alī al-Akbar, was the first amongst the relatives of Imām al-Ḥusayn to join the battlefield. When he bid farewell to his father, Imām al-Ḥusayn looked at him, and then turned his face toward the heavens, and made the above sermon quoted in (a), he recited the Qur'ānic verses of the Sūrah Āl-i 'Imrān: 33-34.

When 'Alī al-Akbar intended to leave the encampment and join the battlefield, Imām al-Ḥusayn addressed and cursed 'Umar b. Sa'd as indicated in (b) above. [49]

When 'Alī al-Akbar initiated attacking the enemy, he cried out following *rajaz* (war poem):

"I am 'Alī b. al-Ḥusayn b. 'Alī.
By the House of Allāh [50], we deserve the Prophet the most,
By Allāh, the illegitimate one [51] will never govern us,
I will hit you with this spear so hard that it will bend,
I will hit you so hard with this sword that it will twist,
The strike of a Hāshimid, 'Alīd youth."

According to Sheikh al-Mufīd in *Kitāb al-Irshād* and al-Ṭabarasī in *I'lām al-Warā*, 'Alī al-Akbar kept reciting this *rajaz* (war poem) and attacked the enemy incessantly. However, the enemies were reluctant to kill him and withdrew.

There are several interpretations of the above observation. Briefly, a principal reason for the enemy withdrawal was his extraordinary handsomeness, as this is recorded by Sheikh al-Mufīd in that 'Alī al-Akbar's description goes thus: "He was the most handsome man." This is confirmed by Imām al-Ḥusayn's description cited above.

According to al-Khwārazmī, despite his intense thirst, 'Alī al-Akbar fought bravely and killed about one hundred and twenty enemy soldiers. He returned to the encampment and after a short while returned to the battlefield for the second time. After battling for a while, he was struck and fell to the ground. Then he cried out: "O Father! Now my ancestor, the Prophet of Allāh, has just quenched my thirst with a cup of Paradise water after which there will never be any thirst."

Imām al-Ḥusayn rushed towards him. At the sight of his son's mutilated body, he made the statements quoted in (c) above. In the words of Imām al-Ḥusayn, the world was not worth living in after the martyrdom of 'Alī al-Akbar. [52]

Two Issues

There have been two issues concerning 'Alī al-Akbar among the experts in the field and historians. The first concerns his precise age at the time of his martyrdom and the second is whether or not his mother was present in Karbalā.

As for the first issue, it must be noted that 'Alī al-Akbar's *kunya* (filial byname) was Abū al-Ḥasan and, on the account of *Anīs al-Shī'a* [53], his date of birth was 33 AH/ 655, which is two years before death of 'Uthmān as he was killed in 35 AH/657. In addition, Ibn Idrīs's view in his *Maẓār al-Sarā'ir* is that: " 'Alī al-Akbar was born during the reign of 'Uthmān 23-35 AH/ 645-657." This supports *Anīs al-Shī'a*'s view.

On the basis of the above evidence, if 'Alī al-Akbar was born at the end of 'Uthmān's reign, he would have been almost twenty-seven at the time of his martyrdom. Additionally, historians and genealogists hold that 'Alī al-Akbar was older than Imām 'Alī al-Sajjād who was twenty-three years old at the time; his son, Imām Muḥammad al-Bāqir was only four years old at the time.

Other views about the age of 'Alī al-Akbar do not seem to be supported with enough evidence. Some other scholararly opinons in this regard include: The late Iraqi scholar Fakhr al-Dīn al-Ṭurayḥī in *al-Muntakhab* who records 'Alī al-Akbar's age as seventeen; al-Mufīd in *Kitāb al-Irshād*, al-Ṭabarasī in *I'lām al-Warā*, and Ibn Shahr Āshūb al-Sarawī's *Manāqib Āl Abī Ṭālib*, who record his age as nineteen.

Quite surprisingly, Ibn Namā al-Ḥillī in *Muthīr al-Aḥzān*, holds that 'Alī al-Akbar's age in the Battle of Karbalā was just more than ten years. Although it is a succinct statement, such a remark implies that he must be at the age of twelve or thirteen. More surprising is Naṣīr al-Dīn al-Ṭūsī's view that 'Alī al-Akbar was only seven years old on Ashurā. [54]

'Alī al-Akbar enjoyed a high station in the eyes of his father. To Imām al-Ḥusayn, 'Alī al-Akbar was superior to everybody else in the army except Imām al-Ḥusayn's step-brother al-'Abbās. This high regard does not seem appropriate for a person at the age of seven or thirteen. In addition, all historians agree that on the eve of Ashurā, Imām al-Ḥusayn ordered all his companions to stand outside the tent except al-'Abbās and 'Alī al-Akbar and this occurred during a meeting with 'Umar b. Sa'd whose son Ḥafṣ and servant were with him.

Again on Ashurā, when the women and children started crying and sobbing, Imām al-Ḥusayn ordered his step-brother al-'Abbās and his son 'Alī al-Akbar to calm them, for they would certainly be crying much more in the near future.

Other evidence is that on the 8th of Muharram, when Imām al-Ḥusayn ordered some of his companions to go to the river Euphrates to bring water, he chose his son 'Alī al-Akbar as their commander.

In conclusion, 'Alī al-Akbar was indeed older than seven-years of age on Ashurā. However, it is probable that the Arabic word *'asharah* (ten) was probably deleted from the text of Naṣīr al-Dīn al-Ṭūsī, hence in agreement with the view of al-Turayḥī. Although it must be far from acceptable that 'Alī al-Akbar was a seventeen-year-old youth at the time of martyrdom, the occurrence of textual mistakes during copying earlier sources seems highly probable.

Did 'Alī al-Akbar Have any Children?

According to the late Iraqi scholar Sayyid 'Abd al-Razzāq al-Mūsawī al-Muqarram in his work *Maqtal al-Ḥusayn*, 'Alī al-Akbar was at the age of twenty-seven and had a wife and a child. In support of his view, he quotes a *ziyārah* dictated by Imām Ja'far al-Ṣādiq sending salutations on 'Alī al-Akbar. One verse reads: "May the salām of Allāh be bestowed upon you, your family, and your children".

Al-Muqarram surmises that the *kunya* (filial by-name) Abū al-Ḥasan for 'Alī al-Akbar must be due to his son's name, al-Ḥasan.

The present author believes that al-Mūsawī al-Muqarram's assumption was correct. It is not the case that the above Arabic phrase is used only once in the ziyārah-text he quoted. Rather, it is used elsewhere as well. For instance, it is used in the *ziyārah* quoted in Ibn Qūlawayh's *Kāmil al-Zīyārāt* (Najaf ed., 1356 AH/ 1935), Ch. 79, pp. 204 and 239.

In addition to the above discourse, the Grand Ayatollah Najafī Mar'ashī asserts that 'Alī al-Akbar was older than Imām 'Alī al-Sajjād. He mentioned this point in his preface to al-Mūsawi al-Muqarram's book entitled *'Alī al-Akbar.* [55] He cites Ibn Idriss' view as his evidence which is the most convincing argument and expert view within the circles of genealogists.

In summary, 'Alī al-Akbar was older than twenty years and must have been about twenty-seven at the time of martyrdom.

The second issue concerns whether or not 'Alī al-Akbar's mother was present in the Battle of Karbalā. This issue is still a point of debate between historians as there is little evidence for either stance.

The renowned Iranian *hadith*-scholar Ayatollah 'Abbās Qummī maintained that 'Alī al-Akbar's mother was not present in Karbalā as he could not find any evidence in support of her presence in authoritative sources. [56]

On the other hand, the late Iraqi scholar Sheikh Muḥammad al-Samāwī believed that 'Alī al-Akbar's mother was present in Karbalā. He believes that nine of the Ashurā martyr's mothers were present and watching the ongoing battle. Among those nine women was 'Alī al-Akbar's mother, Laylā, who was offering prayers for her son from inside the encampment. [57]

The present author (Najmī) believes that the late al-Samāwī presented no document to support his views. This might be because al-Samāwī relied on the reports available in Ibn Shahr Āshūb's *Manāqib.* [58] It is probable that al-Samāwī might have had access to other sources, too.

To complement the above discussion, below there is a list of other eight Ashurā martyrs whose mothers were present in Karbalā: 1. 'Abd Allāh b. al-Ḥusayn (or 'Alī al-Asghar) whose mother's name was Rabāb; 2. 'Awn b. 'Abd Allāh b. Ja'far whose mother was Lady Zaynab al-Kubra [59]; 3. Qāsim b. al-Ḥasan al-Mujtabā whose mother was Ramla; 4. 'Abd Allāh b. al-Ḥasan al-Mujtabā whose mother was the daughter of Shalīl al-Bijliya; 5. 'Abd Allāh b. Muslim b. 'Aqīl, whose mother Ruqaya, a daughter of Imām 'Alī; 6. Muḥammad b. Abī Sa'īd b. 'Aqīl, a little boy who, extremely scared, was holding firmly the pole of a tent, but an enemy soldier, called Luqayt or Hanī, attacked him and martyred him right in front of his mother; 7. 'Umar b. Junāda whose mother was present in Karbalā and encouraged him to fight the enemy; he was martyred while his mother was watching him; 8. According to Ibn Ṭāwūs, another martyr was 'Abd Allāh al-Kalbī whose mother and wife encouraged him to fight the enemy and he was martyred.

Addressing the Sons of Abū Ṭālib

صبرا على الموت يا بنى عمومتى! صبراً يا اهلبيتى! والله لا رايتم هوانا بعد هذا اليوم!

"Be patient with death, O my cousins' sons! Be patient, O my *Ahl al-Bayt.* By Allāh! You shall never face condemnation after this day." [60]

Context

After 'Alī al-Akbar was martyred, 'Abd Allāh, the teenage son of Muslim b. 'Aqīl and Ruqaya, daughter of Imām 'Alī, attacked the enemy three times and killed many of them each time. During his attacks he recited the following *rajaz* (war poem):

"Today I shall meet Muslim, my father, and the enthusiasts
Who gave their lives for the religion of the Prophet."

Finally, an enemy soldier by the name of Yazīd b. al-Raqqād shot an arrow towards him. To guard himself, 'Abd Allāh put his palm on his forehead. However, the arrow pierced his hand and went into his forehead; he soon fell down on the ground. At the same time, an enemy soldier attacked and killed him. Yazīd b. al-Raqqād rushed forward and pulled out the arrow from 'Abd Allāh's forehead; however, the metal head of the arrow remained in 'Abd Allāh's forehead.

Following this tragedy, a group of Hāshimid youths and some descendants of Abū Ṭālib, including Muḥammad and 'Awn, and other sons of 'Abd Allāh b. Ja'far and Muḥammad b. Muslim, raided the enemy forces. During their brave attack, Imām al-Ḥusayn made the above comment to encourage them.

By the Body of al-Qāsim b. al-Ḥasan

a) بعداً لقوم قتلوك! ومن خصمهم يوم القيامة فيك جدّك وابوك. عزّ و اللّٰه على عمّك ان تدعوه فلا يجيبك او يجيبك ثمّ لا ينفعك. صوت. واللّٰه! كثر واتره وقلّ ناصره ...

b) اللّهمّ! احصهم عددا ولا تغادر منهم احدا ولا تغفر لهم ابدا! صبرا يا اهل بيتى! لا رايتم هوانا بعد هذا اليوم ابدا.

(a) "May your killers be far away from the grace of Allāh! And, on the Resurrection Day your grandfather – Prophet Muḥammad – and your father – Imām al-Ḥasan – shall be their enemy. By Allāh! It is unbearable for your uncle [Imām al-Ḥusayn] that you call on him, but he cannot answer you, or you call on him, but if when he answers, it does not benefit you. By Allāh! This is a voice whose assaulters have been abundant and whose helpers have decreased."

(b) "O Allāh! Make them dispersed, never help any of them, and never forgive them forever. Be patient, O my *Ahl al-Bayt*! You shall never face condemnation after this day!" [61]

Context

After a group of youths from the *Ahl al-Bayt* were martyred, al-Qāsim, son of the Imām al-Ḥasan al-Mujtabā, decided to join the battleground. Having barely reached puberty, he was extremely handsome, wearing a long Arab robe and a pair of slippers. With a sword in his hand, he raided the enemy forces. Finally, an enemy soldier by the name of ʻAmr b. Saʻd attacked him and pulled him to the ground.

At that moment, al-Qāsim cried out for help and called on his uncle, Imām al-Ḥusayn. While carefully watching al-Qāsim, Imām al-Ḥusayn rushed toward him; at the sight of his injured and mutilated body, he made the statement quoted in (a) above.

According to al-Ṭabarī, Imām al-Ḥusayn carried al-Qāsim's body to the tent specially designed for preserving the martyrs' bodies. There he laid al-Qāsim's body beside his son ʻAlī al-Akbar.

Then Imām al-Ḥusayn cursed the Kūfan enemy army in the way indicated in (b) above.

At the Martyrdom of the Little Child

a) هل من ذابّ يذبّ عن حرم رسول الله؟ هل من موحّد يخاف الله فينا؟ هل من مغيث يرجو الله فى اغاثتنا؟ هل من معين يرجو ما عندالله فى اعانتنا؟ ربّ! ان تك حبست عنّا النّصر من السّماء فاجعل ذلك لما هو خير وانتقم لنا واجعل ما حلّ بنا فى العاجل ذخيرة لنا فى الآ جل ...

b) هون علىّ ما نزل بى و انّه بعين الله .

(a) "Is there any devotee to sacrifice his/her life in favour of the *ḥarām* of the Prophet of Allāh? Is there any monotheist who fears Allāh (out of concern) for us? Is there any helper who considers Allāh by helping us? Is there any helper who is hopeful for what is available before Allāh by helping us? [62] O Lord! If You wish to deny us Your victory from the heavens, put it in the way that is graceful, take vengeance for us, and put the reward of (enduring) what is immediately destined for us as a deposit for us in the Hereafter."

(b) "It is easy for me to endure because Allāh observes it." [63]

Context

According to al-Ṭabarī, one day a man named 'Uqba b. Bashīr al-Asadī met Imām Muḥammad al-Bāqir. During their conversation, Imām Muḥammad al-Bāqir reminded 'Uqba that someone of his tribe shed the blood of a person from the Prophet's lineage. Then Imām Muḥammad al-Bāqir explained as follows: "On Ashurā, a baby boy of my grandfather [Imām al-Ḥusayn] was given to him, and while the baby was in his arms, someone from your tribe tore his throat with an arrow." [64]

Imām al-Ḥusayn filled his palm with the baby's blood and threw it up towards the sky. After that Imām al-Ḥusayn prayed as quoted above – that if Allāh had denied him the Divine victory, he was hopeful to receive a reward better than victory in the Hereafter and hoped revenge would be taken against those tyrannical people.

Al-Khwārazmī narrates a more detailed account but does not give any documentation. He narrates: "After all combatants and companions of Imām al-Ḥusayn were martyred except for the women, children, and Imām 'Alī al-Sajjād, Imām al-Ḥusayn recited [the above call as mentioned in (a)]"

The women and children began to cry and weep loudly. Imām al-Ḥusayn then returned to the encampment and requested his baby son 'Alī to be brought to him to bid farewell. While the baby was in Imām al-Ḥusayn's arms, Ḥarmala b. Kāhil al-Asadī killed him by shooting an arrow. At that time, Imām al-Ḥusayn collected the martyred baby's blood and threw it above towards the heavens. Then he offered the prayer mentioned above.

On the authority of Ibn Ṭāwūs, Imām al-Ḥusayn threw his son's blood to the heavens and cried out the prayer mentioned above in (b).

It is timely to mention that other than ʻAlī al-Asghar, four other boys who had not reached puberty were martyred in Karbalā. They were as follows: (1) al-Qāsim b. al-Ḥasan al-Mujtabā whose account was given in the preceding section; (2) ʻAbd Allāh b. al-Ḥasan al-Mujtabā whose account will be given elsewhere; (3) Muḥammad b. Abī Saʻīd, whose account was rendered right after that of ʻAlī al-Akbar; and (4) ʻUmar b. Junāda whose account was given previously.

On the Martyrdom of al-ʻAbbās b. ʻAlī

انت صاحب لوائی!

تعدّیتم یا شرّ قوم ببغیکم   وخالفتموا فینا النّبیّ محمّدا

اما کان خیرالخلق اوصاکم بنا   اما کان جدّی خیرة الله حمدا

اما کانت الزّهرا امّی ووالدی   علیّ اخا خیرالانام مسدّدا

لعنتم واخزیتم بما قد جنیتم   ستصلون نارا حرّها قد توقّدا

"You are my standard-bearer"
"With your wickedness, O People, you have acted cruelly
And expressed hostility to us and to Prophet Muḥammad
Didn't the best person recommend us to you?
Wasn't my grandfather Ahmad [Muḥammad] the best person?
Wasn't al-Zahrā my mother?
And, my father, ʻAlī the Guided, the brother of the best person, Muḥammad?
You have been cursed and will be punished for the crime you have committed,
You shall be dragged to the Fire whose flames soar!" [65]

Context

Imām al-Ḥusayn's step-brother al-ʻAbbās b. ʻAlī, also known as Abū al-Faḍl, frequently went to Imām al-Ḥusayn seeking permission to join the battlefield. He was extremely brave, but Imām al-Ḥusayn did not let him go. To change his mind, Imām al-Ḥusayn told him each time that he was the standard-bearer of his army, as indicated in (a) and his martyrdom, would mean the fall of the standard, the defeat of the Divine army and the triumph of Satan's horde.

After all the companions of Imām al-Ḥusayn were martyred, al-'Abbās b. 'Alī attempted to obtain Imām al-Ḥusayn's consent to go to the battlefield. After some insistence, Imām al-Ḥusayn agreed with his request. He asked his step-brother al-'Abbās to go to the river Euphrates to bring water for the thirsty women and children of the camp. Al-'Abbās obeyed the order right away. However, when he reached the water, he refrained from drinking it out of sympathy to the thirsty camp of Imām al-Ḥusayn, although he himself was suffering from extreme thirst. When the enemy cut off his hand, he cried out epic poems indicative of his faith and lofty objectives.

The above narration is rendered in the following way in al-Samāwī's *Ibṣār al-'Ayn*: "Having received negative answers from Imām al-Ḥusayn to go to the battlefield, al-'Abbās b. 'Alī said: 'I have turned impatient and got fed up with life!' "

After hearing this, Imām al-Ḥusayn told him that if he intended to join the battlefield, he wanted him to obtain some water for the thirsty women and children. Accordingly, al-'Abbās set out towards the river Euphrates and, on his way, he caused agitation and disorder in the enemy lines. Having filled the leather flask with water, it crossed his mind to quench his thirst, so he filled his hands with water and raised it near his dry lips. Reminding himself of the raging thirst of Imām al-Ḥusayn's side, he did not drink a drop of water and instead threw it aside. At that time, he addressed himself in the following way:

"O soul! May you be despised after al-Ḥusayn,
May you not live after him.
This is al-Ḥusayn approaching death,
And you are going to drink cool water?
By Allāh! My faith never allows me this deed!" [66]

When he was on the way back toward the tents, he was faced with a huge number of the enemy forces. At the sight of them, he recited:

"I do not fear death when it screeches,
Until I am found hidden amongst the swords.
May my soul be sacrificed for the noble grandson of Muṣṭafā.
I am al-'Abbās and take water by the leather flask,
And on the day of the battle, I do not care about death."

While he was galloping to the tents with the water flask, an enemy soldier by the name of Zayd b. Raqqād who was lying in ambush behind a tree jumped out, attacked him, and severed his right arm; al-'Abbās declared his intent in the form of the following *rajaz:*

"By Allāh! If you cut off my right arm,
I shall always defend my religion and the truthful Imām,
Who is the Grandson of the trustworthy, noble Prophet."

Disregarding the fact that his right arm had just been cut off, al-'Abbās persisted and rushed towards the tents. Meanwhile, another enemy soldier by the name of Ḥukaym b. al-Ṭufayl al-Sinbisī leapt out of an ambush and cut off al-'Abbās's left arm. A torrent of arrows were fired toward him; an arrow pierced his leather water-flask and another sunk into his chest. At this moment, another enemy soldier approached him with a pole and shattered his skull. Having fallen on the ground, al-'Abbās cried out: "Farewell to you, O Abā 'Abd Allāh [Imām al-Ḥusayn]."

Hearing the final cry of al-'Abbās, Imām al-Ḥusayn instantly rushed towards him. By the injured and mutilated body of al-'Abbās, Imām al-Ḥusayn cried out the above poem mentioned above.

A significant number of statements have been quoted from Imām al-Ḥusayn at the time of martyrdom of al-'Abbās; likewise, several poems have been quoted from al-'Abbās in maqtal texts (martyrdom accounts), including al-Ṭurayhī's *al-Muntakhab*. However, none of these statements and poems have been quoted in the present volume as they have not been found present in authoritative sources.

Despite the short remarks from al-'Abbās quoted above, they sufficiently describe his lofty aim, staunch belief, and profound conviction. Due to these noble characteristics, al-'Abbās threw off water from his palms and regarded drinking water in that situation a conduct devoid of any religious and moral value. In the heat of several clashes, he expressed his willingness to sacrifice his soul in support of Islam and Imām al-Ḥusayn. When he glanced at his severed arm, he declared that he would continue to support his faith and religious conviction for eternity.

Likewise, when Imām al-Ḥusayn reached the severely injured body of al-'Abbās, such a uniquely loyal brother, he addressed the enemies saying they had done an utterly dispicable crime. For doing so, they would certainly be seperated from the Divine mercy and would be dragged to the scorching Hell.

Al-'Abbās as Viewed by the Infallibles

The Infallible Imāms praised the bravery of al-'Abbās b. 'Alī. In the previous section, some remarks made by Imām al-Ḥusayn have been mentioned. Now, the views of other Infallible Imāms will be mentioned confirming that al-'Abbās' bravery which originated from his profound religious and spiritual personality is truly unique. .

Religious and Spiritual Growth under Imām 'Alī

No doubt the education one receives from one's parents, family, and the home environment plays a significant role in shaping one's personality: al-'Abbās was not an exception. Growing up with a mother like Umm al-Banīn [67] and receiving religious and moral principles from his father, Imām 'Alī, and having such step-brothers like Imām al-Ḥasan and Imām al-Ḥusayn, coupled with such step-sisters like Lady Zaynab and Lady Umm Kulthūm, led to the crystallization of such a unique personality like al-'Abbās. As such, al-'Abbās was not only credited with fine virtues, he was also endowed with many admirable qualities. Careful scrutiny of the life and development of al-'Abbās, as reflected in the Infallible Imām's praises, indicate that his praiseworthy qualities, knowledge, piety, religiosity, courage and above all, his sacrifice could not be due only to the environmental influences on his personality. He did not acquire all of them through learning, rather a portion of these virtues were inherited genetically from his esteemed father.

These indications are supported by a beautiful *hadith* narrated in al-Nūrī al-Ṭabarsī's *Mustadrak al-Wasā'il* and al-Khwārazmī's *Maqtal al-Ḥusayn*: As a child, al-'Abbās was sitting before his father, Imām 'Alī. Imām 'Alī asked him to say "one", and he did so. Then Imām 'Alī, in a language suitable to a child, asked him to say "two". Al-'Abbās begged his pardon and said that he felt ashamed to pronounce "two" with a tongue with which he has just said "one". On such a wise answer from a child, Imām 'Alī embraced and kissed him. [68]

The above worldview is expected only from the Infallible household. Such a worldview recognises unity exclusively for the Creator of the heavens and earth. The fruits of the blessed tree of the descendants of Prophet Muḥammad speak only what is worthy of the Almighty. Such an advanced way of thinking is not common among ordinary children and even many adolescents fall short of reaching this stage. This proves that this type of knowledge is instinctive and God-given. He must have inherited it from such a father like Imām 'Alī whose remark was that if the veils of cognition be removed his certitude would not be affected, meaning that he has reached the zenith of mystical certitude. [69]

Having mentioned the above introductory account, in the following section, the views of three Infallible Imāms on al-'Abbās b. 'Alī are presented: Firstly, Imām Ja'far al-Ṣādiq made the following remark about al-'Abbās b. 'Alī: "Our uncle al-'Abbās b. 'Alī was sharp-sighted and a staunch believer, he undertook *jihad* in company with his brother [Imām] al-Ḥusayn, successfully passed an examination [participation in *jihad*], and passed away through martyrdom." [70]

Elsewhere, Imām Ja'far al-Ṣādiq eulogized al-'Abbās b. 'Alī in a ziyārah he taught Abū Ḥamza al-Thumālī [71] in the following way: "I testify that you strived hard with loyalty and put forth all your efforts (in the way of Allah)" and elsewhere " I testify that you were not weakened and you did not lose heart (while facing the enemies). Indeed, you died with insight about your affairs while following the Righteous Ones and the [Divine] Prophets." [72-73]

These verses highlight his complete devotion, high spirit, and ultimate sacrifice to strengthen the sublime aim of the prophets.

Secondly, Imām 'Alī al-Sajjād's description reads as follows: According to Abū Ḥamza al-Thumālī, one day Imām 'Alī al-Sajjād's eyes became filled with tears on seeing 'Ubayd Allāh b. al-'Abbās b. 'Alī. Imām 'Alī al-Sajjād went on to say that the Battles of Uḥud and Mu'tah were the most challenging and critical days for Prophet Muḥammad, for in the Battle of Uḥud Ḥamzah, an uncle of Prophet Muḥammad, was martyred. During the Battle of Mu'tah Ja'far b. Abū Ṭālib, Prophet Muḥammad's cousin, was martyred. However, the Day of Ashurā was even more agonising because on Ashurā, 30,000 soldiers surrounded Imām al-Ḥusayn, while all of them regarded themselves as Muslims and intended to get nearer to Allāh through killing the grandson of Prophet Muḥammad. Even though Imām al-Ḥusayn advised them, they never gained an understanding and martyred him.

Then Imām 'Alī al-Sajjād talked about al-'Abbās b. 'Alī and said: "May Allāh bless my uncle al-'Abbās who passed his difficult test successfully and sacrificed his life for his brother until both of his arms were severed. In return, Allāh has granted him two wings so, like Ja'far al-Ṭayyār, he flies in Paradise together with the angels." Then Imām 'Alī al-Sajjād added: "Al-'Abbās enjoys such a high status before Allāh that on the Day of Resurrection, all martyrs shall envy him."[74]

Finally, the true character of al-'Abbās b. 'Alī becomes clear in view of Imām al-Ḥusayn's address toward him. When Imām al-Ḥusayn noticed that the enemy soldiers were about to attack the encampment in the afternoon of 9th Muharram, commonly called Tāsū'ā, he addressed al-'Abbās saying: "Ride [on the horse]! O Brother! May my life be sacrificed for you! Go and meet them and enquire if anything [news] might have reached them". [75, 76]

Imām al-Ḥusayn's devotion to his brother is astounding. It is difficult to imagine his position, considering the infallible Imām who is described as: "Through you Allāh opens up all possibilities and at your will He closes". [77] He addressed al-'Abbās with the respectful saying: "May my life be sacrificed for you!"

Four other sons of Imām 'Alī were also martyred on the day of Ashurā. These four, whose names are given below, together with Imām al-Ḥusayn and 'Abbās b. 'Alī, make six sons of Imām 'Alī who were martyred in the Battle of Karbalā. The other four sons of Imām 'Alī were as follows: 'Abd Allāh b. 'Alī, who was nine years younger than al-'Abbās b. 'Alī, was martyred at the age of twenty-five; 'Uthmān b. 'Alī was martyred at the age of twenty-three; and Ja'far b. 'Alī was martyred at the age of twenty-one. 'Abbās b. 'Alī and these three martyers were the sons Imām 'Alī and Fāṭima "Umm al-Banīn".

The fifth son of Imām 'Alī who was martyred on the Day of Ashurā was Muḥammad b. 'Alī whose mother was Laylā bt. Mas'ūd b. Khālid; his age at the time has not been ascertained. Their names are recorded in historical texts and in *Ziyārah al-Nāḥīya al-Muqaddasa* next to which their killers' names are also given. [78, 79]

At the Martyrdom of 'Abd Allāh b. al-Ḥasan al-Mujtabā

a) يا ابن اخى! اصبر على ما نزل بك! فانّ الله يلحقك على ابائك الطّاهرين الصّالحين برسول الله وعليّ وحمزة وجعفر والحسن ...

b) اللّهمّ! امسك عنهم قطر السّماء و امنعهم بركات الارض! فان متّعتهم الى حين ففرّقهم فرقا واجعلهم طرائق قددا ولا ترض عنهم الولاة ابدا فانّهم دعونا لينصرونا فعدوا علينا فقتلونا.

(a) "O (my) nephew! Be patient over what has happened to you, for Allāh will make you meet your noble and pious ancestors, the Prophet of Allāh, 'Alī, Ḥamza, Ja'far, and al-Ḥasan."

(b) "O Allāh! Deny them any rain and the graces of the earth, and if You provide them with respite, make them disunited and dispersed apart, and never make their rulers pleased with them for eternity, for they had invited us to help us but expressed animosity against us and then fought us." [80]

Context

According to Ibn al-Athīr's *al-Kāmil fī al-Ta'rīkh* and al-Mufīd's *Kitāb al-Irshād*, after engaging in a lengthy and tiring battle, Imām al-Ḥusayn was thrown off his horse and surrounded by the enemy. A little boy from his relatives rushed out of the tents, and Lady Zaynab bt. 'Alī ran after him to make him return. The little boy cried out:

"No! By Allāh! I will never leave my uncle [Imām al-Ḥusayn] alone and unassisted!"

In the meantime, an enemy soldier by the name of Baḥr b. Ka'b b. Tayyim rushed with a sword towards Imām al-Ḥusayn. At the sight of this sudden raid, that boy shouted at him: "O son of a notorious woman! Are you going to kill my uncle?" He then raised his arm to protect Imām al-Ḥusayn against the enemy's sword.

Baḥr b. Ka'b attacked both of them with his sword. The boy's hand was severely cut, hanging by the skin from the arm.

The injured boy turned to Imām al-Ḥusayn and cried out: "O uncle! Help me and relieve me from this pain!"

Imām al-Ḥusayn embraced him and addressed him in the way indicated in (a) above. Then Imām al-Ḥusayn cursed the enemy as in (b) above.

There were three sons of the Imām al-Ḥasan al-Mujtabā among the Ashurā martyrs. There were: 'Abd Allāh, whose mother was the daughter of Shalīl b. 'Abd Allāh al-Bijlī, al- Qāsim, and Abū Bakr whose mother was Ramla.

Notes to Chapter 62
Imām al-Ḥusayn's Statements at the Time of His Companions' Martyrdom

1. 'Abd Allāh b. Nūr al-Dīn al-Baḥrānī, *Maqtal al-'Awālim*, p. 91; and Muḥammad Ṭāhir al-Samāwī, *Ibṣār al-'Ayn fī Anṣār al-Ḥusayn*, p. 85.
2. *Dhakhīra al-Dārayn*, qtd. in al-Mūsawī al-Muqarram, *Maqtal al-Ḥusayn*, p. 301.
3. The Qur'ān, Sūrah al-Aḥzāb [33:23].
4. According to Ibn Sa'd in his *al-Ṭabaqāt*, Muslim b. 'Awsaja was a companion of Prophet Muḥammad. A brave resident of al-Kūfa, he was one of those who wrote a letter of invitation to Imām al-Ḥusayn. After the arrival of 'Ubayd Allāh b. Zīyād to

al-Kūfa and Muslim b. 'Aqīl's martyrdom, Muslim b. 'Awsaja left al-Kūfa with his family and remained loyal to Imām al-Ḥusayn to the last drop of his blood.

5. Al-Khwārazmī, *Maqtal al-Ḥusayn*, vol. 2, p. 22; al-Majlisī, ed., *Biḥār al-Anwār*, vol. 45; p. 27; al-Samāwī, *Ibṣār al-'Ayn*, p. 107.

6. Ibn Ṭāwūs never mentions 'Abd Allāh b. 'Umayr in his *al-Luhūf*; however, part of his account is ascribed to that of Wahab b. Jināḥ al-Kalbī, all mixed with some accounts of Wahab the Christian.

7. The *Ziyārah al-Nāḥīya al-Muqaddasa* can be found in Ibn Ṭāwūs's *Iqbāl al-A'māl*, ed. Ḥusayn al-A'lamī (Beirut, 1417 AH/ 1996), pp. 48-52. This is also known as the *ziyārah* addressing the Ashurā martyrs of the Battle of Karbalā.

8. Al-Ṭabarī, *Ta'rīkh*, the Events of the Year 61 AH; and Ibn al-Athīr, *al-Kāmil fī al-Ta'rīkh*, vol. 3, p. 29.

9. Ibn Ṭāwūs, *al-Luhūf*, p. 96.

10. The Battle of Ṣiffīn took place during the Imāmate of Imām 'Alī around the middle of the month Ṣafar 37AH/ 656.

11. The Eve of Whining (Arabic, *Layla al-Ḥarīr*) was a night when it was extremely cold during the Battle of Ṣiffīn such that the dogs of the region were whining owing to the unbearable cold. On such an extremely cold night Imām 'Alī performed his midnight *salat*. It was known as such because some 10,000 soldiers were killed from both armies.

12. See al-Ḥurr al-'Āmilī, *Wasā'il al-Shī'a*, vol. 1, Ch. 1: The Times of *Salat*.

13. For a life of Abū Thumāma, see al-Māmiqānī, *Tanqīḥ al-Maqāl*, and Muḥammad al-Samāwī, *Ibṣār al-'Ayn fī Anṣār al-Ḥusayn*.

14. 'Abd Allāh b. Nūr al-Dīn al-Baḥrānī, *Maqtal al-'Awālim*, p. 88; Ibn Ṭāwūs, *al-Luhūf*, p. 95; Ibn Namā al-Ḥillī, *Muthīr al-Aḥzān*; Ibn al-Athīr, *al-Kāmil fī al-Ta'rīkh*, vol. 3, p. 290.

15. This concept is mentioned in several verses in the Holy Qur'ān,

among them, in the Sūrah Yūnus [10:31].

16. For more information about Qurẓa b. Ka'b, see *al-Iṣāba fī Ma'rifa al-Ṣaḥāba* of Ibn Ḥajr al-'Asqalānī. Regarding his sons, see al-Māmiqānī, *Tanqīḥ al-Maqāl,* vol. 2, p. 332, as well as the letter Q, p. 28; and al-Samāwī, *Ibṣār al-'Ayn fī Anṣār al-Ḥusayn*, p. 92.

17. Al-Muqarram, *Maqtal al-Ḥusayn*, p. 297.

18. The correct form seems to be Muẓāhir, although Maẓāhir is more commonly used.

19. Al-Ṭabarī, *Ta'rīkh,* vol. 7, p. 349.

20. An additional comment is needed concerning Ḥabīb b. Maẓāhir: He was a companion of the Prophet, and a close comrade of Imām 'Alī from whom he learned a lot. On the authority of Fuḍayl b. al-Zubayr, the late al-Kashshī reported that once Maytham al-Tammār encountered a group of people of the Banū Asad tribe with Ḥabīb b. Maẓāhir. They had a conversation and Ḥabīb mentioned that he was forseeing an old fat and bald man, who was selling melons at Dār al-Rizq, would be hung due to his devotion to the progeny of Prophet Muḥammad. By this remark, he meant that, Maytham al-Tammār, would have such a fate. Maytham al-Tammār replied that he in turn was forseeing an old man, with dense hair and red face, who would endeavor to help a grandson of Prophet Muḥammad, would be killed and his severed head will be taken around al-Kūfa. By this prediction, he indicated Ḥabīb b. Maẓāhir's tragic fate. Shortly after this dialogue, they left that place. Some of those who were noticing the exchanges of these two disciples of Imām 'Alī remarked that they had not seen anyone to be more of liar than them. A few moments later, Rushayd al-Ḥujarī reached the same place and asked about Ḥabīb and Maytham. The people around there told him that they had been there and reported to him their exchanges. Rushayd then commented: "May Allāh bless Maytham. He must have forgotten to add the following remark about Ḥabīb that the bearer of his severed head would be given 100 dirhams more." The bystanders were perplexed and quite astonished,

they described Rushayd to be the biggest liar of them all. Later on, Fuḍayl reported that shortly after that conversation he witnessed Maytham al-Tammār being hung from the gate of 'Amr b. Ḥurayth and, much later, he realised that Ḥabīb's severed head was taken into al-Kūfa.

21. Al-Ṭabarī, *Ta'rīkh*, the Events of the Year 61 AH; al-Ṣadūq, *al-Amālī*, Session 30.

22. Banu Rīyah was the name of a prominent Arab tribe.

23. At the peak of the war.

24. Supposing the word nādā (called) is replaced with fādā (sacrificed for), the translation would read as: "... when he sacrificed himself for al-Ḥusayn."

25. Al-Ḥurr belonged to a noble Arab family in al-Kūfa and he was also the chief of his tribe. 'Ubayd Allāh b. Zīyād appointed him the commander of 1,000 soldiers to intercept Imām al-Ḥusayn's route. According to Ibn Namā, the author of *Muthīr al-Aḥzān*, after al-Ḥurr was assured that his repentance had been accepted, he reported to Imām al-Ḥusayn that when leaving the Dār al-'Imārah (Government House) after being appointed by 'Ubayd Allāh b. Zīyād to confront Imām al-Ḥusayn, he heard a caller giving him the good tidings of reaching Paradise. When he turned around, he saw nobody there. Until he joined Imām al-Ḥusayn, he was confused about what the call meant. While he knew very well that he was going to stand on the side opposite to that of Imām al-Ḥusayn, he could not imagine that he would finally join Imām al-Ḥusayn.

26. Al-Ṭabarī, *Ta'rīkh*, the Events of Year 61 AH; Ibn al-Athīr, *al-Kāmil fī al-Ta'rīkh*, vol. 3, pp. 288.

27. Ibn Kathīr al-Dimashqī, *al-Bidāyah wa al-Nihāyaya*, vol. 8, pp. 183- 184.

28. The tent for the martyrs' bodies was placed at the end of the encampment toward the battlefield where the bodies were deposited.

29. Some historians ascribe the poems quoted to Imām al-Ḥusayn,

while some attribute it to Imām 'Alī b. al-Ḥusayn al-Sajjād, or yet to another companion of Imām al-Ḥusayn. For further details, see al-Majlisī, ed., *Biḥār al-Anwār*, vol. 45, p. 14; al-Ṣadūq, *al-Amālī*, Session 30; 'Abd Allāh b. Nūr al-Dīn al-Baḥrānī, *Maqtal al-'Awālim*, p. 85; and al-Khwārazmī, *Maqtal al-Ḥusayn*, vol. 2, p. 11.

30. This was the slogan of the Kharijites.

31. For biographies of the two brothers Sa'd and Abū al-Ḥutuf, see al-Māmiqānī, *Tanqīḥ al-Maqāl*, vol. 2, p. 12; Muhsin al-Amīn, *A'yān al-Shī'a*, new ed., vol. 2, p. 319; and al-Qummī, *al-Kunā wa al-Alqāb*, vol. 1, p. 43.

32. Al-Khwārazmī, *Maqtal al-Ḥusayn*, vol. 2, p. 20; al-Samāwī, *Ibṣār al-'Ayn fī Anṣār al-Ḥusayn*, p. 99.

33. Zuhayr b. al-Qayn was a prominent figure of his tribe in al-Kūfa. He used to be a follower of 'Uthmān, the third caliph. In the year 60 AH/ 680, he performed Ḥajj with his wife. On the way back home, he happened to meet Imām al-Ḥusayn and turned into a true Shi'i. He composed the poems mentioned in the text. For a biography, see *Zuhayr b. al-Qayn* (Karbalā, 1430 AH/ 2009).

34. The Holy Qur'an, Sūrah Ṭāhā [20: 120].

35. Al-Samāwī, *Ibṣār al-'Ayn fī Anṣār al-Ḥusayn*, ed. Muḥammad Ja'far al-Ṭabasī, p. 118.

36. Some texts record his name as al-Shamī which is not correct. The correct from is al-Shibāmī.

37. The Holy Qur'ān, Sūrah al-Ghāfir [40:32-33].

38. Al-Ṭabarī, *Ta'rīkh*, the Events of the Year 61 AH/ 680, p. 352; and Ibn al-Athīr, al-Kāmil fī al-Ta'rīkh, vol. 3, p. 292.

39. For the life story and martyrdom of Seyf and Mālik, see al-Ṭabarī, *Ta'rīkh*, vol. 6, pp. 353-54; al-Māmiqānī, *Tanqīh al-Maqāl*, vol. 2, p. 78; Ibn al-Athīr, *al-Kāmil fī al-Ta'rīkh*, vol. 3, p. 292; and al-Samāwī, *Ibṣār al-'Ayn fī Anṣār al-Ḥusayn*, p. 78.

40. Al-Khwārazmī in *Maqtal al-Ḥusayn*, vol. 2, p. 23, attributes the

above account to two other martyrs, namely, 'Abd Allāh and 'Abd al-Raḥmān, both of Banū Ghifār tribe; however, due to the authority of al-Ṭabarī and al-Māmiqānī, these two works prove more authoritative, hence regarded as references for the account given here.

41. The Holy Qur'ān, Sūrah al-Muṭaffifīn [83:26, 42];

42. Ibn Ṭāwūs, *al-Luhūf*, p. 95; al-Samāwī, *Ibṣār al-'Ayn fī Anṣār al-Ḥusayn*, p. 105; and Ibn Namā al-Ḥillı, *Muthīr al-Aḥzān*, p. 63.

43. Abū Dhar al-Ghifārī (d. 652) was a close companion of Prophet Muḥammad.

44. The designations "the herald" (al-Bashīr) and "the warner" (al-Nadhīr) refer to Prophet Muḥammad.

45. Al-Khwārazmī, *Maqtal al-Ḥusayn*, vol. 2, p. 22; al-Majlisī, *Biḥār al-Anwār*, vol. 45, p. 27; and Ibn Shahr Āshūb, *al-Manāqib*, vol. 3, p. 219.

46. The Holy Qur'ān, Sūrah al-Jinn [72:11].

47. The Holy Qur'ān, Sūrah Āl-i 'Imran [3:33-34].

48. Literally, Imām al-Ḥusayn's remark is translated as follows: "May dust be showered on the world."

49. Imām al-Ḥusayn's curse was so broad that 'Umar b. Sa'd's line of descendants stopped at his grandson Abū Bakr who did not live much longer than his father Ḥafṣ. According to two genealogy books, that is, al-Zubayrī's *Nasab* and Ibn Ḥazm's *Jamḥara*, 'Umar b. Sa'd's grandson had no offspring. Had he had any offspring, they would have been recorded in genealogy books. The second part of Imām al-Ḥusayn's curse indicates that the line of Imāmate would continue through 'Alī al-Akbar, as Imām al-Ḥusayn's statement is an evidence that he expected his lineage to spread in the world though him.

50. That is, the Ka'bah at Mecca.

51. That is, Zīyād b. Abīh, the then governor of al-Kūfa.

52. Al-Khwārazmī, *Maqtal al-Ḥusayn*, vol. 2, p. 30; Ibn Namā al-

Ḥillī, *Muthīr al-Aḥzān*; Ibn Ṭāwūs, *al-Luhūf*, p. 100; al-Ṭabarī, *Ta'rīkh*, the Events of the Year 61 AH; Ibn al-Athīr, *al-Kāmil fī al-Ta'rīkh*, vol. 3, p. 293; al-Mufīd, *Kitāb al-Irshād*, p. 238.

53. *Anīs al-Shī'a* was a book authored by Sayyid Muḥammad Ja'farī Ṭayyārī Hindī in 1241 AH/ 1825. According to Aqā Buzurg al-Tehrānī in *al-Dharī'a*, vol. 2, p. 458, he saw a copy of it, in Persian, with Sayyid Āqā Tustarī at Najaf.

54. *Naqd al-Muḥaṣṣal*, p. 179.

55. The volume in question is the late Sayyid 'Abd al-Razāq al-Mūsawī al-Muqarram's *'Alī al-Akbar*, 2nd ed. (Najaf, 1368 AH/ 1957).

56. 'Abbās al-Qummī, *Muntahā al-Āmāl*.

57. Al-Samāwī, *Ibṣār al-'Ayn fī Anṣār al-Ḥusayn*, p. 130.

58. Ibn Shahr Āshub, *Manāqib*, vol. 4, p. 99.

59. There was another son of 'Abd Allāh b. Ja'far who was martyred in the Battle of Ashurā: his name was Muḥammad and his mother's name was Khawṣā'.

60. Ibn Ṭāwūs, *al-Luhūf*, p. 101; al-Mūsawī al-Muqarram, *Maqtal al-Ḥusayn*, p. 318.

61. Al-Ṭabarī, *Ta'rīkh*, vol. 7, p. 359; Ibn al-Athīr, *al-Kāmil fī al-Ta'rīkh*, vol. 3, p. 293; Ibn Sa'd, *al-Ṭabaqāt al-Kubrā*, vol.1, p. 471; al-Mufīd, *Kitāb al-Irshād*, p. 239; al-Tabrasī, *I'lām al-Warā*; al-Khwārazmī, *Maqtal al-Ḥusayn*, vol. 2, p. 27.

62. Al-Khwārazmī, *Maqtal al-Ḥusayn*, vol. 2, p. 32.

63. Al-Ṭabarī, *Ta'rīkh*, the Events of the Year 61 AH; Ibn Sa'd, *al-Ṭabaqāt al-Kubrā*, and al-Mufīd, *Kitāb al-Irshād*.

64. Al-Baḥrānī, *Maqtal al-'Awālim*, p. 94.

65. Ibn Shahr Āshūb, *Manāqib*, vol. 4, p. 108; al-Qunduzī, Yanābī' al-Mawaddah, p. 340.

66. Al-Samāwī, *Ibṣār al-'Ayn fī Anṣār al-Ḥusayn*, p. 30.

67. Umm al-Banīn is the byname of Fāṭima bt. Ḥizām b. Khālid

al-Kilābī. Her grave is in Medina.

68. Al-Nūrī al-Tabarasī, *Mustadrak al-Wasā'il al-Shī'a*, vol. 2, p. 635; vol. 3, p. 815; and al-Khwārazmī, *Maqtal al-Ḥusayn*, vol. 1, p. 122.

69. Al-Ḥillī, *al-Alfayn* (Qom, 1409 AH/ 1997), Ch. 53, p. 147.

70. Al-Māmiqānī, *Tanqīḥ al-Maqāl.*

71. Abū Ḥamza al-Thumālī was a great figure in Islamic history; he was honoured to be a companion of the Infallible Imāms 'Alī al-Sajjād, Muḥammad al-Bāqir, and Ja'far al-Ṣādiq. According to Imām Ja'far al-Ṣādiq he was a personality comparable to Salmān the Persian with regard to his piety.

72. Abū al-Qāsim Ja'far b. Muḥammad b. Qūlawayh al-Qummī, *Kāmil al-Zīyārāt*, ed. 'Abd al-Ḥusayn al-Amīnī al-Tabrīzī (Najaf, 1356 AH/ 1935), Ch. 85, p. 257.

73. The English translation is taken from Abū al-Qāsim, Ja'far b. Muḥammad b. Ja'far b. Mūsā b. Qūlawayh al-Qummī, *Kāmil al-Zīyārāt*, English tr. Sayyid Mohsen al-Ḥusaynī al-Mīlanī (Miami, FL, 2008), p. 526.

74. Al-Ṣadūq, *al-Khisāl*, ed. 'Alī Akbār al-Ghaffārī (Qom, 1403 AH/ 1362 Sh/ 1983), vol. 1, p. 68, *hadith* No. 101.

75. See Ch. 46.

76. One might assume that in the passage of the ziyārah issued by the Imām Ja'far al-Ṣādiq the sentence "May my parents [everything] be sacrificed for you!" was used in addressing all the Ashurā martyrs. However, in this ziyārah Imām Ja'far al-Ṣādiq did not address the Ashurā martyrs in this way; rather, it is the way he taught Ṣafwān al-Jammāl on how to perform a ziyārah to the Ashurā martyrs. For further details, see al-Ṭūsī, *Miṣbāḥ al-Mutahajjid*, p. 660.

77. This is a fragment of "*Zīyāra al-Jāmi'a al-Kabīra*", as quoted in al-Qummī, ed., *Mafātīḥ al-Jinān*, var. eds.

78. The full text of "*Zīyāra al-Nāḥīya al-Muqaddasa*" in which the names of the Ashurā martyrs and their killers are mentioned can be found in a range of authoritative texts and collections,

for example in al-Majlisī, ed., *Tuḥfa al-Zā'ir* (Qom, 1386 Sh/ 2007), pp. 391-398; *Mawsū'a Zīyārāt al-Ma'sūmīn*, vol. 3, pp. 514-529; and al-Tabasī, *al-Maqtal al-Ḥusaynī* al-Ma'thūr (2nd ed.; Tehran, 2007), pp. 143-151, where the text is ascribed to Imām 'Alī al-Hādī.

79. Historical evidence suggests that the title "*al-Nāḥīya al-Muqaddasa*" (lit., the sacred area) was a metaphorical and prudent title used to refer to the texts and instructions issued by the Infallible Imāms 'Alī al-Jawād, al-Ḥasan al-'Askarī, and al-Mahdī, mainly for security reasons. For some literature in this regard, see M.-R. Jabbārī, *Sazmān-i Wikālat wa Naqsh-i ān dar 'Aṣr-i A'imma 'Alayhim al-Salām* (Qom, 1382 Sh/ 2003).

80. Ibn al-Athīr, *al-Kāmil fī al-Ta'rīkh*, vol. 3, p. 294; al-Mufīd, *Kitāb al-Irshād*, p. 241.

63

The Final Departure

ثمّ انّه ودّع عياله وامرهم بالصّبر ولبس الازر وقال : استعدّوا للبلاء! واعلموا انّ الله حاميكم وحافظكم وسينجيكم من شرّ الاعدا ويجعل عاقبة امركم الى خير ويعذّب عدوّكم بانواع العذاب ويعوّضكم عن هذه البليّة بانواع النّعم والكرامة فلا تشكوا ولا تقولوا بالسنتكم ما ينقص من قدركم.

Then he [Imām al-Ḥusayn] bid farewell to his wife, (family) and advised them to be patient and put on outer clothes [1], and (thus) remarked: "Get ready for the calamity [2] and know that Allāh is indeed your support and preserver, He will rescue you from the evil of the enemy and make the end of your affair toward the good. He will punish your enemy in different ways, and will grant you in compensation for this calamity [3] various (types of) blessings and honour; therefore, never complain or express what might harm your status." [4]

Context

The final departure of Imām al-Ḥusayn was one of the most crucial moments on the Day of Ashurā for himself, the women in his camp, and Imām 'Alī al-Sajjād. This was because the granddaughters of Prophet Muḥammad realised that their sole support, hope, and leader was leaving them and would not return. They became destitute in the scorching desert plains. They were fearful of their vulnerable position and how they could express their deep, inconsolable grief. They could not help but gather around him and appeal for his advice and consolation. Imām al-Ḥusayn, who was a symbol of kindness and bravery, was surrounded by a group of children who were incessantly sobbing, and an orphan girl who was suffering from raging thirst. He was surrounded by many women, choked with grief by the overwhelming calamities they had faced and the fear of what might befall them after his departure.

One can only imagine Imām al-Ḥusayn's reaction to this heartbreaking scene. He could not loose control of his emotions and neglect his sublime objective, even for a short while. What follows is an account of Imām al-Ḥusayn's reaction narrated by other Infallible Imāms and leading 'Ulamā'.

At the sight of the culmination of the above calamities, Imām al-Ḥusayn addressed the women and his own family at his second farewell. The text reads as indicated in the beginning of this chapter.

The late Allama Muḥammad-Bāqir al-Majlisī quoted the above text from a *hadith* narrated by Imām Muḥammad al-Bāqir; the above text seems to be in continuation of the same *hadith*. The text of Imām al-Ḥusayn's farewell might be a separate *hadith*, but it was also in another *hadith* which the late al-Majlisī regarded as authoritative. [5] Due to the significant authority of al-Majlisī's text, the late Iraqī scholar Sayyid 'Abd al-Razzāq al-Mūsawī al-Muqarram [6] quoted it from al-Majlisī's *Jalā' al-'Uyūn* as as one continious text, with the following comment:. "Imām al-Ḥusayn's conversation contains two previously unnoticed messages: that he intended to inform the surviving women that they would not be killed by the enemies and would return home safely, and that their clothes and outer covers would not be looted [7].

Al-Mūsawī al-Muqarram also added a further linguistic exposition of Imām al-Ḥusayn's speech. That Imām al-Ḥusayn ordered the survivors "to be patient and put on outer clothes" and this confirms the two messages inferred above. Furthermore, his remark "that Allāh is indeed your support and preserver" was an indication that the survivors would remain in the Divine protection against the enemy looting and that they would not be killed.

Farewell to Imām 'Alī al-Sajjād

a) وعن زين العابدين عليه السلام قال : ضمنى والدى عليه السلام الى صدره يوم قتل و الدماء تغلى وهو يقول: يا بنى! احفظ عنى دعاء علّمتنيه فاطمة عليها السلام و علّمها رسول الله صلّى الله عليه و اله وعلّمه جبرئيل عليه السلام فى الحاجة والمهمّ والغمّ والنازلة اذا نزلت والامر العظيم الفادح. قال ادع : بحق يس والقران الحكيم وبحق طه والقران العظيم يا من يقدر على حوائج السائلين يا من يعلم ما فى الضّمير يا منفّس عن المكروبين يا مفرّج عن المغمومين يا راحم الشّيخ الكبير يا رازق الطّفل الصغير يا من لايحتاج الى التّفسير صلّ على محمد وال محمد وافعل بى كذا وكذا.

b) عن ابى جعفر عليه السلام قال لما حضرت على بن الحسين الوفاة ضمنى الى صدره ثم قال . يا بنىّ اوصيك بما اوصانى به ابى حين حضرته الوفاة وبما ذكر ان اباه اوصاه به. يا بنىّ! ايّاك وظلم من لا يجد عليك ناصرا الا الله!

a) Imām 'Alī al-Sajjād narrates: "My father [Imām al-Ḥusayn] held me to his chest on the day he was killed, while it was a critical situation, and then he said: 'O My dear son! Learn from me a prayer that my mother Fāṭima instructed me (of which) she had been instructed by the Prophet of Allāh who was taught in turn by the Archangel Gabriel, that when one is in need [for help], or has encountered an important case, intense grief, a calamity, or an unbearable disaster, he must invoke thus: "By the honour of "Yāsīn". By the wise Qur'an [8] and "Ṭāhā" [9] and by the Sublime Qur'ān! O One Who determines and fulfills what the enquirers wish! O One Who knows the contents of the soul! O Reliever of the distressed! O Soother of the grieved! O One Who is merciful to an old person! O Sustainer of a little baby! O One Who never needs any interpretation! Bless Muḥammad and the progeny of Muḥammad and provide me with so and so."' [10]

b) Imām Muḥammad al-Bāqir narrates: "When Imām 'Alī b. al-Ḥusayn [Imām Muḥammad al-Bāqir's father] approached death, he held me to his chest and then said: 'O My dear son! I advise you a statement which my father gave me when approaching death, that he received in turn from his father. "O my dear son! Never commit any crime against a person who has no supporter save Allāh." ' " [11]

Context

Imām al-Ḥusayn first bid farewell to the women of the *ḥarām* [his encampment] and then went to the tent of his son and successor Imām 'Alī al-Sajjād. It is not clear what happened between the two Imāms at that critical moment. According to al-Mas'ūdī's account, Imām al-Ḥusayn advised him of all the recommendations concerning Imāmate and asked him to obtain the special Imāmate heritage such as the documents and weapons, from Lady Umm Salamah [12] upon returning back to Medina. [13]

However, the text of the *hadith* quoted above is narrated from Imām 'Alī al-Sajjād, who was one of the two Infallible Imāms who was present at the farewell.

The *hadith* quoted above contains several lessons. Firstly, that one must pay attention to Allāh and rely on Him alone. Imām 'Alī al-Sajjād related the *hadith* mentioned in part (1) above; it was Imām al-Ḥusayn's instruction to him to pay close attention to Allāh in critical and stressful situations. Secondly, one must keep away from committing extreme cruelty. Abū Ḥamza al-Thumālī related from Imām Muḥammad al-Bāqir that his father, Imām 'Alī al-Sajjād, upon his death, embraced him and informed him of the seconf *hadith*, quoted above.

The above statements quoted are two of the wills and recommendations of Imām al-Ḥusayn when he bid farewell to Imām 'Alī b. al-Ḥusayn. These recommendations could have been issued at two separate meetings, and the remarks "on the day he was martyred" and "when martyrdom approached him" might confirm the above inference.

Conclusion

The above three wills and recommendations are indicative of Imām al-Ḥusayn's firm resolve. He never doubted his decision to challenge blasphemy, from the moment that he decided to challenge the illegitimate ruler until the last moment of his life. Rather, he progressed systematically, in the best way according to temporal, situational, and geographical circumstances. To him, the moment of farewell was no different from his life at his hometown, Medina, where he enjoyed peace, tranquility, and full respect. He was as peaceful and content at the moment of farewell as he was in Mecca by the secure House of Allāh or when he was moving across the Hejaz desert toward Karbalā. Rather, the Day of Ashurā was the climax of his journey from Medina to Karbalā.

Imām al-Ḥusayn had a divine aim throughout his movement. When he was by the tomb of Prophet Muḥammad he said that he favoured the right, divinely-commanded acts and hated what is prohibited; in the beginning of his movement he declared that Yazīd was always in the habit of drinking wine, hence he would not pledge allegiance to him; when he anticipated the end of Islamic leadership as soon as Yazīd was declared the head of the Islamic state; when he declared that he would not succumb to such a mean person like Yazīd; when he depicted the future of his movement by the Ka'bah; when he declared that it was his duty to oppose Yazīd on the basis of a Prophetic *hadith*, and at every moment. Now, he directed the women of the camp to put on suitable clothes, not to be seen and to be protected from the enemy's attacks. He meant that the whole movement was divine in nature. Hence, he directed the women to get ready for captivity soon after his martyrdom, and that they should not complain, for the ultimate aim was divine.

Readiness for hardships is a requisite for attaining lofty aims. It is a requisite for enjoining good and prohibiting evil and for not cooperating with tyrants and rejecting pressures, tortures, and captivity. More importantly, the person must be so steadfast that he would not utter even a word which might be taken as a sign of discontentment, instability, and dubiousness for presenting so many sacrifices and martyrdom in the way of Allāh. Any sign of unhappiness in the cause of Allāh would devalue the efforts.

There are two important aspects in the final recommendation of Imām al-Ḥusayn. On an individual level, the words of Imām al-Ḥusayn in these testing times are soothing and a comfort to all people who hear them. This is because Imām al-Ḥusayn reminded Imām 'Alī al-Sajjād of the sublime status of Allāh, hence disconnecting his regard to all the previous events. He also informed him of the severe punishment destined for the tyrants of al-Kūfa.

There is also a general aspect observable in Imām al-Ḥusayn's recommendations. Regarding the critical role of Imāmate that Imām 'Alī al-Sajjād would assume after his father, Imām al-Ḥusayn instructed the whole human community in general and the *Shī'is* and his followers specifically. He did this in the form of a prayer he taught Imām 'Alī al-Sajjād, to be attentive to the real mode of monotheism and attentive to Allāh, as this invitation has been the cornerstone of all Divine missions. It is in the form of a prayer that he reminds us of the omnipotence of Allāh and His supreme knowledge of all secrets of the world and everybody's intent, with His Divine tenderness and Provision.

In another recommendation, Imām al-Ḥusayn warns all people against the worst type of oppression. This is doing injustice to the poor and utterly helpless people, a crime being committed every day all over the world. This instruction of Imām al-Ḥusayn prevents us from committing it.

The general scope of the content of Imām al-Ḥusayn's advice takes precedence over its private and personal aspect. The evidence for this lies firstly in the authority of Imāmate and religious leadership which entails informing everybody of a public duty. Secondly, the advice not to do injustice cannot be restricted to the next Infallible Imām, for his infallibility entails being away from committing any crime or injustice, hence it must address a wider audience.

Although both pieces of advice were entrusted to Imām 'Alī al-Sajjād, they were targetted at the whole of mankind, particularly the Muslims, as it is the case in all directives and recommendations issued by the Qur'ān and all the Infallibles.

Reminders for the Real Devotees of Imām al-Ḥusayn

The above pieces are the recommendations of Imām al-Ḥusayn, as he bid farewell for the last time according to reliable sources and mentioned within some narrations of other Imāms. There must be other recommendations that have not reached us. However, the steadfast and resolute character of Imām al-Ḥusayn is accurately portrayed in these three short statements. They are indicative of Imām al-Ḥusayn's resolution and firm decision in his choice.

Unfortunately, there are some baseless statements in certain unauthoritative *maqtal*-books [14] and in the oral descriptions made by uneducated composers of eulogies concerning the farewell of Imām al-Ḥusayn. Such materials are not recorded in authoritative texts, nor are they harmonious with the high status of the Infallible Imām al-Ḥusayn, the Prince of Martyrs. Such statements and depictions orginate from those who have constructed such materials while only paying attention to the rewards of shedding tears, or making others shed tears [15] over the afflictions Imām al-Ḥusayn endured. They were either ignorant of the sin of fabricating false accounts or were simply unaware of their fabrication. Simply quoting such groundless materials is evidence that those who fabricated them did not have a good understanding or profound appreciation of the exalted and high status of Imāmate. Hence, it must be regarded as a doctrinal drawback and flaw to which learned 'Ulamā' must pay attention for safeguarding the doctrinal precinct of Islamic articles of faith and statements.

There are several insightful remarks in this regard. The late Ayatollah Mirzā Ḥusayn Nūrī, the author of *Mustadrak al-Wasā'il al-Shī'a* [16] who spent his life conducting research on *hadiths* and taught such renowned scholars like Sheikh 'Abbās Qummī and Aqā Buzurg Tehranī, made very constructive remarks about fabricating false accounts. In his book *Lu'lu' wa Marjān*, Nūrī discusses some types of lies and the punishments for this grave sin, maintaining that the punishment will be more severe if the lie concerns quoting *hadiths*.

According to Nūrī, those who intend to recount the eulogies and the heart-rending Ashurā events must be very careful. They should not rely entirely on other preachers' oral presentations, nor should they regard every Arabic fragment as authoritative. They must be very careful regarding the books they quote, as being mentioned in a book is not a mark of authority. This is because the author of a book might be an unknown or a famous person, but he might not have the skill of differentiation to distinguish between accurate accounts. Or it could be the case that a renowned author might have written a book when he had not reached academic maturity, but after becoming famous, his books have become best-sellers. While introducing a few instances of such books, Nūrī mentions a case in point. He relates that: "It is reported that on Ashurā when all the companions of Imām al-Ḥusayn were martyred, he went to the tent of Imām 'Alī al-Sajjād and sat by his bed. Then Imām 'Alī al-Sajjād enquired about the enemies and received the answer that the affair led to a battle. Upon enquiring about the companions, he received the answer "Slain!", "Slain!" Upon enquiring about 'Alī al-Akbar and al-'Abbās, he received the same answer. The final comment of Imām al-Ḥusayn was that there were no men left in the encampment except them two."

The late Nūrī's comment concerning the above account is that it is a fabricated story. It was not the case that Imām 'Alī al-Sajjād was entirely unaware of what was happening on the battlefield. In support of Nūrī's view, it is sufficient to remark that Imām 'Alī al-Sajjād's illness was not severe enough to make him completely unaware of what was happening. There are at least two reasons for this. Firsly, many of the incidents of Ashurā were reported by Imām 'Alī al-Sajjād. This fact indicates that he was fully aware of whatever happened. Secondly, on the basis of a reliable report, when all the companions of Imām al-Ḥusayn were martyred, Imām 'Alī al-Sajjād attempted to get out of his tent to attack the enemy, despite being seriously ill, hence unable to carry a weapon. At that time, Lady Umm Kulthūm [17] ran after him to return him to his tent. In spite of his illness, Imām 'Alī al-Sajjād was determined to join the battlefield, crying out, "O my aunt! Let me fight in company with the Prophet's grandson – Imām al-Ḥusayn." In the meantime, Imām al-Ḥusayn cried out and ordered his sister Lady Umm Kulthūm, "O sister! Return him to the tents so that the earth would not remain without the Prophet's progeny." [18]

The above account is yet another evidence that Imām 'Alī al-Sajjād witnessed the events on the Day of Ashurā, although he was unwell.

Hence, when he found Imām al-Ḥusayn was left alone, he tried to attack the enemy in support of him.

In summary, one of the reasons of mixing the true accounts with the untrue ones is that they are all narrated in Arabic. As mentioned by Nūrī, some people regard the presence of narrations in Arabic as evidence for their reliability.

The above remindful comments of the late Nūrī are a great lesson for those who are in pursuit of the truth. This is because there are many Arabic sentences, poems, and expressions attributed to Imām al-Ḥusayn where he is quoted begging for mercy from his enemies which have no authentic basis at all. What follows is a few instances of the above three types:

1. It is reported that one of the war poems and slogans of Imām al-Ḥusayn on Ashurā while attacking the enemy was: "In case the religion of Muḥammad would not survive save by killing me, so come to me, O swords!"
2. It is ascribed to Imām al-Ḥusayn that he used to put emphasis on the significance of opposing Yazīd and conducting *jihad* against the Umayyads. As such he used to remark: "Life consists of only belief and *jihad*."

As for his poem, it is said that Imām al-Ḥusayn composed the following lines by the body of his son 'Alī al-Akbar:

"O star! How short has been your life
As such is the life of morning stars
In what I speak of you are my first subject
And, when I am silent, you are in my mind."

In addition, concerning pleading for mercy, it is reported that Imām al-Ḥusayn used to ask for water from the Kūfans by saying: "O People! Quench my thirst with a drop of water, for my liver has become burnt out of thirst."

Critique

The two slogans, (1 and 2), cannot be found in any reference book, whether reliable or unreliable. This quote is mentioned only in popular magazines and newspapers. Regarding the above two-*bayt* (four-line) poems, they are taken from rhymed *qaṣīdah* of Abū al-Ḥasan 'Alī b. Muḥammad al-Tihamī, a *Shi'i* literary figure who was killed in Egypt in 416 AH/ 1052. He composed an 84-*bayt* (168-line) qasida in memory of his beloved son who died when he was a young child. The above two-line poems are taken from his *qasida*. [19]

Imām al-Ḥusayn never pleaded the enemy for water as mentioned in some unreliable sources. No authoritative reference has recorded it. It seems that this inaccuracy has appeared in texts due to a lack of awareness of the wider context. More specifically, Imām al-Ḥusayn's request for water is mentioned in three accounts of which two have no relation whatsoever to requesting water from the Kūfans. The account is as follows: "The Kūfans attacked Imām al-Ḥusayn while he was trying to reach water, and as he tried to make his way to the river Euphrates, they all attacked him and pushed him away from it." [20]

In another instance, the account is: "[Imām] al-Ḥusayn was in quest of water, and Shimr cried out: 'By Allāh! You will never reach it until you enter into the Fire.' " [21]

The accounts above indicate Imām al-Ḥusayn's purpose to reach the Euphrates. The contents never mention requesting water from the Kūfans. Rather, by seeking water, it means seeking water by means of having access to the Euphrates.

The third case is the only context where, according to Nāfi' b. Hilāl's report, Imām al-Ḥusayn sought water at the time of martyrdom. [22]

Interestingly, a *fiqh* oriented question arises from this account: What would be the effect of attributing the report of Nāfi' b. Hilāl to Imām al-Ḥusayn for a person who is in a state of fasting, while the attributed statement may be "Give me a drop of water because my liver has become burnt with thirst?" [23]

Notes to Chapter 63
The Final Departure

1. By "outer clothes" it is meant the clothes that were highly protective, especially in wartime.

2. The word "calamity" is taken as an equivalent of "*al-balā*'" which also means 'test'.

3. Ibid.

4. Al-Mūsawī al-Muqarram, *Maqtal al-Ḥusayn*, p. 337; and al-Qummī, *Nafas al-Mahmūm*, p. 355. Both of them quoted the above passage from Majlisī's *Jalā' al-'Uyūn*. Al-Qummī's reference to Majlisī volume reads as follows: "1323 AH ed., p. 201". See his *Nafas al-Mahmūm*, ed. R. Ustadī (Qom, 1405 AH/ 1974 AD), p. 355, note 3. However, al-Mūsawī al-Muqarram indicated no chapter-and-verse reference to Majlisī's book.

5. The farewell speech is quoted from Majlisī's book *Jalā al-'Uyūn*, a volume on the lives of the 14 Infallibles. According to him, he drew up the scholarly accounts of the lives of the 14 Infallibles because he had noticed some flaws in the reliability of certain books.

6. For a short biographical account of the late al-Mūsawī al-Muqarram (1316 AH/ 1894 – 1391AH/ 1971), see his book *Maqtal al-Ḥusayn* (5th imp., Beirut, 1399 AH/ 1979), pp. 5-21, contributed by his son Sayyid Muḥammad Ḥusayn al-Muqarram.

7. There is no reference to this point in Ayatollah Najmī's account in Persian. However, the present translator has found its reference in al-Mūsawī al-Muqarram's volume (as cited above in Note 6), p. 276, note 2. Fortunately, the late Ayatollah Sayyid Shahab al-Dīn al-Mar'ashī al-Najafī's preface to the late Sayyid 'Abd al-Razzāq al-Mūsawī al-Muqarram has been reprinted; the reference is as follows: Grand Ayatollah Sayyid Shahab al-Dīn al-Mar'ashī, *Mawsu'a al-Āllama al-Mar'ashī*, ed. Sayyid Muḥammad al-Mar'ashī al-Najafī, Muḥammad Isfandīyārī, and Husayn Taqizadeh (Qom, 1432 AH/ 1389 Sh/ 2011), vol. 3, p. 134.

8. Enclosed within the quotes are the first two verses of the Sūrah Yāsīn, Sūrah 36 of the Holy Qur'ān.
9. These are the mysterious letters with which the Sūrah ṬāHā, the Sūrah 20 of the Holy Qur'ān, begins.
10. In the end of the prayer the Arabic phrase "*kadhā wa kadhā*" means "so and so". When the reader reaches these words, they may mention their requests.
11. This prayer is quoted in al-Majlisī's *Biḥār al-Anwār* (vol. 95, p. 196) from Qutb al-Dīn Sa'īd b. Hiba Allāh al-Rāwandī's *Kitāb al-Da'awāt al-Kabīr*, p. 54. The latter was one of the research resources of al-Majlisī's *Biḥār al-Anwār* as well as al-Nūrī's *Mustadrak al-Wasā'il al-Shī'a*; at the end of the latter there are some praises about it. Al-Qummī in *Hadīyya al-Aḥbāb* describes al-Rāwandī as an expert, critic, exegete, and scholar. Al-Rāwandī passed away in Qom in 573 AH/ 1177 and his tomb is located in the greater courtyard of Lady Fāṭima al-Ma'sūma's Sacred Sanctuary, Qom.
12. Al-Ṣadūq, *al-Khisāl*, ed. 'Alī Akbar al-Ghaffārī (Qom, 1403 AH/ 1362 Sh/ 2003), vol. 1. p. 16, *hadith* No. 59; al-Harrānī, *Tuhaf al-'Uqūl*, p. 176. Lady Umm Salamah was the byname of Hind. She was one of the immigrants to Abyssinia who, after returning back to Hejaz, migrated to Medina. After her husband was injured and martyred in the Battle of Uḥud, she married Prophet Muḥammad before the Battle of al-Aḥzāb. She was entrusted to take care of the Prophet's daughter Fāṭima al-Zahrā. When Imām al-Ḥusayn was born, she was fortunate to become in charge of taking care of him. Lady Umm Salamah remained loyal to the *Ahl al-Bayt* and realated Prophetic *hadiths*. Imām al-Ḥusayn respected her very much such that before leaving Medina, he deposited some Imāmate heritage with her, and she passed them on to Imām 'Alī al-Sajjād. Lady Umm Salamah had long been informed of Imām al-Ḥusayn's martyrdom by Prophet Muḥammad several years ahead of the Ashurā tragedy. She passed away at the age of 84 in Medina and is buried in al-Baqī' Cemetery.
13. Al-Mas'ūdī, *Ithbāt al-Wasīyya*, p. 164.

14. Maqtal books typically describe how someone was killed. However, in the Shi'i tradition, there are mainly concered with the martyrdom account of Imām al-Ḥusayn. For some research literature on maqtal-books, see S. Guenther, "Maqātil literature in Medieval Islam", *Journal of Arabic Literature*, 25 (1994): 192-212, and M.-R. Fakhr-Rohani, "The maqtal genre: A preliminary inquiry and typology", *Payam-e Mehr/ Message of Cordiality*, 1.2 (October-December 2009/ Mehr-Azar 1388 Sḥ: 114-130.

15. Shedding tears and making others shed tears over the hardships Imām al-Ḥusayn endured is highly recommended. For a thorough study in this regard, see Sayyid Muḥammad-Ḥasan Mīr-Jahānī Isfahānī, *al-Bukā' li-al-Ḥusayn,* ed. R. 'Abbāsi (Qom, 1386 Sh/ 2007).

16. The first edition of this book was in three large volumes, containing 23,000 *hadiths* of the Infallibles. This book is arranged according to the chapters and headings of al-Ḥurr al-'Āmilī's *Wasā'il al-Shī'a*.

17. Lady Umm Kulthūm's name was Zaynab al-Sughra; she was Imām al-Ḥusayn's sister.

18. Al-Majlisī, ed., *Biḥār al-Anwār*, vol. 45, p. 46; al-Qummī, *Nafas al-Mahmūm*, p. 348; and al-Khwārazmī, *Maqtal al-Ḥusayn*, vol. 2, p. 32.

19. For some information about al-Tihāmī, see Ibn Khallakān, *Wafayāt al-A'yān*, vol. 3, p. 378; al-Ziriklī, *al-A'lām*, vol. 3, p. 1710; al-Qummī, *al-Kunā wa al-Alqāb*, vol. 1, p. 46; Mudarris-Tabrīzī, *Rayḥāna al-Adāb*, vol.1, p. 356.

20. Al-Khwārazmī, *Maqtal al-Ḥusayn*, vol. 2, pp. 33-34: and al-Majlisī, ed., *Biḥar al-Anwār*, vol. 45, p. 51.

21. Al-Isfahānī, *Maqātil al-Talibīyyīn*, p. 86; and al-Majlisī, ed., *Biḥār al-Anwār*, vol. 45, p. 51.

22. Al-Majlisī, ed., *Biḥār al-Anwār*, vol. 45, p. 57.

23. The religious rule is that deliberate attribution of a false statement to Allāh, the Prophet and the rest of the Infallibles invalidates the fast.

64

Imām al-Ḥusayn's War Poems
on the Battlefield

Imām al-Ḥusayn recited a couple of war poems when he began to fight on the battlefield. Earlier they were referred to as "martyrdom songs" [1, 2].

(a

الموت اولى من ركوب العار   والعار اولى من دخول النّار

انا الحسين بن علي   اليت ان لا انثنى

احمى عيالات ابى   امضى على دين النّبى

(b

انا ابن علي الخير من ال هاشم   كفانى بهذا مفخرا حين افخر

وجدّى رسول اللّه ، اكرم من مضى   ونحن سراج اللّه فى الارض نزهر

وفاطمة امّى ابنة الطّهر احمد   وعمّى يدعى ذوالجناحين جعفر

وفينا كتاب اللّه انزل صادعا   وفينا الهدى والوحي بالخير يذكر

ونحن امان اللّه فى الخلق كلّهم   نسّر بهذا فى الانام ونجهر

ونحن ولاة الحوض نسقى محبّنا   بكاس وذاك الحوض للسقى كوثر

فيسعد فينا فى القيام محبّنا   ومبغضنا يوم القيمة يخسر

(c

كفر القوم وقدما رغبوا   عن ثواب الله ربّ الثّقلين

قتلوا قدما علّيا وابنه   حسن الخير وجاءوا للحسين

خيره الله من الخلق ابى   بعد جدّى وانا ابن الخيرتين

"Death is preferred to accepting abasement
And abasement is better than entering the Fire. [3]
I am al-Ḥusayn, son of 'Alī
Swore not to succumb
I protect my father's descendants;
I sacrifice my life in defending the religion of the Prophet." [4]

According to al-Khwārazmī, Imām al-Ḥusayn attacked the enemy on horseback, with a sword in his hand, while he was ready for martyrdom. At that time, he called out the lines quoted below:

"I am son of 'Alī, the Hāshimid nobleman
As an honour, this is enough for me
And my grandfather was the Prophet, the best of the past.
And we are the lights of Allāh that always shine.
And my mother, Fāṭima, was the chaste daughter of Aḥmad [5]
And my uncle Ja'far has 'two wings'. [6]
And among us is the Book of Allāh explicative
And among us is the Guidance and Revelation, mentioned nicely
And we are Allāh's protection for all the public
That we keep it sometimes overtly and sometimes covertly
And we are the Pond's owner whereat we give water to our devotee
With a cup, and the Pond [7] *is bounteous on Resurrection [Day], our devotees will ascend high*
And our enemies will be the losers on the Resurrection [Day]." [8]

According to al-Khwārazmī, after this Imām al-Ḥusayn cried out:

"The people turned blasphemous in the past
And turned away from the reward of Allāh, the Lord of the two precious entities [9]
Formerly they killed [Imām] 'Alī and his son [10]
The select people of Allāh; my father is
Next to my grandfather [11], *and I am the son of two choices."* [12]

Notes to Chapter 64
Imām al-Ḥusayn's War Poems on the Battlefield

1. See Ch. 62, the section on "Addressing the Descendants of Abū Ṭālib."

2. *Rajaz* was a poem that Arab combatants used to cry out. In such a "war or battlefield poem", the warrior praises his own family, clan, or ancestor, and despises the enemy. It was meant to exert psychological effects: to restate one's own merits, and to scare the enemy.

3. Ibn Namā al-Ḥillī, *Muthīr al-Aḥzān*; al-Baḥrānī, *Maqtal al-'Awālim*.

4. Al-Khwārazmī, *Maqtal al-Ḥusayn*, vol. 2, p. 33.

5. Aḥmad is another designation of Prophet Muḥammad; it is mentioned only once in the Holy Qur'ān, [61:6].

6. Ja'far b. Abī Ṭālib was a brother of Imām 'Alī, since Ja'far lost his two arms and was martyred in the Battle of Mū'ta, Allāh has provided him with two wings instead in Paradise.

7. According to Islamic teachings. The pious will be given water in Paradise by the Bounteous Pond, al-Ḥawḍ al-Kawthar.

8. Op. cit., note 4.

9. *Al-Thaqalayn*. 'The Two Precious Entities' refers to the Holy Qur'ān, the Greater Entity, and the *Ahl al-Bayt*, the Lesser Entity.

10. Imām al-Ḥasan, the elder brother of Imām al-Ḥusayn.

11. Prophet Muḥammad.

12. The "two choices" refers to Imām 'Alī, and Fāṭima al-Zahrā, Prophet Muḥammad's daughter.

65

A World Charter

a) يا شيعة ال ابي سفيان! ان لم يكن لكم دين وكنتم لا تخافون المعاد فكونوا احرارا في دنياكم! وارجعوا الى احسابكم ان كنتم عربا كما تزعمون!

b) انا الّذى اقاتلكم وتقاتلونى والنّساء ليس عليهنّ جناح فامنعوا عتاتكم عن التّعرّض لحرمى مادمت حيّا.

(a) "O followers of the House of Abū Sufyān [1]. If you do not have any faith whatsoever and are not scared of the Resurrection, at least act with dignity in your life and look back at your family backgrounds if you regard yourselves as Arabs, as you claim." [2]

(b) "I am the one who is fighting you, and you have decided to kill me; the women have done nothing wrong, so prevent your offenders from attacking my *ḥarām* [family] so long as I am alive." [3]

Context

According to al-Khwārazmī, Imām al-Ḥusayn bravely attacked the enemy and killed many of them in each attack. All of a sudden, they decided to exert psychological pressure on the Imām in an attempt to make him stop fighting: they rushed toward his encampment. At such a critical moment, Imām al-Ḥusayn cried out as mentioned in (a) above.

Then Shimr replied: "What do you mean, O Ḥusayn?" In response to him, Imām al-Ḥusayn made the statement indicated in (b) above.

Following the above exchange, Shimr said: "You do have this right, O son of Fāṭima!" Then he addressed his group: "Stop rushing toward the encampment of this man; attack him. Indeed, he is a noble combatant!"

A World Charter

The above brief statement of Imām al-Ḥusayn has in fact proven to be a world charter. Although it seems to be an address specific to the Day of Ashurā when the Kūfan army initiated a savage raid on Imām al-Ḥusayn's encampment, it is in fact a universal message. This message is that even if people do not believe in any religion or Divine rules, they must at least observe their national human duty, and universal moral laws.

Islam condemns any aggression against human rights. This applies to the case of war or defense, and even when the enemy has started the war. The Holy Qur'ān is explicit in this regard: "Fight in the cause of Allāh those who fight you, but do not transgress. Indeed Allāh does not like transgressors."[4]

The above charter has several implications and interpretations in the modern world. It means that one should only fight those who initiated the war, and not others from the opposition. Never destroy the enemy's houses, nor uproot their trees. Never deny them water. Give medical treatment to the enemy forces who are injured. Never chase those who run away from the battlefield; never make any trouble for the women and old men and never abuse and insult the attackers.

Several centuries after the revelation of the "do-not-transgress" rule and after Imām al-Ḥusayn's announcement of the above charter, the modern, so-called civilized world has offered some rules for wars. A question that remains is whether the selfish man can restrict himself to such positive rules, messages, and regulations without having received a religious education and absorbing the true human qualifications – a trait obtainable through following the teachings of the prophets. As observed above, Shimr ordered his army to withdraw temporarily, all due to the effect of Imām al-Ḥusayn's speech. However, after Imām al-Ḥusayn's martyrdom they started to attack the women and children and looted the tents.

Notes to Chapter 65
A World Charter

1. Abū Sufyān, Yazīd's grandfather, was an enemy of Prophet Muḥammad. The Umayyad dynasty are all his descendants. His given name was Ṣakhr.
2. Al-Khwārazmī, *Maqtal al-Ḥusayn*, vol. 2, p. 3.
3. Ibid.
4. The Holy Qur'ān, Sūrah al-Baqara [2:190].

66

The Last Supplication of Imām al-Ḥusayn

a) اللّهمّ! متعالى المكان عظيم الجبروت شديد المحال غنىّ عن الخلائق عريض الكبرياء قادر على ما تشاء قريب الرّحمة صادق الوعد سابغ النّعمة حسن البلاء قريب اذا دعيت محيط بما خلقت قابل التّوبة لمن تاب اليك قادر على ما اردت تدرك ما طلبت شكور اذا شكرت ذكور اذا ذكرت ادعوك محتاجا وارغب اليك فقيرا وافزع اليك خائفا وابكى مكروبا واستعين بك ضعيفا و اتوكّل عليك كافيا. اللّهمّ! احكم بيننا وبين قومنا فانّهم غرّونا وخذلونا وغدروا بنا وقتلونا ونحن عترة نبيّك و ولد حبيبك محمّد صلى الله عليه و اله الّذى اصطفيته بالرّسالة وائتمنته على الوحى فاجعل لنا من امرنا فرجا ومخرجا يا ارحم الراحمين.

b) صبرا على قضائك يا ربّ! لا اله سواك يا غياث المستغيثين! ما لى ربّ سواك ولا معبود غيرك. صبرا على حكمك يا غياث من لا غياث له! يا دائما لا نفاد له! يا محيى الموتى! يا قائما على كلّ نفس بما كسبت! احكم بينى وبينهم وانت خيرا لحاكمين.

a) "O Allāh! Your status is sublime, and Your power is great, Your strategy is profound and you are independent of all creation. Your grandeur is magnificient, You are capable of whatever You wish, compassionate, and true to the promise of abundant grace, Who sets a fine test. You are close to the one who calls you, the Supervisor, Controller of whatever You have created, Acceptant of whoever repents (or returns) to You; Capable of (doing) whatever You desire.

You remember those who remember You. I pray to You earnestly; I request You appealingly; I appeal to You apprehensively; I shed tears in distress; I seek Your help feebly; and I rely on You out of Your sufficiency. O Allāh! Judge between us and our people, for they beguiled and left us, and they betrayed and fought us, while we are the house and descendants of Your Prophet Muḥammad – May Allāh bestow blessing on him and his progeny – whom You selected for prophethood and entrusted with the Revelation. Therefore, O Most Merciful of the merciful! Provide for us a rescue and a way out of this affair."

(b) ... "O Lord! I am patient with Your Will. There is no deity other than You, O Helper of those who seek help! To me there is no Lord except You and no one deserves to be worshipped save You! I am patient with Your decision, O Helper for Whom there is no helper! O Omnipresent for Whom there is no exhaustion! O Reviver of the dead! O Authority on every soul of whatever it has gained. Judge between me and them, for You are the best of all judges." [1]

Context

According to al-Ṭūsī in *Miṣbāḥ al-Mutahajjid* and Ibn Ṭāwūs in *Iqbāl al-A'māl*, Imām al-Ḥusayn opened his eyes in the last moments of his life and looked up to the heavens. He whispered his last supplication in the way indicated in (a) above. He then recited the supplication cited in (b) above.

In the last moment of his blessed life, he put his face on the ground, and offered the following prayer: "In the Name of Allāh, through the help of Allāh, in the cause of Allāh, and in respect to the faithful community of the followers of the Prophet of Allāh". [2]

Notes to Chapter 66
The Last Supplication of Imām al-Ḥusayn

1. This last supplication of Imām al-Ḥusayn is in fact a compact lesson in Islamic basic articles of faith and particularly in Islamic monotheism. The following sentences, as indicated in the translation, are markworthy: "I shed tears distressfully: I seek Your help feebly." This shedding tears is by no means out of the afflictions Imām al-Ḥusayn endured on Ashurā. Rather, this shows, Imām al-Ḥusayn's awareness of the sublime status of Allāh and his state of prayer, asking whether he had exercised all he could do to sincerly sacrifice what he had in the cause of Allāh. This supplication deserves a thorough and detailed exegesis.
2. Ibn Ṭāwūs, *al-Luhūf*, p. 110.

Select Bibliographies

Below two Select Bibliographies are provided. The first Select Bibliography provides a list of works the late Ayatollah Muḥammad-Ṣādiq Najmi used to develop the present book in Persian. To provide bibliographical details of the books he used, I had to visit his private library a couple of times. I am grateful to his son, Mr. Aḥmad Najmi, for providing me with such a unique opportunity. I made every effort to make this bibliography as complete as possible, although in some cases no more details seemed obtainable. The second Select Bibliography lists the works used in producing the present English translation.

First Select Bibliography

Al-ʿĀmilī, al-Ḥurr [d. 1104 AH/1692], *Wasā'il al-Shīʿa* (Tehran, n.d.).

Al-ʿAsqalānī, Aḥmad b. ʿAlī b. Ḥajar [d. 852 AH/ 1448], *al-Iṣāba fī Maʿrifa al-Ṣaḥāba*, 4 vols (Beirut, 1328 AH/ 1907).

-----, *Fatḥ al-Bārī fī Sharḥ Ṣaḥīḥ al-Bukāhrī*, 2nd ed., 13 vols (Cairo, 1300 AH/1879).

-----, *Tahdhīb al-Tahdīb* (Hyderabad, A. P., India, 1326 AH/ 1905).

Al-Baḥrānī, ʿAbd Allāh b. Nūr al-Dīn [d. 12th/ 18th], *Maqtal al-ʿAwālim* (Tehran, 1295 AH/ 1253 Sh/ 1874).

Al-Balādhurī, Aḥmad b. Yaḥyā [d. 279 AH/892], *Ansāb al-Ashrāf* (Beirut, 1397 AH/ 1977).

Al-Bukhārī, Muḥammad b. Ismāʿīl, comp. [d. 310 AH/ 922], *al-Ṣaḥīḥ* (N.p., n.d.).

Al-Dhahabī, Muḥammad b. Aḥmad [d. 748 AH/ 1374], *Siyar Aʿlām al-Nubalā'*, 9th ed., 25 vols (Beirut, 1413 AH/ 1993).

-----, *Ta'rīkh al-Islam*, 26 vols, ed. ʿUmar ʿAbd al-Salām Tadmurī (Beirut, 1407 AH/ 1987).

Al-Dīnawarī, Aḥmad b. Dāwūd [d. 282 AH/ 895], *al-Akhbār al-Tuwāl*, ed. 'Iṣām Muḥammad al-Ḥaj Alī (Beirut, 1421 AH/ 2001).

Al-Dīnawarī, Ibn Qutayba ʿAbd Allāh [d. 276 AH/ 889], *al-Imāma wa al-Sīyāsa* (Cairo, 1388 AH/ 1967).

Al-Ḥākim al-Nayshābūrī, Abū ʿAbd Allāh [d. 405 AH/ 1014], *al-Mustadrak ʿAlā al-Ṣaḥīḥayn*, 4 vols (Aleppo, Syria; and Beirut, n.d.).

Al-Ḥarrānī, Ḥasan b. Shuʿba [d. 381AH/ 991], *Tuḥaf al-ʿUqūl* (Qom, 1394 AH/ 1974).

Āl-i Iʿtimād, Sayyid Muṣṭafā, *Balāgha al-Ḥusayn*, 2nd ed., tr. ʿAlī Kazemi (Qom, 1406 AH/ 1985).

Al-Jawzī, Sibṭ b., *Tadhkira al-Khawāṣ* (Najaf, 1369 AH/ 1948).

Al-Kātib al-Wāqidī, Muḥammad b. Sa'd [d. 230 AH/ 845], *al-Ṭabaqt Ibn Sa'd* (N. p., n.d.).

Al-Khwārazmī, Abī al-Mu'ayyid [d. 568 AH/ 1172], *al-Manāqib*, ed. M.-R. al-Mūsawī al-Khirsān (Tehran, 1365/ 1946).

-----, *Maqtal al-Ḥusayn*, ed. M.T. al-Samāwi (Qom, 1367 AH/ 1947).

Al-Kulaynī, Muḥammad b. Ya'qūb [d. 329 AH/ 941], *Uṣūl al-Kāfī* (Tehran, 1388 AH/ 1967).

Al-Majlisī, Muḥammad Bāqir [d. 1110 AH/ 1698], *Biḥār al-Anāwr*, 110 vols (Tehran, n.d.).

Al-Māmiqānī, 'Abd Allāh [d. 1351 AH/ 1930], *Tanqīḥ al-Maqāl* (Najaf, 1350 AH/ 1929).

Al-Mas'ūdī, 'Alī b. al-Ḥusayn [d. 346 AH/ 957], *Ithbāt al-Waṣīyya li al-Imām 'Alī b. Abī Ṭālib 'Alayh al-Salām* (Qom, 1304 AH/ 1883).

-----, *Murūj al-Dhahab*, 2nd ed., 4 vols, ed. Muḥammad M. 'Abd al-Ḥamīd (Cairo, 1384 AH/ 1964).

Al-Māzandarānī al-Ḥā'irī, Muḥammad Mahdī, *Ma'ālī al-Sibṭayn fī Aḥwāl al-Ḥasan wa al-Ḥusayn* (Tabriz, Iran, 1356 AH/ 1937).

Al-Mufīd, Muḥammad b. Muḥammad b. Nu'mān [d. 413 AH/ 1022], *Kitāb al-Irshād* (Najaf, n.d.).

Al-Mūsawī al-Muqarram, 'Abd al-Razzāq, *Maqtal al-Ḥusayn* (Najaf, 1392 AH/ 1971).

Al-Muttaqī al-Hindī, 'Alī [d. 975 AH/ 1567], *Kanz al-'Ummāl* (Beirut, 1399 AH/ 1978).

Al-Nūrī al-Ṭabarasī, Ḥusayn [d. 1320 AH/ 1899], *Mustadrak al-Wasā'il* (Najaf, n.d.).

Al-Qummī, 'Abbās, *Safīna al-Biḥār* (Tehran, n.d.).

Al-Qundūzī, Sulaymān [d. 1294 AH/ 1877], *Yanābī' al-Maqadda* (Baghdad, 1385 AH/ 1964).

Al-Rāwandī, Quṭb al-Dīn [d. 573 AH/ 1177], *al-Da'awāt* (Qom, n.d.).

Al-Ṣadūq, Muḥammad b. 'Alī [d. 381 AH/ 991], *al-Amālī* (Tehran, n.d.).

-----, *'Iqāb al-A'māl*, ed. A.-A. Ghaffārī (Tehran, 1367 Sh/ 1989).

Al-Ṣaffār, Muḥammad b. al-Ḥasan b. Farrūkh, *Basā'ir al-Darajāt* (Tabrīz, Iran, 1380 AH/ 1959).

Al-Samāwī, Muḥammad Ṭāhir, *Ibṣr al-'Ayn fī Anṣr al-Ḥusayn* (Najaf, 1341 AH/ 1920; Qom, n.d.).

Al-Suyūṭī, Jalāl al-Dīn [d. 911 AH/ 1505], *Ta'rīkh al-Khulafā'* (Beirut, 1394 AH/ 1974).

Al-Ṭabarasī, Faḍl b. al-Ḥasan [d. 548 AH/ 1153], *I'lām al-Warā bi Ā'lām al-Hudā* (Tehran, 1338 AH/ 1917).

Al-Ṭabarī, Muḥammad b. Jarīr [d. 310 AH/ 922], *Ta'rīkh al-Ṭabarī* (Leiden n.d.).

Al-'Ubaydlī, Yaḥy b. al-Ḥasan, *Akhbār al-Zaynabāt* (Qom, 1401 AH/ 1359 Sh/ 1981).

Al-Ya'qūbī, Ibn Wāḍiḥ [d. 284 AH/ 897], *Ta'rīkh al-Ya'qūbī* (Beirut, 1379 AH/ 1958).

Ibn Abī al-Ḥadīd [d. 656 AH/ 1258], *Sharḥ Nahj al-Balāgha* (Cairo, 1378 AH/ 1957).

Ibn 'Asākir al-Dimashqī [d. 571 AH/ 1175], *Ta'rīkh Ibn 'Asākir* (Beirut, 1398 AH/ 1977).

-----, *Ta'rīkh Ibn 'Asākir*, 2nd ed., ed. Muḥammad-Baqir al-Maḥmūdī (Qom, 1414 AH/ 1993).

Ibn al-Athīr, Mu'izz al-Dīn [d. 630 AH/ 1233], *al-Kāmil fī al-Ta'rīkh*, 9 vols (Beirut, 1387 AH/ 1967).

Ibn Jum'ah al-Ḥuwayzī, 'Abd 'Alī [d. 1112 AH/ 1700], *Tafsīr Nūr al-Thaqalayn* (Tehran, n.d.).

Ibn Kathīr al-Dimashqī [d. 774 AH/ 1372], *al-Bidāya wa al-Nihāya* (Beirut, 1387 AH/ 1966).

-----, *al-Bidāya wa al-Nihāya*, 2nd ed., 15 vols (Beirut, 1977).

Ibn Muzāḥim, Naṣr [d. 212 AH/ 827], *Waqa'a Ṣiffīn* (Cairo, n.d.).

Ibn Namā al-Ḥillī [d. 645 AH/ 1247], *Muthīr al-Aḥzān*, 2nd ed. (Qom, 1406 AH/ 1985)

Ibn Qūlawayh al-Qummī, Ja'far b. Muḥammad [d. 367 AH/ 977], *Kāmil al-Zīyārāt*, ed. 'Abd al-Ḥusayn al-Amīnī al-Najafī (Najaf, 1356 AH/ 1944).

Ibn Shahr Āshūb, Muḥammad b. 'Alī [d. 588 AH/ 1192], *Manāqib Āl-i Abī Ṭālib*, 4 vols. (Qom, n.d.).

Ibn Ṭāwūs, 'Alī b. Mūsā [d. 673 AH/ 1274], *al-Luhūf 'alā Qatl al-Ṭufūf* (Tehran, 1321 AH/ 1900).

Ṣāberī al-Hamadānī, Aḥmad, *Adab al-Ḥusayn wa Ḥimāsatuh* (Qom, 1395 AH/ 1974).

Second Select Bibliography

English Translations of the Holy Qur'ān

Abdel Haleem, M. A. S., tr., *The Qur'an* (Oxford, 2004)

Ali, A., tr., *al-Qur'ān: A Contemporary Translation: Arabic-English Edition* (Karachi, 1984; Delhi, 1987).

Ali, 'A. Y., tr., *The Holy Qur'ān, English Translation of the Meanings and Commentary* (Medina, 1410 AH/ 1990).

Ali, 'A. Y., tr., *The Meaning of the Holy Qur'an*, new ed. rev. (Brentwood, MD, 1412 AH/ 1992).

Ali, S. V. Mir Aḥmad, tr., *The Holy Qur'ān*, English Translation with Arabic Text (Karachi, 1975).

Arberry, A. J., tr., *The Koran Interpreted* (1955; Oxford, 1964).

Asad, M., tr., *The Message of the Qur'ān* (1980; Bitton, UK, 2003).

Pickthal, M. M., tr., *The Qur'ān Translated: Message for Humanity* (Washington, D.C., 2005).

Qara'i, 'A.-Q., tr., *The Qur'an, with a Phrase-by-Phrase English Translation* (London, 2004).

Zafrulla Khan, M., tr., *The Qur'ān*, 3rd ed. rev. (London, 1981).

Dictionaries

An Advanced Arabic-English Dictionary, Including an English Index, by H. Anthony Salmoné (London, 1889; Beirut, 1978).

An Arabic-English Lexicon, 8 vols., E.W. Lane (London, 1863-1893; Beirut, 1980).

Al-Munjid, 33rd ed. (Beirut, 2000)

Chambers Biographical Dictionary, 6th ed., ed. M. Parry (Edinburgh, 1997).

A Comprehensive Persian-English Dictionary, by F. Steingass (London, 1892).

The Concise Dictionary of World Place-Names, ed. J. Everett-Heath (Oxford, 2005).

The Concise Oxford Dictionary of World Religions, ed. J. Bowker (Oxford, 2000; 2005).

Concise Oxford English Dictionary, 12th ed., ed. A. Stevenson, and M. Waite (Oxford, 2011).

Dictionary of Islam, by T. P. Hughes (London, 1885; New Delhi, 1999).

A Dictionary of Modern Written Arabic, Arabic-English, by H. Wehr; 4th ed., enl., ed. J. Milton Cowan (Wiesbaden, Germany, 1979; New York, 1994).

Islamic Desk Reference, Compiled from The Encyclopaedia of Islam, by E. van Donzel (Leiden, 1994).

A Learner's Arabic-English Dictionary, by F. Steingass (London, 1884; Beirut, 1989).

Merriam Webster's Geographical Dictionary, 3rd ed. (Springfield, MA, 2001).

Oxford Dictionary of English, 2nd ed. rev., ed. C. Soanes, and A. Stevenson (Oxford, 2005).

The Oxford Dictionary of Islam, ed. J. L. Esposito (New York, 2003).

The Oxford Dictionary of World Religions, ed. J. Bowker (Oxford, 1997).

The Oxford English Dictionary, 2nd ed., 20 vols, ed. J. A. Simpson, and E. S. C. Weiner (Oxford, 1989).

Shorter Oxford English Dictionary on Historical Principles, 6th ed., 2 vols, ed. A. Stevenson (Oxford, 2007).

Atlas

Baba-Askari, A., *Atlas-e Ghadir va Ashurā/ The Atlas of Ghadir and Ashurā* (Qom, 1391 Sh/ 2012).

Other Works

Al-Amīnī al-Najafī, A.-H. A., *al-Ghadīr*, 10 vols. (Tehran, 1372 AH/ 1971).

Al-ʿAshshāsh, T., *Dīwān Ashʿār al-Tashayyuʿ ʾilā al-Qarn al-Thālith/ al-Tāsiʿ* (Beirut, 1997).

Al-Ḥamawī, Y. [d. 626 AH/ 1228], *Muʿjam al-Buldān*, 7 vols. (Beirut, 1957).

Al-Ḥusaynī, S. J. B., *Tāʾrīkh al-Adab al-ʿArabī: Adab Ṣadr al-Islām* (Qom, 1416 AH/ 1995).

Āl-i Yāsīn, R., *Ṣulḥ al-Ḥasan* (Baghdad, 1372 AH/ 1953).

Āl-i Yāsīn, R., *Solh-e Imām Ḥasan ʿAlayh al-Salm*, tr. S. A. Khameneie, 8th ed. (1348 Sh/ 1969; Tehran, 1388 Sh/ 2009).

Al-Jumaḥī, M. b. S. [d. 231 AH/ 846], *Ṭabaqt Fuḥkl al-Shuʿar*, 2 vols., ed. M. M. Shākir (Jeddah, 1974).

Al-Khwārazmī, M. [d. 568 AH/ 1172], *Maqtal al-Ḥusayn*, ed. M. al-Samāwī (Qom, 1428 AH/ 2007).

Al-Kiliddār, A.-J., *Taʾrīkh Karbalā wa Ḥāʾir al-Ḥusayn ʿAlayh al-Salām* (1368 AH/ 1947; Qom, 1418 AH/ 1376 Sh/ 1998).

Al-Mufīd, M. b. M. [d. 413 AH/ 1022], *al-Irshād*, tr. A. Khān Boluki, 2nd ed. (Qom, 1389 Sh/ 2010).

-----, *Kitāb al-Irshād: The Book of Guidance into the Lives of the Twelve Imāms*, Eng. tr. I. K. A. Howard (London, 1981; Qom, 1383 Sh/ 1425 AH/ 2004).

Al-Mūsawī al-Muqarram, S. A.-R., *ʿAlī al-Akbar* (Najaf 1368 AH/ 1957).

-----, *ʿAlī al-Akbar*, 2nd ed., ed. S. S. al-Ḥusaynī al-Marʿashī al-Najafī (Qom, 1401 AH/ 1980).

-----, *Maqtal al-Ḥusayn* (Beirut, 1399 AH/ 1979).

-----, *Maqtal al-Ḥusayn* (Beirut, 1423 AH/ 2002).

-----, *Maqtal al-Husain: Martyrdom Epic of Imām al-Husain*, Eng. tr. Y. T. al-Jibouri, MS. Also available online.

Al-Qurayshī, 'A.-A., *al-Bālighūn al-Fatḥ fī Karbalā* (Beirut, 1429 AH/ 2008).

Al-Qarashī, B. S., *Ḥayt al-Imām al-Ḥusayn*, 10th ed., 3 vols. (Qom, 1427 AH/ 2006).

-----, *The life of Imām Husain*, Eng. tr. S. A. H. S. H. Rizvi (Qom, 1386 Sh/ 1428 AH/ 2007).

Al-Qasīr, S. A., *Ḥayt Ḥabīb b. Maẓāhir al-Asadī* (Karbalā, 1431 AH/ 2010).

Al-Saberi al-Hamadani, A., *Adab al-Ḥusayn wa Ḥimsatuh*, 3rd ed. (Qom, 1415 AH/ 1994).

Al-Ṣadūq, M. b. A. [d. 381 AH/ 991], *al-Khiṣl*, ed. A.-A. Ghaffārī (Qom, 1403 AH/ 1362 Sh/ 2003).

-----, *Kitāb al-Hidāya*, 2 vols. (Qom, 1384 Sh/ 1426 AH/ 2005).

Al-Samāwī, M. Ṭ., *Ibṣār al-'Ayn fī Anṣār al-Ḥusayn*, ed. 'A. J. al-Ḥassānī (Najaf, 1341 AH/ 1920; Beirut, 1427 AH/ 2003).

-----, *Ibṣār al-'Ayn fī Anṣār al-Ḥusayn*, ed. M.-J. al-Ṭabasī (Qom, 1384 Sh/ 2006).

Al-Ṭabasī, M.-J., *al-Maqtal al-Ḥusaynī al-Ma'thūr*, 2nd ed. (Tehran, 1428 AH/ 1386 Sh/ 2007).

Āl-Tu'ma, S. S. H., *Karbalā fī al-Dhākira* (Baghdad, 1988).

-----, *Mu'jam Rijāl al-Fikr wa al-Adab fī Karbalā* (Beirut, 1420 AH/ 1999).

-----, *Ta'rīkh Marqad al-Ḥusayn wa al-'Abbās* (Beirut, 1416 AH/ 1996).

-----, *Turāth Karbalā*, 2nd ed. (Beirut, 1403 AH/ 1983).

Fakhr-Rohani, M.-R., "Ashura literature: Its status amongst the world literatures and for comparative studies," *Hussein Revivalism*, 8 (2008): 32.

-----, A Concise Dictionary of Ashura and Karbala, forthcoming.

-----, "The maqtal genre: A preliminary inquiry and typology," *Payam-e Mehr/ Message of Cordiality*, 1.2 (October-December 2009/ Mehr-Azar 1388 Sh): 114-130.

-----, "Reflections on Ashura-oriented literature," *Message of Thaqalayn*, 12.3 (2011): 95-101.

-----, "The ziarat-texts issued in favor of Imām al-Ḥusayn," *Hussein Revivalism*, 9 (2012): 12.

-----, ed., *Ashura Poems in English, Explained and Annotated*, 2nd ed., 2 vols. (Karbala and Qom, 2011).

Fu'ādiyiān, M.-H., and F. Ḥasasnlouyi, *Sharḥ wa Taḥlīl Rajaz-hye Ḥemse farīnn Karbalā dar Rkz-e Ashurā*, 2nd ed. (Tehran, 1389 Sh/ 2010).

Guenther, S., "Maqātil literature in Medieval Islam", *Journal of Arabic Literature*, 25 (1994): 192-212.

Haddū, H. M., and S. J. Kazim, *Dufanā' fī al-'Ataba al-Ḥusaynīyya al-Muqaddasa* (Karbalā, 1432 AH/ 2011).

Ḥusaynī-Tehrnī, S. M.-Ḥ, *Lama'āt al-Ḥusayn* (Mashhad, 1429 AH/ 2008).

Ibn Ḥazm al-Undulusī, 'A. b. A. b. S. [d. 456 AH/ 1064], *Jamhara Ansāb al-'Arab*, 6th ed., ed. 'A. M. Hārūn (Cairo, 1999).

Ibn Manẓūr al-Afrīqī, M. b. M. [d. 711 AH/ 1311], *Lisān al-'Arab*, 2 vols, ed. Y. al-Baqā'ī, I. Shams al-Dīn, and N. 'Alī (Beirut, 1426 AH/ 2005).

Ibn Qūlawayh al-Qummī, J. b. M. [d. 367 AH/ 977], *Kāmil al-Zīyārāt*, ed. 'A.-Ḥ. al-Amīnī (Najaf, 1356 AH/ 1935).

-----, *Kāmil al-Zīyārāt*, ed. J. al-Qayyūmī (Qom, 1424 AH/ 2003).

-----, *Kāmil al-Zīyārāt*, Eng. tr. S. M. al-Husayni al-Milani (Miami, FL, 2008).

Ibn Ṭāwūs, 'A. b. M. [d. 664 AH/ 1266], *Iqbāl al-A'māl*, ed. H. al-A'lamī (Beirut, 1417 AH/ 1996).

Jafri, S. H. M., *The Origins and Early Development of Shi'a Islam* (London and Beirut, 1979; Oxford and Karachi, 2000).

Majlisī, M.-B. [d. 1110 AH/ 1698], *Jalā' al-'Uyūn*, 2nd imp (Tehran, 1390 Sh/ 2011).

Mawsū'a Zīyārāt al-Ma'sūmīn, 7 vols (Qom, 1425 AH/ 1383 Sh/ 2005).

Mīr-Jahānī Isfahanī, S. M.-Ḥ., *al-Bukā' li-al-Ḥusayn*, ed. R. Abbasi (Qom, 1386 Sh/ 2007).

Mohaddethi, J., *Farhang-e Ashurā*, 8th ed. (Qom, 1385 Sh/ 2006).

Muhammadi-Reyshahri, M., ed., *Daneshnameh-ye Imām Husayn 'Alayh al-Salām*, 14 vols. (Qom, 1388 Sh/ 1430 AH/ 2010).

Muhsin Khan, M., *The Translation of the Meanings of Ṣaḥīḥ al-Bukhrī, Arabic-English*, 4th ed., 9 vols (Beirut, 1405 AH/ 1985).

Mūsawi-Garmaroudi, S. M. S., et al., *Farhang-e Ashurā* (Tehran, 1384 Sh/ 2005).

Pour-Amini M.-B., *Chehreha dar Ḥemase-ye Karbalā* (Qom, 1382 Sh/ 2002).

Qummī, A., *Nafas al-Mahmūm*, ed. R. Ustadi (Qom, 1405AH/ 1974).

Sharīfī, M., et al., *Mawsū'a Kalimāt al-Imām al-Ḥusayn 'Alayh al-Salām*, (Qom, 1373 Sh/ 1415 AH/ 1995).

Shomali, M.-A. *Discovering Shi'i Islam*, 7th ed. (London, 2010).

——, *Shi'i Islam: Origins, Faith, and Practices* (London, 2003; Qom, 2010).

Tabatabaie, S. M.-Ḥ., *A Shiite Anthology*, tr. W. C. Chittick (London, 1980; Qom, 2003).

Zuhayr b. al-Qayn (Karbalā, 1430 AH/ 2009).

Index

J

K

L

M

CPSIA information can be obtained
at www.ICGtesting.com
Printed in the USA
BVHW060955260820
587378BV00009B/447